Fútbol!

UNIVERSITY PRESS OF FLORIDA

Florida A&M University, Tallahassee
Florida Atlantic University, Boca Raton
Florida Gulf Coast University, Ft. Myers
Florida International University, Miami
Florida State University, Tallahassee
New College of Florida, Sarasota
University of Central Florida, Orlando
University of Florida, Gainesville
University of North Florida, Jacksonville
University of South Florida, Tampa
University of West Florida, Pensacola

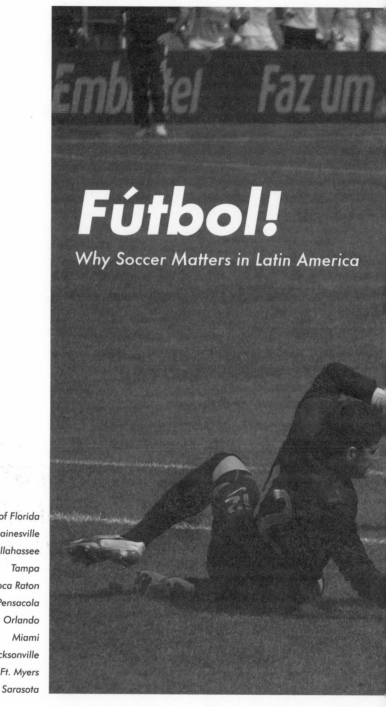

Fútbol!

Why Soccer Matters in Latin America

University Press of Florida
Gainesville
Tallahassee
Tampa
Boca Raton
Pensacola
Orlando
Miami
Jacksonville
Ft. Myers
Sarasota

Joshua H. Nadel

Title page: Lionel Messi. Lee Dos Santos/ModernWorldPhotography.com

This book may be available in an electronic edition.

19 18 17 16 15 14   6 5 4 3 2 1

Library of Congress Cataloging-in-Publication Data
Nadel, Joshua H. author.
Fútbol! : why soccer matters in Latin America / Joshua H. Nadel.
pages cm
ISBN 978-0-8130-4938-0
1. Soccer—Latin America—History. 2. Soccer—Social aspects—Latin America.
I. Title.
GV944.L3N34 2014
796.334098—dc23
2013038964

University Press of Florida
15 Northwest 15th Street
Gainesville, FL 32611-2079
http://www.upf.com

For Evanthia, Sofia Ariadne, and Rafael Nikolaos

Contents

Introduction

Soccer Narratives

> If we want to talk about the masses, of popular interest and enthusiasm, of uniting an entire country behind a cause, we are talking about soccer. Please, let's not talk about anything else. Simply talk about soccer.
>
> Daniel Matamala, *Goles y autogoles*

Fútbol (or *futebol*) *is* Latin America. People live for it. They kill for it. It is a source of hope and a reason for suicide. It is a way out of poverty and misery for a very few and an intangible escape for millions more. Since its arrival in the late nineteenth century, soccer has served as a vessel into which Latin Americans pour their hopes. It has been both a reflection and an idealized projection of the countries in the region. As such it is much more than a game: soccer helps build the nation and forges between disparate groups of people a unity difficult to find else-where. At first glance, it transcends politics and is embraced by both military dictators and leftist militants. It mutes racial and class differences, suspending for anywhere between ninety minutes (the length of a match) and one month (the length of the World Cup tournament) social, political, and economic tensions.

It is easy to overstate soccer's ability to bridge conflicts that cross traditional social boundaries. Nevertheless, soccer's potential to heal national wounds and boost national pride is a powerful reason for the sport's popularity. This book explores soccer's importance in Latin

America. But instead of seeking answers to *how* it matters, it looks for answers to the question of *why* it matters. Why has this imported sport, born of British boarding schools, taken such firm root in Latin America's distant soil? Soccer matters because it is woven into regional identities and the historical narratives of Latin American nations. Soccer, in other words, is a crucial element in the stories that Argentines and Brazilians, Hondurans and Chileans, tell themselves about who they are.

Soccer did not arrive in Latin America in a vacuum. It arrived at a particular moment (or moments) in time: the late 1800s, just as the countries of the region were beginning to consolidate themselves as modern nations. Massive immigration from Europe altered the demography and with it some of the "traditional" social norms. Immigrants helped to grow the popularity of soccer, just as the sport aided in integrating new populations into the nation. New constitutions offered new rights. Men and women, people from all social classes, agitated for more inclusive notions of citizenship, in so doing changing Latin American self-perception. Many of these changes were intended to make Latin America look more like Europe, both socially and culturally. At the time, national leaders in the region tried to superimpose a modern European mentality on their nations. These ideas were supposed to lift the countries of the region out of ignorance and put them in the flow of European development, and they revealed something of an inferiority complex in the region.

Soccer arrived at just this moment of political, economic, and cultural consolidation, what one prominent sports theorist has called a "critical juncture." Soccer and country became fused in the minds of many so that the sport came to embody the nation. As a result, modern Latin American nations and soccer grew and evolved together. Soccer clubs and stadiums acted as spaces where Latin American societies could grapple with the complexities of nationhood, citizenship, politics, gender, and race. The sport eventually allowed Latin American countries to show that, far from being inferior to Europe, they could match their colonial and neocolonial masters through sport. While soccer arrived at a crucial moment in Latin American national histories, the sport and the nation have remained intertwined in important ways until the present day. The nation at play continues to bind people together and highlights the strength of regional cultures.

Just as the context helps to explain soccer's importance to the region, the inverse is also true: soccer can help explain the history of modern Latin America. Soccer's history—from its arrival and popularization through to the continued hold it has in the region today—tells the story of modern Latin America as well. And that is the goal of this book: it is an episodic account that highlights the importance of soccer in the region. In so doing, it helps explain the history of modern Latin America through soccer. Since soccer arrived when nations were consolidating, the sport became a way for new local and national identities to be expressed. Since it remained a crucial way to discuss the nation, it also played an important role at other critical junctures in regional history. From ongoing debates about gender to moments of intense political change, discussions about soccer remain a way for citizens to talk about their nation, its people, and its politics.

A Game of Passion?

It has been said so many times that it is almost a cliché: Latin Americans are passionate about soccer. Perhaps it is sacrilege to say, but Latin Americans are no more passionate about soccer than fans in any other region of the world. Yes, Brazilians and Argentines weep when their team loses, and once Honduras and El Salvador went to war at the end of a match. (It was a short war, and the World Cup qualifier merely acted as a spark to long-simmering border tensions.) But Germans and Englishmen also cry after defeats. And while there has never been a war in Europe over soccer, certainly there has been intense violence, and games have taken on deep political meaning.

If Latin Americans are no more passionate about their soccer than people from other regions, why are they *perceived* to be so? Here discussion could lead us into stereotypes of the non-European world held by Europeans. Latin Americans—whether Colombian or Argentine, Cuban or Mexican—are thought to be passionate while Europeans and North Americans are stereotyped as rational. Without doubt, there is an element of old-school racial ideology in the way that people from the West view the rest of the world and the ways that non-Europeans love their games. Nevertheless, it cannot be denied that by and large, Latin Americans love soccer, and that the sport carries with it immense importance in the region.

Why? Academics who look at sport have come up with myriad answers, few of which help us understand the passion for soccer. Some have argued that sport is a way for capitalism to discipline workers, teaching them the importance of teamwork and sacrifice, inculcating time management, and offering a healthy way to spend free time. Others have argued that sport distracts the masses from the daily hardship of their lives. For other analysts, sport is a vehicle for nationalist sentiment: to paraphrase Eric Hobsbawm, the nation is more palpable as eleven men on a field than in almost any other form. It can also serve as a way to unite the far-flung corners of a country into an "imagined community," to turn to an oft-used yet compelling cliché about nation building. Still others show how soccer teaches men to be men, while soccer's growing economic importance and political influence in a globalizing world forms the basis of much scholarship.

All of these analyses have helped our understanding of why soccer matters in Latin America, yet we academics rarely succeed in two ways: to adequately show *how*, practically, the sport and the nation connect; and to capture the pleasure of sport, the joy of sport. Journalists are better at conveying the latter, but the answers that they give are in many ways just as incomplete as those found by academics. Journalists ascribe Latin Americans' passion to the success of their teams. People in the United States do not have to look far to see where this argument fails: the Boston Red Sox spent eighty-six years chasing an elusive World Series title and their fans adored them for it. Indeed, after finally winning, "real" Boston fans distinguished themselves from bandwagon fans by asserting that they followed the team in their lean years. The rabid fans of Chile, Paraguay, Mexico, Bolivia, Ecuador, Colombia, Costa Rica, Honduras, El Salvador, and Guatemala have never seen the senior men's team succeed in a world tournament, yet they continue to be passionately supportive of their teams.

Actually, national teams fail most of the time. In regional and international tournaments, they lose. Thus, success at soccer on an international stage cannot explain Latin American fascination with the sport. Only eight nations have won the World Cup: five from Europe (Italy [four times], Germany [three times], England, France, and Spain) and three from Latin America (Brazil [five times], Uruguay [twice], and Argentina [twice]). European countries have won ten titles to Latin America's nine. If we take into account the 1924 and 1928 Olympics, as the Fédération Internationale de Football Association (FIFA) does, then South America has won eleven world championships to Europe's ten. So are Latin American nations as a whole better at soccer than other nations? Hardly. In fact, the majority of Latin American countries rarely taste success on soccer's international stage. In South American regional championships, results show that there is little success beyond the big three (Argentina, Brazil, and Uruguay). Of the forty-three South American Championships held since 1916, Uruguay, Argentina, and Brazil have won thirty-seven. So too in North and Central America and the Caribbean, success is limited. Mexico has won nine of twenty-two regional titles; the United States, five; Costa Rica, three; Canada, two; and Guatemala, Haiti, and Honduras, one each. In other words, we cannot ascribe Latin American love for soccer to national team success.

Nor can we say that professional success keeps people interested in the game. Sixteen teams, out of literally hundreds that have existed over time, have won the Argentine championship; seventeen have won a chaotic mélange of Brazilian titles; ten Uruguayan teams (with two winning an astonishing eighty-nine between them); and twenty-three Mexican clubs have captured their countries' championships. In other words, most teams in Latin America *never* win championships. At best, soccer fans can hope not to wait too long between victories. The point here is that Latin Americans do not love soccer only because they excel at it. Rather, soccer matters in Latin America not because of how well a nation performs in international tournaments or club teams perform in national championships but because of why, how, and when play started, and how the sport has continued to play a crucial role in initiating, reflecting, and mitigating changes in Latin American societies. Because of when soccer arrived and how it has evolved with the nation, it has come to reflect identities—be they local, regional, or national—in ways that other institutions do not. This makes soccer incredibly powerful.

Clubs and Nations

The focus of this book is on the intersections between soccer and the nation. It examines anecdotes and histories of national teams (*selecciónes* or *seleções*), of club teams and leagues, and of players. Why? Because these sites offer fertile ground for analyzing how soccer and nation fused. National teams reveal a great deal about narratives and representations of the nation, but they are not always the most fruitful place to look. For instance, in the 1920s Mexicans were too busy reuniting their country after long years of revolution for international soccer competitions to matter. Club soccer, on the other hand, played within Mexico and across the region, witnessed a massive growth in numbers of both players and spectatorship after 1920, demonstrating soccer's ability to knit people together after conflict.

Indeed, love of the game is often first learned, memorized, and internalized at the club level since clubs are a strong force in consolidating local identities. Latin American soccer teams were born in neighborhoods and were based on ethnicity, class, and other particularistic affinities. They served as both sports and social clubs, playing the additional role of mutual aid societies for their members. Today many large clubs still have kindergartens and schools, and they sponsor youth activities. They offer free movies, dance classes, and other events to members that reflect and reinforce the cultural identities of their members. And they have political functions as well, sometimes becoming jumping-off points for members with political aspirations. Campaigns for club leadership often have political undertones as *socios* (members) of one political party compete against socios of another party for control of the club. Club leadership campaigns in Buenos Aires, for example, appear similar to political races, with posters and murals pasted across the city complete with smiling headshots and slogans.

Clubs, then, form a crucial nexus of soccer and neighborhood life, and as such, tell a great deal about soccer and the construction of local identities. But to get at the bigger picture—why, for example, Brazil shuts down during the World Cup or why Uruguayan employers gave workers a holiday for the finals of the 2011 Copa América—national teams give us more insight. At the local level, clubs play the seminal role of getting people involved in the game, socializing them to the rules of the sport and the norms of fandom like the history, chants, glories, and failures of the team. This embeds the idea of soccer's importance. Competition against other clubs creates greater loyalty to the *patria chica*, the little fatherland to which the club is attached, be it a physical neighborhood, city, or region, or a less tangible loyalty like social class or ethnic heritage. International competition, on the other hand, brings together rival fans from different clubs and cities, mobilizing entire nations across the very same social and political lines that club teams played a role in creating. In other words, even if the hardcore fans might choose club over nation, club teams cannot galvanize the population in the same ways that the national team can.

Just as club teams operate as extensions of a neighborhood, national teams become extensions of the country. Much more seems to rest on the outcome of a World Cup or a Copa América match than a win or a loss. In the international arena, national pride is on the line, gauged against other nations. This gives the opportunity for neighbors to stake claims of superiority, for former colonies like Brazil or Mexico to take a measure of revenge from their former European masters.

Narratives, Soccer, and the Nation

Typically when we watch a sporting event—whether the World Cup or the Olympics, the Super Bowl or the World Series—the farthest thing from our minds is how the game ties into the "real world." Occasionally, a network will air a human-interest story that shows how an athlete overcame adversity and arrived at the pinnacle of her sport. These depictions are essentially selected versions of events put together in a compelling way to provide drama or a sense of predestined glory, as though every moment naturally led to this finale. These are narratives. They are consciously constructed to evoke powerful emotions of awe, empathy, or national pride. Narratives are the stories that we, as individuals or as part of a group, tell about ourselves and our past. In short, they are part and parcel of our identities, revealing both who we are and who we want to be. Just as individuals have narratives, nations do too, which convey a sense of history, common values, mores, and customs. National narratives serve both to unify the country and to present the country to the wider world.

As much as they serve to project an image to the outside world, however, national narratives are mostly for internal consumption. Each nation has a grand narrative constructed by politicians, historians, reporters, and average citizens—what we could call its textbook history—that seeks to unite its population. This version of national history has to be one that most can agree on, creating what one historian has called "the deforming mirror of truth": a historical narrative accurate enough to be believable by all (or most) groups in a society.[1] The grand narrative, we might say, is two parts history and one part optimism. It is an articulation of what a nation imagines itself to be. But it is hardly inclusive, complete, or fully accurate.

So alongside the dominant history, multiple subnarratives exist that tell a part of the larger one: we call these women's history, black history, working-class history, and so on. Some of these act as counternarratives, stories that challenge constructed national identities and question the grand story. For example, Honduras is supposedly a mestizo (mixed indigenous and European ancestry) nation, yet half of the Honduran soccer team is of African descent; officially about 2 percent of the population is black. Brazil illustrates the counternarrative potential of soccer as well. There women allegedly only began playing soccer in the past four decades. In fact, however, they started playing in the 1920s, when women were considered too fragile and weak for such a physical sport. In short, the game sometimes forced people (and continues to force people) to question the dominant narrative of their nations. Soccer, in other words, can act as a window into both the dominant and hidden histories of Latin America.

Soccer is among the last places we might think to look for national narratives and counternarratives. For a long time sport was seen as something apart from the things that mattered in history. If considered at all, historians perhaps studied how it could be a modern version of the Roman bread and circuses, when Roman leaders provided food and entertainment as a way to win favor with the population. Fascist leaders such as Benito Mussolini and Adolf Hitler exploited the popularity of sport to garner support for their rule by sponsoring national and international competitions such as the World Cup and the Olympics. These events lent legitimacy to the regimes and served to bolster national pride. But within the last thirty years historians have begun to look at what sports might tell us about society. If sports could be used to mobilize a population to craft a new image of the nation, then they must have some potential to reflect the tensions, conflicts, and challenges of a particular society.

No sport is better suited for this, on a worldwide scale, than soccer. After all, more than three hundred million people worldwide play the game. Soccer was, and remains, a way to examine all manner of issues, from new immigrants to national identity, from gender to social class and race. For example, much as baseball became a way to integrate new arrivals into American culture, soccer helped assimilate new immigrants to Latin America. National teams not only came to represent their nation in the World Cup or the Olympics but they also supposedly represented the "personality" of their country. German players—and European players in general—were said to play a rational and strategic style while Latin Americans played more uninhibited and improvisational soccer that reflected something deep in the players' psyches. So not only did players become national heroes, but sporting victories were also seen as victories for the nation's way of life.

A Narrative of Soccer

The dominant narrative of soccer has been handed down across generations as a birthright, an act of faith akin to a creation myth. First, the game evolved in Britain from the late Middle Ages: a rough-and-tumble version with few rules that would pit town against town. A ball could be carried, hurled, kicked, or otherwise transported from one place to another, almost like capture the flag in reverse. Hundreds of people might be involved. It became so disruptive that King Edward III and, later, King James I of Scotland ordered it banned. The game continued. By the 1800s it had been mildly civilized, and two versions caught on at the elite public schools across England. In one, the use of the hands was the perfectly legal—in fact, often preferred—way to move the ball toward the goal, though once in possession of the ball a player was not supposed to run with it in his hands. One kicked the ball to move it up field, and the idea was either to kick the ball through the goals or to touch the ball down across the goal line. Tackling was permitted, and the game was quite rough. In the other, players could use any part of their body except the hands and arms. The aim was to move the ball by kicking it into a goal composed of two wooden poles (which at this point in time had no crossbar). Tackling and holding were not permitted, but players could use their shoulders to try to push opponents off the ball.

By the middle of the nineteenth century these games became seen as integral in the creation of civilized Englishmen, who were to be educated, refined, and masculine. Games such as football provided the sons of the elite with opportunities for physical exertion that other elite sports of the time, such as cricket, did not. Moreover, sports taught modern skills of teamwork and physical discipline. But tensions arose between the adherents of the two different kinds of football. Each sport wanted to dominate the public school landscape, and as a result different schools became advocates of one form of the sport or the other. Those who liked to carry the ball in their hands, tackle, and score across the touchline gravitated around Rugby School in Warwickshire, while those who favored kicking centered around Cambridge, which had drawn up rules in 1848. In October 1863 representatives from a number of schools gathered in a London pub to agree on a set of rules that would officially demarcate one form of the sport or the other: Association Football was born, based largely on the 1848 Cambridge rules. By the end of 1863 the new Football Association (FA) had banned any form of hitting or tackling. Those who wanted to play soccer (English shorthand for "association") ascribed to the FA rules while those who used their hands followed Rugby rules (codified in 1870, allowing running while carrying the ball).

This narrative elides certain inconvenient truths, such as the fact that earlier iterations of a ball game played without hands exist around the world. In Mesoamerica, ancient societies played the ballgame, as it is known, prior to the arrival of Europeans. Played with a small rubber ball on a stone court, the game allowed touching of the ball with any part of the body except the hands. The physical purpose of the game was to shoot the ball through a round hole, but historians and anthropologists also believe that the game possessed religious and political meaning. So too in China, thousands of years ago, both men and women played a game called *t'su chu* that involved kicking a leather ball through a hole. It is certainly possible, though unlikely, that later European explorers saw the Chinese playing the "sport of kings" and brought some version of it back, but again, history—and creation myths—has a way of reorganizing truth. And the British have been fond of claiming provenance of all things modern.

In all fairness the similarities between the ancient and modern games seem slight, if suggestive. But one thing that they do share is a spiritual power: Mesoamerican and Asian ball games had explicitly religious purposes. In today's world, soccer is often described as a secular religion. People place faith in their soccer teams—whether from the barrio or the nation—and attend "ceremonies" in specially built megachurches to what one geographer has called the "earthbound gods" of soccer. And, while all myths highlight the shape shifting qualities of history, they also contain elements of truth. So if England was not the sole birthplace of what we today call football or soccer, it certainly played the crucial role in its reincarnation as a modern sport, replete with codified rules, an organizing federation, and the desire to spread the sport.

Indeed, few debate the veracity of England's claim as progenitor of the world's game. The branches of the story—how the game developed in countries around the world—bear striking resemblance to one another: British sailors, merchants, engineers, bankers, or some combination of all of these began to play among themselves while abroad and, having connections to the local social elite, began to pass the game on to them. At the same time people from the working classes saw these "crazy Englishmen," as they were called in Argentina and Uruguay, kicking a ball around and began to mimic their actions, teaching themselves the rudiments of the game.

This was how the game arrived throughout Latin America in the late nineteenth century. The sport appeared in Argentina a scant five years after the creation of the Football Association rulebook. British sailors brought the sport to the Chilean port city of Valparaíso, and it is there rather than the capital city of Santiago that soccer developed in the late 1890s. In Brazil most agree that the true birth of Brazilian futebol branches off of the same British trunk as all other soccer. Charles Miller, an Anglo-Brazilian who spent ten years at school in England, is generally seen as the father of the sport. Indeed, the only place in South America that soccer did not come from the British is Paraguay, a country that always does things just a little differently. There William Paats, a Dutch schoolmaster, introduced the game in Asunción, from whence it rapidly spread throughout the city and into the rural surroundings. In Uruguay, across the Rio de la Plata from Argentina, the sport also received an early impulse from the British community. The foreign-born elite of the Montevideo Cricket Club created a team in the 1870s, and the two English high schools, the British School and the English School, introduced the sport into their curricula in the 1890s.

One question that we might fruitfully ask is, why soccer? Why not cricket or rowing, both of which were popular among expatriates as well? Indeed, both sports arrived earlier than soccer and had adepts not only among the foreign community but also among local elites. Both were "modern" in that they adhered to a set of rules and perceived of competition as both physically and psychologically strengthening. Some have suggested that the simplicity of soccer's rules, fourteen in all, made the game more alluring than its competitors. Simple to learn and simple to play, the game had another advantage over others: to play, one needed only a ball. Someone to play with helped but, barring companions, one could kick a ball against a wall and, as I have seen my children do countless times, dribble around imaginary opponents.

Whatever the reason for its popularity, when soccer came to Latin America, it wore ideology on its sleeve. Not the regional political affiliations of the day, Liberal and Conservative, but the ideologies of progress and civilization, which were dominant at the end of the nineteenth century. Political and intellectual leaders throughout Latin America felt that northern Europe's wealth indicated its cultural and social superiority over the world, and they sought not only to adopt the political attitudes but also to emulate the cultural and social practices of England, France, and Germany. As a result, a growing trend toward more open political structures, more rational economic organization, and more modern social activities developed in the region. Soccer's arrival, then, coincided with a series of other changes—known generally as the neocolonial period—that swept Latin America in the late nineteenth century. In other words, soccer appeared and gained popularity as Latin American narratives were in the process of being formed, and for that reason the sport became an integral part of those national stories. Soccer remained intertwined with these narratives as they evolved and shifted across the twentieth century, and as a result retains a great deal of explanatory power up until the present day.

Latin American Soccer: Seven Snapshots

This book develops as a series of snapshots that focus on intersections between soccer and national narratives and counternarratives in Latin America. It is meant to be suggestive rather than conclusive, to generate discussion on the ties between soccer and the nation. The book is consciously constructed to be read in one of two ways. The chapters follow a loose chronology from the arrival of the sport in Latin America in the 1800s to the present day. At the same time, they can be read thematically or nationally, as each chapter is a self-contained episode that highlights one aspect of the relationship between sport and country. These themes are crucial to understanding Latin America in the twentieth century and underscore how soccer can help give an identity to a newly forming nation, unite countries fractured by war, show the devastating effects of corruption and poverty, and be used both by and against dictators.

The arrival of the sport in Uruguay occurred during what is called Latin America's neocolonial period. During that era, Uruguay and other nations in the region depended heavily on foreign—particularly British—capital to drive economic growth. They also received large numbers of immigrants and aspired to European cultural norms. Uruguay is at once representative and unique, as the general contours of neocolonialism held, but the shape of national development differed. European finance and immigrants helped to reshape the country, but state consolidation happened much later than elsewhere in the region. In Uruguay, soccer ended up playing an important role in fostering a sense of national community amid rapid economic, political, and demographic changes.

Reinforcing nationalist sentiment through sport was visible in a number of ways, including the creation of "national styles." Mythic creations that rested in part on history and in part on the assumption of national traits, playing styles helped to shape the discussion both about the nation and about soccer in early-twentieth-century Argentina and Brazil. A particular way of playing soccer composed a key piece of the grand narratives being shaped at the time. For example, in the 1930s authors began writing about a distinctive Brazilian style that reflected Brazil's African heritage. This in turn allowed for the construction of narrative of the nation that relied heavily on its African roots. Argentine journalists and fans also claimed that the *criollo* style highlighted Argentine guile and improvisation over European rationality and training. Here again the narrative of the criollo style expressed superiority over Europeans on the cultural front and helped to consolidate national identity in the early century.

Crafting a unified identity was crucial in the aftermath of the Mexican Revolution (1910–20), and soccer played an important role in weaving together one nation out of Mexico's many regions. Postrevolutionary leaders sponsored tournaments that brought teams from around the country together to compete toward a common goal. Mexico is an example of the difficulty of this process, given the country's lost opportunities for economic and sporting development. In the long run, however, soccer has become one of the cultural symbols of the Mexican nation.

While Mexican political leaders used soccer as a tool to bring the nation together, political leaders in Paraguay arguably impeded the sport by failing to develop the nation. The Latin American historical narrative suggests that in the period immediately after independence

(1810–25), most nations fell under the sway of strong military leaders called caudillos. While the caudillo era ended in the 1860s, some say that they never left Paraguay. And their continued rule left a marked impact on the country and on soccer: patronage and corruption led to intense poverty for much of the population while leaders enriched themselves. Soccer offers another avenue to examine the impact of caudillos while exposing that networks of corruption and personalist politics exist in soccer as well.

Direct links between soccer and politics are even more clearly visible in the case of Chile, which offers the opportunity to examine soccer as a site of political resistance. Historians have written about how governments used soccer to bolster their regimes (for example, the Argentine government and the 1978 World Cup). The Chilean story questions that link by looking at how soccer was used to protest against the military dictatorship of Augusto Pinochet, who ruled the country from 1973–89. Protestors used soccer stadiums around the world to register their disagreement with his regime. At the same time players used their positions as national heroes to speak against the regime. Along with earlier examples of politicians failing to harness soccer to their own political ends, the story of Chile questions the dominant narrative of rulers successfully using soccer to control populations, highlighting the sport's counternarrative potential.

Counternarratives exist in every country, and Honduran soccer provides insight into a counternarrative of race. Honduras, for example, claims to be a mestizo—mixed indigenous and European—nation, and in the early twentieth century nationalist leaders spent a good deal of energy constructing this image. Even today Honduran education and social structure highlight the mestizo nature of the country. But looking at soccer suggests a very different picture of Honduran racial identity. We see how blackness was systematically erased from Honduran identity by examining the history of the Honduran national team, which calls into question the dominant Honduran racial narrative.

If there is one place where the dominant Latin American narratives of both soccer and the nation can be challenged, it is women's soccer. While most soccer histories suggest that women had no interest in playing the sport, in fact this could not be farther from the truth. All over the region, especially in Brazil, Costa Rica, and Mexico, women found ways to play soccer in the face of institutional and social obstacles. Popular theories suggested that women soccer players would be unfit mothers and would risk their own health. Marginalized from the outset, women have been intentionally left out of national soccer narratives. Women's soccer has been seen as a threat not just to the national game but to the nation as well. Even now the persistence of opposition to women's play has meant that women players face many of the same obstacles today that they did in the last century.

Exploring soccer in Latin America helps us understand the social importance of sport as well as the histories of individual countries. We can learn how soccer came to be so popular, how and why people of African descent were written out of their countries' histories, and how politicians used soccer to their advantage. The beauty of national (and soccer) narratives is that facts have almost no bearing on their power. That we can tell these stories through soccer reflects just how important soccer is in the region. The seven chapters here focus on the seven countries that qualified for the World Cup in 2010. More importantly, however, in one way or another they all shed light on the intertwining of soccer and national narratives. In other words, they help explain soccer's prominent place in Latin America.

1

Uruguayan Arrivals

From Shadow to the Sun

On paper it was a match for the ages. On October 14, 2009, in Montevideo the two oldest soccer-playing nations in the region, Argentina and Uruguay, played for the 177th time for a spot in the 2010 World Cup. Lionel Messi, FIFA player of the year, faced off against Diego Forlán, Europe's Golden Boot winner for most goals in the 2008–9 season. Although the losing team would still have a chance to qualify for South Africa, their road would be more difficult: a home and away playoff series against a strong and confident Costa Rican side awaited.

On the field the game was uninspired, and spectators would have been forgiven for thinking that the match was nothing more than a meaningless "friendly." Both teams used defensive strategies and appeared to fear losing more than they wanted to win, perhaps Argentina more than Uruguay. Why? With Ecuador one point behind in the standings, the Celeste, as the Uruguayan team is known for its sky blue uniforms, needed a win to guarantee qualification for South Africa. But the famed Uruguayan fighting spirit, called the *garra charrúa*, seemed to be missing. Uruguay's garra had brought the country four world championships between 1924 and 1950, but since then it had been conspicuously absent. This team, however, was supposed to embody the heart of the small country again, mixing a never-say-die attitude with the technical skills of Forlán and strike partner Luís Suárez.

The sole spark of excitement came when Argentine substitute Mario Bolatti scored the game's lone goal in the eighty-second minute off a sloppy set piece. Argentina was on its way to South Africa, beating the team that for much of the twentieth century had been its regional nemesis. At the time, the match devastated Uruguay. While the Celeste would go on to qualify for the World Cup, losing to archrival Argentina at home was a particularly harsh blow. The loss appeared to be one more example of Uruguay's decline in soccer, a sport that had historically done much to elevate national pride.

There is no better place to start the story of Latin American soccer than the Río de la Plata, the region named for the estuary that separates Argentina and Uruguay, where the sport first arrived on Latin American shores. And soccer history in the region rests heavily on competition between the two countries, among the oldest rivalries in the world. While play began first in Argentina, Uruguay quickly outpaced its larger neighbor. The Celeste won the first two South American Championships and four of the first six world championships to become the first soccer power in the world.

We would do well to ask why soccer caught on so quickly in Uruguay. One answer is that ties between England and Uruguay were particularly close. Another answer suggests that the development and consolidation of the Uruguayan state occurred slightly later than in other countries, thus coinciding more closely with the popularization of soccer in the country. Indeed, the context of soccer's arrival in Uruguay is important to understanding its power over the Uruguayan national psyche. Equally important is the narrative that grew up around soccer's development. Uruguay's soccer history posits a nationalization of the English sport (exhibited by beating expatriate teams) and an ability to defeat larger neighbors in international play as sources of pride and a representation of Uruguayan nationalism.

Soccer arrived in Uruguay at a particular time in regional history. During the late nineteenth century Latin American countries entered what historians call the neocolonial period, which heralded major changes in the region. National governments sought to modernize agriculture, industrialize, establish educational systems, develop infrastructure, foster immigration, and court foreign investment from Europe. Soccer came along with these changes. Other cultural forms—from clothing styles to consumer goods and membership in social clubs—required either money or connections, or both. But soccer easily diffused to the working classes. To paraphrase Uruguayan historian Eduardo Galeano, soccer quickly became a universal language spoken equally well by poor immigrants from Europe and rural migrants to the capital city. For national leaders, soccer had other benefits as well: it generated unity around the selected eleven. Ethnic, political, and class difference could be set aside in cheering on the national team. From a nation of many, then, soccer could help unite the country.

Galeano titled his iconic book about soccer *El fútbol a sol y sombra—Soccer in Sun and Shadow*. Although he discussed the sport around the world, nevertheless the title inadvertently alludes to soccer's role in Uruguay. From a "tiny spot on a map" wedged in the shadows between two larger and more powerful neighbors (Argentina and Brazil), soccer helped Uruguay emerge into the sun as one of the most respected sporting nations in the world. Success on the field in turn helped bolster Uruguayans' sense of pride in their nation.

Uruguayan Contexts

If people in the United States thought of Uruguay prior to the 2010 World Cup, they might have thought of the beaches of Punta del Este or perhaps expensive grass-fed beef. More likely they would have said something along the lines of, "Isn't that a small Latin American country?" Most would not have thought about it as a soccer powerhouse, nor as a highly developed, modern nation. Yet Uruguay has been both an Olympic and World Cup champion and one of the wealthiest Latin American nations, whether measured by per capita gross domestic product, educational attainment and literacy, infant mortality, or life expectancy. Indeed, for much of the twentieth century Uruguay stood apart from its neighbors in terms of social spending and social development. At the beginning of the century it also stood above most of the region in soccer.

Uruguay has no right to be a soccer power. Nor should it ever have been one. It is a small nation. At a little over sixty-eight thousand square miles, Uruguay is roughly the size of Missouri, or half the size of Italy. Uruguay also has few people. Its population was slightly more than 1.5 million people when José Nasazzi led the Celeste to the gold medal in the 1924 Olympics, and just over 1.7 million people lived there six years later, when Uruguay hosted and won the first World Cup. Uruguay was also a predominantly rural country—in 1908 about 30 percent of the national population lived in the capital city, Montevideo—and soccer was seen as growing best in urban and suburban environments. In other words, conditions in Uruguay would not seem to have been ideal for the development of soccer.

Nevertheless, in other ways the conditions were ripe for soccer's development into the national game: foreign investment and influence, immigration, a growing working and middle class, and political stability. That these phenomena occurred contemporaneously with soccer's popularization powerfully tied the game to a sense of progress in Uruguay at the turn of the century. Moreover, the sport played a crucial role in bringing the country together after nearly a century of political infighting and instability.

When soccer arrived in Uruguay in the 1870s, the country was just emerging from a prolonged period of political strife. Independence in 1815 was delayed by Portuguese invasion a year later, and Uruguay became a province of Brazil until 1828. That year England brokered a treaty to ensure Uruguayan independence. At that point the population of Uruguay stood at seventy-four thousand, smaller than the *cities* of Buenos Aires and Rio de Janeiro. Even with British backing, political turmoil continued as Uruguay was used as a pawn in a struggle for regional hegemony between Argentina and Brazil. The Guerra Grande (1839–52), a civil war that saw Brazil and Argentina support opposing Uruguayan factions, created further political upheaval. Into the 1870s Uruguayan political leaders complained about their neighbors'

The Uruguayan National Team in 1929, between victories in the 1928 Amsterdam Olympics and the first World Cup. © DPA/ZUMAPress.com

influence on internal affairs, noting that Uruguay was a "toy . . . today of these [Argentina] and tomorrow of those [Brazil]," which kept the country in a state of "permanent anarchy."[1] Argentine and Brazilian political interests in the *Banda Oriental* ultimately stunted the growth of autonomous political parties and delayed Uruguayan economic development.

Still, England's presence in the Río de la Plata ensured Uruguayan independence and helped its economy grow. But it could not stop the regular internecine fighting between the two Uruguayan political forces: *Blancos* and *Colorados*. To the extent that ideologies mattered, these parties hewed closely to the ideas of their regional counterparts. The conservative Blancos sought to hold on to the old order as much as possible by retaining social and economic structures from the colonial period and maintaining close ties between church and state. The liberal Colorados, on the other hand, rhetorically sought to broaden the notion of citizenship, to separate church and state, and to modernize trade and economic activity. Likewise, they fostered stronger economic and cultural ties with northern Europe.

José Nasazzi Yarza

Perhaps the most feared player of his generation, José Nasazzi Yarza had unrivalled success as the captain of the Celeste during their heyday in the 1920s and '30s. A right fullback capable of outrunning, outwitting, and intimidating his opponents—a true personification of Uruguayan grit—Nasazzi won every championship imaginable at the time: two Olympic gold medals, one World Cup, and four South American Championships. As a professional, he won two league championships with the professional club Nacional. In all he played fifty-one times for Uruguay over a thirteen-year period.

Born in 1901 in Villa Peñarol, Montevideo, Nasazzi embodied Uruguay's need to integrate immigrants in the early twentieth century. Born of immigrant parents—his father, Italian, and his mother, Basque—he grew up in a humble barrio of Montevideo known as Bella Vista, to which he would remain connected throughout his life. At an early age he showed more interest in playing soccer with friends in the streets and empty lots around the city than attending school. Perhaps it is an apocryphal story that one of Nasazzi's nicknames—*el Terrible*—came from a frustrated teacher. It could easily have applied to the way that opposing players felt before games against him.

His other nickname, *el Gran Mariscal* (the grand marshal), came from his leadership skills, which were rarely called into question. The management of the national team passed over many more-qualified and -experienced candidates when they named him captain of the Celeste soon after he joined the squad. It was a decision they would not regret. Many of his teammates credit Nasazzi's calm with helping Uruguay come from behind to win both the 1928 Olympic and the 1930 World Cup finals. Indeed, in major tournaments, Nasazzi's Celeste failed to win only once, in the 1929 South American Championship.

In the days before professional soccer, all players had day jobs to survive, practicing after work or on weekends. José Nasazzi was a marble cutter. He debuted with third division team Club Lito at age seventeen, helping it ascend to the first division before leaving it to join his barrio team, Bella Vista. He remained with the *Papales* for ten years, until the arrival of professionalism. He then moved to Nacional, one of the two oldest clubs in Uruguay. After retiring in 1937 Nasazzi went on to coach the Celeste to the South American Championship in 1942 before retiring from football altogether in 1947.

The end of the Guerra Grande in 1852 brought Colorados to power, but violent uprisings continued to be the favored way to solve political disputes throughout the late nineteenth century. Only when the final Blanco rebellion failed in 1904 was Uruguayan political stability ensured. Nevertheless, by the late 1850s Uruguay began the slow process of consolidation and modernization of its export infrastructure. This led to economic growth and brought foreign investment, expatriate businessmen, and poor immigrants to the country, as was the case in much of the region. Uruguay's overall population more than quadrupled between 1870–1925, and by 1908 nearly 20 percent of Uruguayans were foreign born, and Colorado rule and stability heralded changes in economic production as well. By the 1870s the fencing of the *pampas* (grasslands), required for improving the quality of beef for export, had begun, which constricted the plains of the Uruguayan littoral. This process turned *gauchos* (cowboys) into wage workers, causing many to move to Montevideo and feed its burgeoning population: in 1870 nearly 30 percent of the national population lived in the capital city, a percentage that would jump to 35 percent by 1930.[2] Yet, even as the majority of immigrants remained in Montevideo, Uruguay's exports remained largely pastoral: cattle and sheep drove the economy. By 1912 Uruguay exported over 178 million pounds of raw wool, and in 1923 the little nation became the second-largest beef exporter in the world, accounting for 12 percent of the world's total beef exports.[3]

Soccer arrived in Uruguay in this period of economic, demographic, and social change in the same way as it arrived elsewhere in the region: in the bags of expatriates from England and Scotland. Reports exist of a game played between British sailors and the elite Montevideo Cricket Club as early as 1878. At that time, soccer was already being played across the estuary in Buenos Aires, and the constant boat traffic—not to mention the substantial number of Uruguayans resident in Argentina—could easily have transported the sport even earlier than this. But the first match between Uruguayan clubs for which written records exist took place in June 1881, pitting the expatriate Montevideo Cricket Club against the elite Uruguayan Montevideo Rowing Club. From this point on the sport began its rapid ascent. In 1891 Albion and the Central Uruguay Railroad Cricket Club (CURCC, later known as

Peñarol) formed. The first Uruguayan league, with four teams, began play in 1895. Throughout the final decade of the nineteenth century new clubs continued forming. Club Nacional split away from Albion in 1899, and in 1902 Montevideo Wanderers took the field for the first time.

At the same time that elite teams formed the official Uruguayan league, other clubs formed as neighborhood or working-class associations, which helped to spread the sport to the majority of the population. So too smaller, less formal organizations began as youth playing improvised games on empty lots began to coalesce into teams. Made up of workers instead of management—youths from the poorer immigrant communities and the immediate suburbs of the capital—teams such as Montevideo Defensa, Intrépido, Dublín, Quaker Oats Football Club, and River Plate disseminated the sport down to the lower social classes. In addition to these teams, countless youth played in ad hoc games without any form of organization. Soccer dominated the streets, courtyards, and open spaces in the city and suburbs.

Regardless of the basis on which clubs were formed, Uruguayan soccer teams played a role in bringing the country together. It appears, for instance, that many clubs abandoned their ethnic roots in Uruguay earlier than in other countries. We can only speculate as to the reasons for this. Perhaps the fact that by 1911 17 percent of Uruguay's population and more than 40 percent of Montevideo's population was foreign-born played a role. The children of this immigrant wave, like many second-generation immigrants, may have looked to assimilate rather than differentiate. So too the ability of soccer to bring together disparate groups around cheering on a sport—whether club teams or national teams—would prove decisive in the construction of national identities and the coagulation of a nation made of immigrants. In the same way that baseball scholars argue that the sport helped bring together the United States after the Civil War and incorporate new immigrants to the nation, soccer helped Latin America.

As Uruguay and other nations throughout the region emerged out of the chaos of the postindependence period, soccer narratives helped both to bring together a people divided by political struggles and to unite new migrants behind the idea of the nation. Moreover, the rivalries between the Blancos and Colorados, which found expression on the battlefield throughout the nineteenth century, began to play out in more peaceful competition on the soccer fields instead. Internationally as well, whether against the new regional economic power (England) or the meddling neighbor (Argentina), Uruguayan soccer became a powerful expression of national pride and skill. Indeed, the ability of Uruguayan clubs to defeat British expatriate teams and the national team's early rivalry with Argentina elicited national sentiment and united Blanco and Colorado alike behind the team. This is not to say that political rivalries disappeared but that politics could be left to one side as the nation represented itself on the international stage. As the twentieth century dawned, soccer had become not only the dominant sport in Uruguay but also a powerful marker of a national identity that began to supersede party loyalty for the first time. As such, soccer played an important role in fostering a more unified nationalism.

The success of Uruguayan soccer—both in its domestic popularity and in its international competitiveness—seemed, for many, to confirm Uruguay's bright future.[4] And, indeed, in the first decades of the twentieth century Uruguayans had reason to be optimistic. José Batlle y Ordóñez, the Colorado leader who ruled from 1903–7 and 1911–15, consolidated the development of the 1870s and 1880s and created the first welfare state in Latin America. During the *Batllista* era, Uruguay emerged as a developed, modern nation with infrastructure, education, and social services both modeled on and, arguably, equal to those in Europe. New port construction facilitated increased exports of beef and wool; tramlines and railroads connected the nation (and coincidentally opened new land for suburbs and soccer fields); the government strengthened the public education system (begun in 1877); and new legislation protected workers and created a social safety net.[5] Together, then, Uruguay's considerable development and soccer offered twin poles of national pride. Indeed, according to Luís Prats, the sport "lived to the beat" of the nation, "constituting an experience through which Uruguayans observed the events that shaped their era."[6]

The Myth of Dual Births

In Uruguay, soccer's connection to the nation rested in part on the construction of a soccer narrative. As was the case around the region, the first decades of the 1900s saw a reevaluation of national heritage and a search for homegrown markers of national pride. The British presence in Uruguay, while crucial to the development of the country, by the 1910s had begun to wear on nationalist sentiment. As intellectuals turned inward, they sought to identify the Latin roots of national identity because dominant philosophies of the day suggested that each "race" carried with it innate traits. They believed that inherent differences existed between people of Anglo-Saxon and Latin heritage. Anglo-Saxon veins carried rationality and logic while Latin blood contained passion and improvisation. As in Argentina, in Uruguay the belief in innate racial traits led to the resuscitation and idolization of national types such as the gaucho.[7]

For soccer to serve national purposes, then, the sport itself needed to be nationalized. Since it had arrived with British expatriates and was first played among the economic elite, organic intellectuals—writers, teachers, athletes, and the like—sought ways to bring the sport down to the people. One way to do this was to craft a narrative about the birth of soccer. So commentators in Uruguay began to create a narrative based on two elements: different "racial" types and a sharp divide between the foreign era and the national era in soccer.

According to the narrative of *rioplatense* soccer—which supposedly comprised both the Uruguayan and Argentine styles—English racial characteristics "tended to destroy individual" play and only valued the "uniform action of the team." The Latin game, on the other hand, rested on "dribbling" and "individual effort." As a result, Uruguayan soccer was more "agile and colorful."[8] The difference between these supposedly innate traits led logically to the creation of the other myth-history of soccer's evolution in Uruguay: the sharp definition between two epochs of the game.

National narratives of Uruguayan (and much of Latin American) soccer argue the sport passed through two phases. In the first phase, expatriates brought the sport with them and played it in exclusive social clubs. Local elites soon took up the game and began to play as well, and eventually the sport spread downward. In this early era, according to the story largely crafted by journalists from Argentina and Uruguay, British teams dominated all others. In Uruguay, for example, the CURCC and Montevideo Cricket Club dominated the sport for the first decade. The second era, or the criollo phase, began when the native-born players and teams surpassed their foreign-born teachers. Historians date the beginning of this transition to 1902, when the all-Uruguayan Nacional defeated CURCC for the league championship for the first time. Occasionally historians add a third phase to the narrative—the professional phase, which began in the early 1930s as the sport broke with its amateur past. To be sure, this simple, clean narrative explains the sport well: the British dominated soccer for a decade or so before Uruguayans adapted the game and surpassed the foreigners, thus deepening the connection between the nation and the sport.

If only truth and history coincided so tightly. Instead, soccer's history is filled with inconsistencies and half-truths that hide much of the reality. Many of the early "British" carriers of the game were partly British at best. For example, Charles Miller, the generally accepted father of soccer in Brazil, was born to a Scottish father and an Anglo-Brazilian mother. Unlike many of his peers, Miller chose to remain in Brazil until his death.

As in Brazil, the founding fathers of Uruguayan soccer were a mixed lot. Enrique Lichtenberger is paramount in the Uruguayan soccer pantheon. Son of a Brazilian man and his English wife, Lichtenberger attended the English High School in Montevideo and became an acolyte of William Leslie Poole, the father of the game in Uruguay. Poole promoted soccer through the physical education program at the high school, and many of his pupils went on to have a lasting impact on the sport in Uruguay. In 1891 Lichtenberger and some friends split off from the Montevideo Rowing Club—a bastion of the Uruguayan elite—and formed the first soccer-only club in the country, which became known as Albion.

Lichtenberger was perhaps ideally suited for his role as a founding father of the national sport, as he had one foot in the expatriate community and the other in Uruguayan society. Shortly after forming

Albion, he took charge of forging the Uruguayan Football League, a precursor to the Uruguayan Football Association. Made up of four teams, the Uruguayan league had a distinctly elite feel. The founding clubs were Albion; the Deutscher Fussball Club, which represented the German community; CURCC, which was composed of expatriate employees of the company; and Uruguay Athletic, a team of Uruguayans and expatriates that represented the British-owned and -operated gas company. In 1901 Football Club Nacional, a combination of ex-players from Albion, Uruguay Athletic, and the more plebeian Montevideo Football Club, gained admittance to the league. Because of its more working-class roots, Nacional is often incorrectly considered to be the first truly Uruguayan team.

Here is where the myth of the dual births gets slightly cloudy. In order to suggest a clear break between the expatriate era and the Uruguayan era, sports chroniclers mistakenly placed Albion in the foreign phase of soccer in Uruguay. And perhaps this is understandable. Simply called "Football Association" at its founding in 1891, the club quickly changed its name to Albion, an ancient name for Great Britain. Formed by students and graduates of the English High School, its name made clear reference to England. Likewise, the names of its founders—along with Lichtenberger were Davie, McLean, and Pratt, among others—all sounded foreign. Thus, many historians and soccer aficionados have presumed that the team comprised Englishmen and other expatriates, and Albion was placed clearly in the expatriate wing of Latin American soccer history. A foundational book on the history of the sport in the region noted that Albion was all "English and British-Americans" and named Nacional as the first "completely criollo" club. With rare exception, this is the story that has been passed down from generation to generation of history.[9]

In fact, however, Albion was the first all-*Uruguayan* club. Rather than forming as an exclusively British club, as the historical narrative suggests, Albion formed explicitly as an Uruguayan club. In what some have called a conscious response to the exclusivity of the expatriate clubs, the initial by-laws of the organization banned foreign-born players from its ranks. Though by no means a plebeian team, Albion was nevertheless Uruguayan-born and -bred.[10] Eventually, as a strategy to beat the archrival Montevideo Cricket Club, Albion permitted foreign-born players to join the team. Nevertheless, Albion's original require-ment that players be Uruguayan-born reflected a burgeoning sense of nationalism and at the same time suggested the ease with which soccer could be used for nationalist causes. Yet, because Albion was made up primarily of Anglo-Uruguayans while Nacional comprised Italo- and Hispano-Uruguayans, later commentators stripped Albion of its Uruguayan identity. Sons of immigrants formed both teams, but only those of Latin blood could be included in the national narrative as Uruguayan. If there is any doubt about the inaccuracy of the narrative of twin births, the Lipton Cup should put it to rest.

The Lipton Cup is among the oldest international cup competitions in soccer. First played in Buenos Aires in 1905 and most recently contested in 1992, the Lipton Cup pit the national team of Uruguay against that of Argentina. In his travels to Buenos Aires and Montevideo, tea baron Thomas Lipton saw the passion and skill of soccer in the Río de la Plata and decided to initiate an annual game between the two countries. He provided a silver cup for the winner, and the Argentine and Uruguayan federations decided that any profit from the game would go to charity.

The first Lipton Cup match, in 1905, was not the first game played between teams from Uruguay and Argentina—that took place in 1889 to celebrate Queen Victoria's seventieth birthday and, by most ac-counts, was played exclusively by British expatriates resident in the respective countries. But the first Lipton Cup match would go down as the first official international between the two countries. Many of the players who lined up for the inaugural Lipton Cup match in Bue-nos Aires on August 15, 1905, had memories of two earlier matches. In 1902 and 1903 teams from the two countries faced each other, with Argentina taking the first and Uruguay the second. But this match was different: while the earlier matches comprised players active in the countries regardless of nationality, in 1905 the match required all players to be Argentine or Uruguayan citizens. According to the rules of the Lipton Cup, all participating players had to be native-born.

Little is known of the match that day. Accounts note that it was hard-fought and that the referee disallowed an Uruguayan goal for off-side. Other than that, we know that the squads played a sportsmanlike game and that it ended in a 0–0 draw due to lack of light. Since no date could be fixed for a rematch, the Argentine captain offered the cup to his Uruguayan counterpart in a gesture of goodwill. The following year in Montevideo more than five thousand people came to watch Argentina defeat Uruguay 2–0.

Indeed, after that first 0–0 draw, the Copa Lipton instantly became an international *clásico*—a rivalry match akin to the Yankees–Red Sox in baseball or UNC–Duke in college basketball—until 1929. After that the Lipton Cup lost importance as other international matches, such as the South American Championship, the Olympics, and the World Cup became regular fixtures of the soccer world. But in the first decades of the twentieth century, prior to Olympic and World Cup success in 1924, 1928, 1930, and 1950, the Lipton Cup served as a bellwether for Uruguayan soccer and identity.

And the Lipton Cup also offers the opportunity to confirm the criollo bona fides of Albion. Many of the players who played in the 1902 match between Argentine and Uruguayan teams went on to play in the inaugural Lipton Cup in 1905. In 1902, for example, Argentina's Brown and Buchanan brothers, Morgan, Anderson, Dickinson, and Moore, defeated Uruguay's Sanderson brothers, Carve, and their more criollo-sounding teammates 6–0. If we were to believe the creation myth of Uruguayan—and Argentine—soccer, players from both teams apparently represented the quintessentially "English" clubs that dominated the foreign phase of rioplatense soccer: alumni in the case of Argentina and Albion for Uruguay.

A closer look, however, reveals the myth of dual births of soccer to be little more than fiction. The Argentine squad of 1902 made up the core of the inaugural 1905 Lipton Cup team. Albion players on Uruguay's national team in 1902, notably the Sanderson brothers, went on to form one another of the earliest "Uruguayan" teams, the Montevideo Wanderers. And many players from Albion represented the country in the first Lipton Cup match in 1905. What does this tell us? We know that the Lipton Cup rules required that each country's team be made up of native-born players. If the myth of soccer's dual birth—

Obdulio Varela

The World Cup in 1950 confirmed Uruguay's place at the pinnacle of international soccer. With it, the Celeste had won four of the first six world championships—and all four that it entered. But the *Maracanazo*, as the victory over Brazil in 1950 is called, was not supposed to happen. Prior to the tournament Uruguay was seen as a weak team, unlikely to go far. But those who doubted the Celeste knew little of its captain, Obdulio Varela.

Very few are the men who can shatter the dreams of a country in the afternoon and go out drinking with its citizens all night. Obdulio Varela, captain of the 1950 Uruguayan World Cup–winning squad, is one of them. Uruguay's victory over Brazil in the final match of the 1950 tournament left two hundred thousand Brazilians stunned inside the stadium (and many millions more outside) as Varela led his team back from a 0–1 deficit to win 2–1. This was also the last time that Uruguay won the World Cup.

Obdulio Jacinto Muiños Varela was born in 1917 in Paysandú, a small town on the border with Argentina. Varela was born poor but with a natural confidence. He would need it when leading an Uruguayan squad past its prime against a more powerful Brazilian team. Like the famous Nasazzi before him, the narrative of Uruguayan soccer gives Varela a crucial part in the come from behind victory. After Brazil scored the first goal in the 1950 final, instead of allowing play to continue amid the fans' jubilation, Varela took the ball from the net to calm his side. He then complained to the referee about a phantom offside, insisting that a translator be called to help settle the dispute. When satisfied that his protest was heard, he slowly walked the ball back to the center circle. This long pause in play allowed the Uruguayan squad to gather itself. Moreover, the crowd had quieted before the ensuing kickoff, thereby negating any energy that Brazil could have drawn from its fans. This was garra charrúa at its best.

Varela played in the era before players transferred regularly between clubs and overseas. He spent his entire career with three teams, progressing from low-level clubs until he landed at Peñarol, one of Uruguay's two strongest clubs. With Peñarol he won the league championship six times. With the national team Varela played forty-five times over a fifteen-year period, as captain for thirteen of them, winning one World Cup and one South American Championship. Uruguay never lost a World Cup game in which Varela played.

The Uruguayan National Team at the 1954 World Cup. This would be the final World Cup for Obdulio Varela, captain of the 1950 cup-winning team in Brazil. Varela is pictured third from right. © DPA/ZUMAPress.com

an era of expatriate strength followed by the development of the criollo game—were true, then the players from Albion would have been banned from representing their country. They were not.

The Celeste

Much of soccer's power in Uruguayan history rests on the national team's ability to fight on in the face of certain defeat. This is supposedly the legacy of the indigenous Charrúa, who fought fiercely to defend their territory against the Spanish before being massacred in 1831. And it is easy to see Uruguayans as underdogs in every fight, given that the country is so small and its neighbors—Brazil and Argentina—are so large. In the early twentieth century, as soccer became a way to represent the nation, the Uruguayan national team embodied the Charrúa spirit. Fighting against the giants of Europe and South America, tiny Uruguay, with its garra, always showed its ability to compete with its more powerful opponents.

Indeed, Uruguayan soccer received a great deal of impetus from international play. One Uruguayan commentator noted that Uruguayan soccer was "born in international play."[11] From the outset, Uruguayan teams sought to prove themselves against their larger rioplatense neighbors. By 1902, as we have seen earlier, the first of what would become regular matches between Uruguayan and Argentine teams would begin, first as "friendlies" and then as competitive matches, recognized after the fact by FIFA as official competitions. These games exposed the improvisational Uruguayans to the more refined play of Argentine squads, to whom they regularly lost. Losing, however, failed to diminish Uruguayan love for the game or the national team. Throughout the first decade of the century, crowds of between five thousand and ten thousand fans packed into stadiums whenever the national team played.

In creating Uruguay's soccer identity, perhaps no matches mattered more than those against Argentina. In the early twentieth century Uruguay lost much more often than it won. Between 1902 and 1909, teams from the two nations played thirteen times, with Uruguay winning twice, drawing three times, and losing eight times to its rioplatense rival.[12] These matches were of paramount importance, drawing thousands of spectators to cheer on their compatriots. In 1910, however, momentum began to shift. That year Uruguay's record against Argentina was 2-1-1, and it won the Lipton Cup for the first time.

There is another reason why 1910 stands as a defining moment. In years prior the Uruguayan team dressed in a variety of uniforms, most of which derived from Albion's post-1895 uniform—a combination of red and blue stripes. In 1910, however, the team dressed in sky blue, a throwback to Albion's original jersey from 1891. Success in sports often engenders superstition, and so from 1910 on Uruguay dressed in sky blue and would be known as the Celeste. In five matches against Argentina in 1911 Uruguay went 2-1-2; the sky blue seemed to have power. Indeed, the birth of the Celeste in 1910 stands as another creation myth in Uruguayan soccer.

And then came 1912. If the power of the Celeste was born in 1910, it was set in stone by 1912. It has been suggested that just as "Christianity divides the world into two epochs: before Jesus and after Jesus," in Uruguay there is a "before and after 1912."[13] That year the Celeste went undefeated against their archrivals, with three victories and one draw.

After years in the shadow of its neighbor, the Celeste announced itself as a team to be reckoned with. One Argentine commentator noted after a match in September 1912 that "until today no team has played as perfectly or as clearly" as the Uruguayan squad had.[14] The Celeste was now a source of immense pride for the nation.

And the soccer team kept offering more reasons for optimism. In July 1916 Argentina hosted a tournament to celebrate its centennial of independence. Uruguay easily dispatched Brazil and Chile, setting up a title match against Argentina. On July 16, 1916, at the stadium of the Buenos Aires club Gimnasia y Esgrima, Uruguay needed only a tie to be crowned champions while Argentina needed to win. A few minutes after the start of the match pandemonium erupted. Fans began pouring onto the field. Some say that the organizers sold too many tickets, others suggest that fans without tickets rushed the fence. Shortly thereafter smoke filled the air as a part of the stands went up in flames. The match had to be abandoned. The following day at the Racing Club stadium, Uruguay and Argentina played to a 0–0 draw. Uruguay won the tournament, which was retroactively recognized as the first South American Championship. The Celeste would repeat its victory the following year.

Success in soccer merely paralleled a more general awakening throughout the country. José Batlle y Ordóñez's return to power after a four-year interregnum promised to make Uruguay a middle-class nation. Educational reform spread further throughout the country, exports continued their rapid growth, and the modernizing impetus began to bear fruit outside of Montevideo. Communication with the countryside and the extension of railroads and electricity into the interior reflected and generated optimism in the country. In efforts to make Uruguay a symbol of progressivism, Batlle y Ordóñez introduced a bill for an eight-hour workday, which included mandatory leisure time for workers. This could have been used by workers as time to play soccer—which was in fact encouraged by many employers at this point as a way to ensure healthy workers—but was an attempt on the part of the government to spread Uruguay's wealth throughout society.[15] Indeed, by 1915 Uruguay stood alone in Latin America in attempting to provide for all of its citizens. While most nations in the region were

A jubilant crowd in Montevideo greets the Uruguayan team after its fourth-place finish at the 2010 World Cup in South Africa. © DPA/ZUMApress.com

under the sway of liberal ideologies, only in Uruguay did change seem to go beyond economics and rhetoric. The general welfare of Uruguayans, then, appeared to be on the rise, and success in soccer coincided with the country's peace and prosperity. Not only could Uruguay dominate its rival in soccer, it could also boast enviable political stability and economic development.

What role did soccer play in the stability of Uruguay? It is not a stretch to say that soccer helped smooth the transition from the chaos of the late nineteenth century to the stability of the early twentieth. It helped integrate new populations and provided the nation with a national—as opposed to political—rallying point. Tens of thousands of people attended league matches each week, and the nation stood still when the Celeste won the South American Championship in 1916, 1917, and again in 1922, further swelling the tiny nation with pride. Through competition on the soccer field, Uruguay could exorcise demons of Brazilian occupation and Argentine interference. The sport offered a small country an opportunity for regional pride, and Uruguay took the opportunity as far as it could go.

Uruguayan soccer truly brought the country into the sun in 1924, when the Uruguayan soccer federation sent the Celeste to France to play in the Olympics. By that point political conflict was long since contained by elections, wealth was equitably distributed, and Uruguayans of all political, ethnic, and social backgrounds united behind the team. Still, many Uruguayans considered sending the team to Europe to be folly. Europe was still considered to be the pinnacle of both economic and sporting development, and many believed that Uruguay would be embarrassed by the Celeste's showing. How could Uruguay compete with Europe's best? Beating Argentina and Brazil was one thing, but European teams were something else. As a result of this attitude, the level of surprise mounted each day as news of each new Uruguayan victory was tapped back to the country on transoceanic telegraph cables. First the Celeste won nine warm-up matches in Spain. Then, once the Olympics began, the Uruguayans dismantled Yugoslavia 7–0 and defeated the United States 3–0 and France 3–1. In the semifinals Uruguay beat the Netherlands 2–1 and completed its undefeated run through Europe by overcoming Switzerland 3–1 in the gold medal match. Uruguay erupted when news of the gold medal arrived, and tens of thousands crammed the Montevideo waterfront to greet their new national heroes when they arrived home. "You are the fatherland, boys," wrote a journalist for the newspaper *El Día*, "a symbol of that tiny point, almost invisible on the map . . . which is growing, growing, growing."[16]

What had initially been seen by many as a fool's errand to represent South America in Europe ended up galvanizing the country. Uruguayan soccer—criollo soccer—took the world by storm. Not only could Uruguay defeat its neighbors regularly in South American Championships, it could also beat the best teams in the world. The Celeste came home from Paris as Olympic champions. World champions. Uruguay would go on to win the 1928 Olympics, the inaugural 1930 World Cup, and the 1950 World Cup in Brazil. The little nation whose very existence had seemed precarious less than a century earlier was on top of the world.

At the start of the twentieth century Uruguay was a country in flux. Just emerging from the shadows of its larger neighbors, wracked by

Diego Forlán, winner of the Golden Ball for best player in the 2010 World Cup. © Action Images/ZUMApress.com

internal conflicts, and coping with an influx of immigrants, the Uruguayan state had to find outlets for disaffected political enemies and ways to integrate new populations. On the political and economic front, Batlle y Ordóñez sought to unite the country by spreading education, communication, and transportation to the countryside—in effect extending the reach of the state into rural communities. National pride, however, could not rest on government reforms and prosperity alone. In the first decades of the twentieth century—a critical juncture for Uruguayan nationhood—soccer emerged as a powerful source of Uruguayan identity. The way that Uruguayans played the game, and especially the Celeste's ability to defeat Argentina and European soccer powers, bolstered the country's sense of nationalism.

Feeding off of the national pride, journalists and others crafted a narrative of Uruguayan soccer history. In these stories of the country's

Luis Suárez

El Pistolero

The Celeste's fourth-place finish at the 2010 World Cup placed Uruguay back on the world soccer map after forty years lingering in the shadows. Since 1950 the Celeste had finished fourth twice—in 1954 and 1970—and had failed to qualify for the tournament six times. Yet although many were shocked by Uruguay's deep run in South Africa and its gold medal performance at the 2011 Copa América, the Celeste had been steadily improving for some time, finishing in the top four at the South American championship since 1999. Until 2010 the Celeste made up for its lack of flair with plenty of the Uruguayan garra charrúa—heart, guts, and perseverance. The three Diegos—the stylish striker, Diego Forlán; the gritty (some would say dirty) midfielder, Diego Pérez; and the heart-on-his-sleeve central defender, Diego Lugano—all embody elements of Uruguayan soccer. But perhaps no one personifies the combination of Uruguay's traditional garra with a new sense of panache better than Luís Suárez, *el pistolero*.

The fourth of seven children, Suárez was born in Salto, Uruguay, in 1987. His parents divorced when he was nine, after which time his mother raised him. In an interview with Canal+ in 2010, he commented that he did not have an easy childhood; he once could not attend a training clinic for lack of cleats. At age fourteen Suárez began playing for the youth squad of famed Uruguayan squad Nacional, reaching the senior squad at age seventeen. Within a year he moved to play in Holland. By 2007 he was regular for Ajax, becoming captain of the squad shortly thereafter. In 2009–10 he led the Dutch league in scoring and was named player of the year. As often happens in Europe, the most competitive leagues poach the best players from lesser leagues, so in 2010 Suárez moved to Liverpool. There he led the team in scoring in all competitions, even after he missed part of the season due to suspension.

Indeed, Suárez is often a lightning rod for controversy, which some take as a sign of the supposed Uruguayan fighting spirit. Though humble and easygoing off the field, on the field he is a different animal altogether, willing to do anything to win. He has been suspended for headbutting and biting opponents. During the quarterfinal match against Ghana in the 2010 World Cup he cleared a ball off the goal line with his hand, earning a red

Luís Suárez, El Pistolero, celebrates after scoring a goal in the finals of the 2011 Copa América. Uruguay defeated Paraguay 3–0 for its fifteenth South American Championship. © Marcelo Sayao/EFE/ZUMAPress.com

card and a suspension for the semifinal match against Holland. But Suárez is most infamous for actions during a match between Liverpool and Manchester United in October 2011. After the match Patrice Evra, a French international player, accused Suárez of using a racial slur. Found guilty of the offense, Suárez received an eight-game suspension.

But Uruguayans (and Liverpool fans) forgive him because el pistolero shines on the field. Since making his debut for the Celeste in 2007 he has played in seventy-six matches and scored thirty-nine goals. In 2013 he passed Diego Forlán for most goals ever for the Celeste. During the 2010 World Cup Suárez scored the only goal against Mexico and both goals in the round of sixteen matches against South Korea. In the Copa América Suárez scored four goals and was recognized as the player of the tournament.

Uruguayan captain Diego Lugano (*left*) and his teammate Edinson Cavani celebrate after winning the Copa América. © Eva Fisher/DPA/ZUMAPress. com

soccer past, Uruguayan writers argued for two births of the sport—the foreign and the criollo—leading to soccer supremacy. While one part of the narrative is not fully accurate, however, the other is undeniable: the break between the foreign and criollo phase was not as clear as chroniclers make it, but the Celeste proved to be world champions. This sense of pride, however, came not only from winning. Rather, it came from having Uruguay represented on the world stage as equals with Europe, from Uruguay's stepping out of the shadows of its larger neighbors and into the sun. Indeed, Uruguayan soccer has always rested on the Celeste's ability to stand up to its more powerful neighbors, which made the loss at home to Argentina in October 2009 with which this chapter opened that much more painful. To add insult to injury that day, Uruguay had not lost a home match to Argentina in more than thirty years, through the darkest period of Uruguayan soccer.

In 2010–11 Uruguay would get its revenge on Argentina, first in the World Cup and then in the South American Championship, known as the Copa América. A surprising run in the World Cup led by Diego

Forlán and Luis Suárez saw Uruguay finish fourth (the best Latin American finish and Uruguay's best since 1970); according to FIFA, Argentina finished in the shadow of its smaller neighbor, in fifth place. Then, at the 2011 Copa América in Argentina, the two teams squared off for the first time since the qualifier in Montevideo. This time more was on the line, particularly for Argentina. As host of the championship, the Albiceleste was expected to win. An early goal by Uruguay set the dominant Argentines back, but only temporarily. Gonzalo Higuaín leveled the score in the seventeenth minute, before Uruguayan goalie Fernando Muslera effectively closed the goal, turning away shot after close-range shot. The game progressed to penalties. When Carlos Tévez stepped up to shoot Argentina's third penalty, Muslera dove to his right, easily blocking Tévez' attempt. Muslera guessed right on the next two shots as well, the first just sneaking under his body into the net and the second ricocheting off the crossbar, down off his back, and into the goal. Still, Uruguay had not missed. Argentina, playing at home, watched helplessly as Martín Cáceres stepped up to the penalty spot. As his shot rocketed into the back of the net, the Albiceleste knew that they would watch the rest of the tournament. Uruguay would go on to win its fifteenth South American Championship, breaking a tie for the most wins with—of course—Argentina.

2

La Nuestra and Futebol Arte

National Styles?

Sitting in a bar in Buenos Aires during an unseasonably warm week in the fall of 2009, I could not believe my ears. My fellow patrons expressed no small amount of pleasure at the style of play exhibited by the Albiceleste—so called because of their uniform's sky blue and white stripes—even though they had failed to score on numerous chances. The game, a qualifier for the 2010 World Cup in South Africa, was being played more than nine thousand feet above sea level in Quito, Ecuador. In the first half Argentina displayed crisp passing and incisive runs and barely displayed the fatigue associated with games at high altitude. The crowd groaned collectively as star Lionel Messi pushed a shot just wide in the eleventh minute. Ten minutes later Messi's cross barely escaped the head of Carlos Tévez. Then another Argentine attack. Surely this time Tévez would hit the target. No. Marcelo Elizaga, Ecuador's Argentine-born goalie, saved the shot, and Maxi Rodríguez missed the frame on the rebound. But the referee had awarded a penalty kick for Elizaga's rash charge on "el Apache" Tévez. Eyes glued to the television, I could hear the sharp inhale of nearby smokers as they waited for Tévez to take the spot kick. A good choice—Tévez rarely missed them—although a little odd given Messi's place on the squad. As he began his run-up, we all held our breath in a collective vigil, and then exhaled epithets as the keeper slapped away Tévez' weak attempt. Still, everyone in the bar agreed that Argentina was playing its game— *la nuestra*: artistic; crisp, short passes along the ground; caginess in one-on-one situations; and the extra pass that, eventually, would lead to a goal.

It was not to be. In the second half, the altitude began to affect the Albiceleste. Argentine legs seemed to get heavier with each step. In the seventy-second minute, as Argentina attempted to clear their area, the ball fell to Ecuador's Pablo Palacios. One pass later Walter Ayovi's left-footed shot gave Ecuador a 1–0 lead. Again the bar quieted. No one smiled. Eight minutes later tired legs led to poor defending and an open chance for Palacios. Like that, it was 2–0. No one left the bar happy that night, but the group agreed with one old man who said on his way out, "mejor que el otro dia"—better than the other day. He was referring to Argentina's 1–0 win at home against Colombia a few days earlier. Despite the Albiceleste's 1–0 victory, the game had been a sloppy affair. In the first half Colombia squandered two clear chances at goal and Argentina had been lucky to win. I had been at that game, sitting high above the pitch, and I listened to the vitriol of Argentine fans as a faster and more physical Colombian squad outclassed their team. Diego Maradona, the Argentine coach (and perhaps the most famous Argentine player ever), came in for the most criticism. Fans excoriated him for playing with only three defenders, which opened the wings for Colombia's fast midfielders. Most damning, however, fans and commentators alike argued that the team played a disjointed game that bore no resemblance to la nuestra, Argentina's national style.

Winning soccer matches does not suffice for the Argentine and Brazilian national teams. While players and coaches want to play a technically sound game, fans expect beauty, skill, and panache. Like the people with whom I watched the game in downtown Buenos Aires, many say that they would rather see their team lose playing well than

Argentine Mario Kempes (*left*) scores for a 2–1 lead against Holland in the 1978 World Cup final. This Argentine squad was coached by the freethinking César Menotti, who believed that each nation has a distinct style of play. © DPA/ZUMAPress.com

win playing ugly. Qualifying for the World Cup clearly mattered, of course, but it was crucial to do so playing the Argentine style.

The myth of national soccer styles is almost as old as the sport itself. It is central not only to the idea of Latin American soccer but to the sport around the world. Argentina has "la nuestra," Brazil has "futebol arte," and Uruguay has the "garra charrúa," while the Dutch play "total soccer," and the Spanish "*tiki-taka*" made them nearly untouchable from 2006 until 2013. From very early in the game's history in Latin America, commentators and players have argued that people of different ethnic and national heritage play a different form of the game based more or less on national "types." The roots of national styles were often considered innate, encoded in the ethnic, racial, and class composition of players.

In reality, national styles were actually carefully crafted historical creations invented at the precise moment that Latin American countries were grappling with their national, racial, and ethnic identities. For much of the nineteenth century Latin American countries sought to identify with their European heritage and to "whiten" their nations. To do this they encouraged migration from Europe. The creation of national styles represented a subtle split from these ideas about race. These "distinct" ways of playing soccer began as closely linked and grew apart only with the passage of time.

Originally, Argentina and Uruguay were said to play the same way, and when Brazil burst on the international scene, its game was likened to its two southern neighbors. Early descriptions of both Argentina's la nuestra and Brazil's futebol arte paralleled those used to describe Uruguay's play in the 1920s: rapid, full of individual play, spontaneity, and guile. These supposed national styles were compared to Europe's more phlegmatic and tactical approach, which in turn suggested "racial" differences between Europeans and Latin Americans. As Uruguayan, Argentine, and Brazilian club teams began beating clubs composed of British expatriates and their sons, and as the national teams regularly defeated European opposition, soccer became a source of national pride and evidence of Latin American social development. Moreover, it offered Latin Americans an opportunity to break away from the idea that their countries needed to Europeanize and "whiten" to advance.

Intellectuals around Latin America began looking for non-European sources of national identity once the irrational violence of World War I exposed the ideas of European progress and superiority as a myth. The search for alternatives to whitening led ultimately to a valorizing of the difference between Latin America and Europe, a difference most clearly seen in racial terms. Rather than looking outward to Europe, Latin American thinkers argued that their cultures should look inward for strength. Whereas Europe was white, Latin America was not. Ideas such as *indigenismo, negrismo*, and *mestizaje* celebrated the indigenous, African, or mixed-race heritage of Latin American societies and developed into powerful ideologies. In soccer terms, the intermixing of immigrants from around Europe with the Argentine population supposedly gave birth to the criollo style, while the Brazilian game purportedly rested on the mulatto heritage of the nation. In both cases what mattered was that the national style embodied the composition of the nation and that it was able to surpass the supposedly superior European "race."

The birth of the criollo style—sometimes called Argentine, sometimes Uruguayan, and sometimes rioplatense—dates to the moment that poor youth, called *pibes*, began to imitate the elite game that they watched from the sidelines. Innumerable stories from the early twentieth century recount street children joining in this game or that, in Rosario or Buenos Aires or Montevideo, and stunning the proper, straight-laced elite sportsmen with their skill and guile. Indeed, this was a popular trope throughout not only Argentina and Uruguay but around the region. In Paraguay and Chile, Mexico and Brazil, the power of the message was unmistakable: the people, represented by the poor youth, could surpass the elite. More precisely, the criollo style dates to the 1910s and 1920s, amid the first wave of nationalist fervor in twentieth-century Latin America, when sports journalists began to define a style and juxtapose it with play from other countries. By that time Latin American national teams had had ample opportunity to play against each other—the first continental championship occurred in 1916—and also against touring teams from Europe, primarily England. Exposure to other nations' play allowed commentators to begin defining criollo style against European and other Latin American ways of playing the game.

The rhetoric of the Argentine style focused on new immigrants and their role in constructing a new Argentina and a new style of soccer. Millions of Europeans, predominantly from Italy and Spain, migrated to Argentina in the late nineteenth and early twentieth centuries. Making these immigrants Argentine and creating some sense of national unity became a pressing concern for national elites. As the newly minted national pastime, soccer offered one method of inclusion. Much like baseball in the United States, soccer became a way for Italian, Spanish, Portuguese, and German immigrants, who also formed the bulk of Argentina's new working classes, to become a part of the nation. Moreover, the criollo style allowed for poor "Latin" youth to show their superiority over the elite "Anglos" who were seen as controlling the national economy.

The supposed emotion and skill of the Brazilian game, on the other hand, developed from the amalgamation of European rationality and African creativity that reflected the national makeup. Intellectuals

Daniel Passarella is lifted on the shoulders of compatriots after winning the 1978 World Cup finals in Buenos Aires. © DPA/ZUMAPress.com

linked the game to artistry in defining the Brazilian style in the 1930s. In other words, they believed the experience of being Brazilian fostered a tendency to play soccer a certain way. It is, of course, not just Brazilians who believe this. There is a worldwide sense that Brazilian soccer players don't as much dribble the ball as dance with it. This is no accident. The ideology of the beautiful game, or futebol arte, developed at a particular moment and coincided with conscious efforts on the part of the Brazilian state and intellectuals to craft a new vision of the nation.[1] That vision suggested a more inclusive nation that accepted Brazil's racial and ethnic heritage even as it drew pseudoscientific racist ideas. Defining a distinctly Brazilian style meant addressing the massive population of color and attempting to deal with the legacy of slavery, which ended only in 1888. In Brazil, then, the rhetoric of futebol arte had a political and social role: to help incorporate people of African heritage into the nation and include them as citizens.

Rather than innate practices coming from the soil, then, soccer styles in Latin America were journalistic and intellectual descriptions that portrayed aspects of soccer as "national." These descriptions

Diego Armando Maradona

He is the quintessential pibe, and it sometimes feels as though his whole life has been lived like the mythical Argentine la nuestra—one long improvisation on the field. Feline in his ability for self-preservation, self-destruction, and self-reinvention, Diego Armando Maradona has been loved, hated, banned for more than a year after testing positive for cocaine, sent home in disgrace from a World Cup, tattooed with Che Guevara's likeness on his arm, and suspended for offensive language. He has been both the angel and the devil of Argentine soccer and is the only soccer player to be the subject of a documentary by art-film director Emir Kusturica. It is impossible to discuss Argentine soccer without mentioning him: he was the last player cut from the 1978 World Cup–winning squad, he was captain of the 1986 World Cup winners, and he led Boca Juniors, Barcelona, and Napoli to national club honors. Even after his playing days ended, Maradona has remained close to the national consciousness, a sort of talisman of Argentine soccer.

One of eight children, Diego Armando Maradona was born in 1960 and raised in Villa Fiorito, a slum on the outskirts of Buenos Aires. He began playing with the Argentino Juniors youth squad at age ten and at age fifteen debuted with the senior squad. His prolific play quickly caught the interest of other clubs, and he transferred to Boca Juniors after five years. In 1982 he moved to Europe, where he would play for Barcelona, Napoli, and Sevilla,

paralleled national discourses that sought to create national identities and incorporate new sections of the population into the national imaginary. But this is not to say that the idea of style had no power. Rather, because it emerged at a particular historical juncture, style became embedded in the way that Latin Americans think about both their soccer and themselves.

La nuestra?

Lionel Messi is something of a lightning rod in Argentina. Very few dispute his skill: he has tremendous ball control, field vision, and his passes almost always find their desired target. Not without reason, Messi won the FIFA player of the year award four times in a row winning major titles with both Barcelona and Napoli. In seventeen years, Maradona played for Argentina ninety-one times, scoring thirty-four goals. He captained Argentina's squads in winning the World Youth Championship in 1979 and the World Cup in 1986.

Maradona's post-playing life has been fraught with challenges. His weight ballooned, requiring gastric bypass surgery. Cocaine addiction continued to trouble him. Eventually he began a generally unsuccessful stint as a coach in Argentina with both third and first division teams. In twenty-three matches over two years, Maradona won three, drew eight, and lost twelve, which made it all the more surprising when, in November 2008, he was named to coach the Argentine national team. Maradona met much better on-the-field success with the Albiceleste, winning fourteen and losing five. Even when winning, however, he courted disaster. He used a record number of players in qualifying for the 2010 World Cup, which affected team chemistry. Maradona's tactical weaknesses were constantly exposed. He feuded with the national association and with club directors. Finally, after qualifying for South Africa, in a press conference he verbally attacked his critics, earning a three-match suspension from FIFA. After a dismal 4–0 quarterfinal loss to Germany in South Africa, the writing was on the wall. Yet, like the pibe who dribbles around life's obstacles, he survived: in 2011 he was hired to coach the club Al Wasl in Dubai, becoming a special adviser on sports for the nation in 2012.

between 2009 and 2012. He has been nothing short of brilliant for Barcelona, where he plays professionally, scoring an unprecedented seventy-three goals in 2012. Combined with his goals for the national team, Messi scored ninety-one times that year. Yet until Argentina's qualification campaign for the 2014 World Cup in Brazil, his play for the national team often disappointed. Critics accused him of seeming lost on the field with the national team, sinking to the more pedestrian level of his teammates. So used to playing with the world's best on Barça, these critics said, he was unable to adapt. Others suggested that he expected the game to orbit around him. Pelé, the Brazilian great, expressed disappointment at Messi's lack of scoring for Argentina, noting that he "does nothing for his country." And at home Messi was faulted for not "feeling" the Argentine jersey, evidenced—according to his detractors—by his not singing the national anthem before qualifying matches. In short, Messi did not play the way he was expected to. He did not play *la nuestra*, the Argentine style.[2]

Few people in Argentina would deny Lionel Messi's heritage. A pibe from a lower-middle-class family in Rosario, a city 185 miles northwest of Buenos Aires, Messi's mannerisms bespeak his Rosarino upbringing. He is humble, deferential, and often mumbles his way through interviews. Yet he is often accused of being an *extranjero* (foreigner). To outsiders this accusation seems a bit unfair. Although he moved to Barcelona when he was twelve, Messi turned down Spanish citizenship and a spot on Spain's youth national team in 2004 so that he could play for Argentina. But the "extranjero" label has little to do with Messi. Indeed, it extends to all players on the Argentine national team playing overseas. Many believe that Argentines who play professionally in Europe have all lost Argentina's supposedly innate style of play. Seventeen of the squad's twenty-three players for the World Cup in 2010 were based in Europe, and of the six who played professionally in Argentina only three saw significant playing time. Perhaps more concerning for those who believe that sending players overseas weakens la nuestra, in 2010 Argentina exported 2,204 players to Europe.[3] The idea that locally based players perform better than those playing on foreign teams appeals to some because when Argentina last won the World Cup in 1986, the majority of the team played in Argentina. That team, led by Diego Maradona and victorious over archrival England in the quarterfinal match, was said to incarnate the Argentine style. It used trickery and guile, individual brilliance and intuition to win the Cup. This way of playing, the narrative of Argentine soccer suggests, dated almost to the arrival of the sport in Buenos Aires.

Argentina was the first nation in Latin America to play soccer. The first recorded game was in 1867, and the first league formed in 1891. The predecessor of the Argentine Football Federation, which still oversees the sport, formed two years later in 1893. In part, the early beginnings relate to the predominance of British influence in Buenos Aires.

Lionel Messi gestures to the crowd during a World Cup qualifier against Chile in 2012. © Mario Ruiz/EFE/ZUMA-Press.com

British firms owned most industries and banks in the late nineteenth century, and British financial assistance was crucial to the building of national infrastructure and in the development of Buenos Aires into a modern urban center. Argentine elites sent their children to "British" schools such as the Buenos Aires English High School and the Colégio Comercial Anglicano-Argentino in Rosario, where they were inculcated with Anglophilia and an appreciation for physical activity. From these schools soccer grew and spread among the Argentine population.

Early soccer matches pit British against Anglo-Argentine youth in elite Buenos Aires athletic clubs, providing another field for the development of soccer in Argentina. Eventually, working- and middle-class citizens, immigrants, and native sons (and even some native daughters) began to play the game as well, improvising fields where they could and crafting balls out of anything they could find. From the outset these games differed markedly in style from the game taught in elite schools and athletic clubs. The elite played a proper, gentlemanly game that was well organized and well attended. Everyone else, however, played a rougher, more individual and creative game bred in the streets and embodying all that the street implied: ingenuity, practical intelligence, and improvisation. The street game also reputedly involved the addition of "Latin blood," which imparted the passion that the Anglo version supposedly lacked.

At least this is the way the story goes. In reality, however, the historical narrative created around Argentine soccer in the early twentieth century may have had less to do with actual differences in styles of play and more to do with the political and social needs of the nation. As immigration, urbanization, and industrialization changed the fabric of Argentina, the creation of an "Argentine" style began in the early twentieth century as a way to consolidate national identity in the country.

Immigration to Argentina in the late nineteenth and early twentieth century flooded the nation with new residents. Between 1895 and 1914 the Argentine population nearly doubled, with European immigrants accounting for the majority of the growth. In Buenos Aires, the birthplace of Argentine soccer, the influence of immigrants was especially marked: nearly 50 percent of the city's population was foreign-born at the turn of the twentieth century. Indeed, Buenos Aires itself exploded over the last half of the nineteenth century, going from less than one hundred thousand in 1850 to over 1 million by 1910. The immigrants, and particularly their children, rapidly took to soccer. In turn, the sport became a way to incorporate immigrants into the nation. Concurrent with mass migration, Argentina underwent a wave of modernization and industrialization. Meatpacking and textile production helped to expand Argentine industry, which grew at an average of 8 percent per year between 1875–1913, precisely the period that immigration was at its peak.

Immigrants, in fact, formed the base of the industrial labor force in Argentina, and they also made up the basis of neighborhood soccer clubs that proliferated around Buenos Aires. One Argentine historian estimated that five hundred clubs existed in the capital alone in 1914.[4] For nationalist politicians and intellectuals seeking to mobilize the burgeoning working and middle classes, soccer offered a way to define Argentine identity. As early as the 1910s, writers in the area began to craft an image of two essential types: the pibe and the *crack*. As noted earlier, the pibe was a poor boy who taught himself to play the game on the empty fields in the Buenos Aires suburbs. These fields, known as *potreros*, were rarely smooth. Instead, holes, roots, and rocks created an obstacle course for the pibe, who by playing on this uneven ground learned how to retain possession of the ball. When the pibe grew up and began to play organized football for his neighborhood club, he might become a crack: a star player defined by his ability to keep the ball at his feet and to use a series of feints to go through opposing defenses. By the 1920s cracks were the undisputed kings of Argentine soccer.

That the crack first appeared in Argentine soccer commentary in 1913 is likely no coincidence, as historian Robert Di Giano pointed out. Prior to that year, an Anglo-Argentine team called Alumni (which changed its name to Quilmes in 1912) had won the Buenos Aires championship every season. Although composed mostly of Argentine-born players, Alumni is remembered in the narrative of Argentine soccer as a British team due to the ethnic heritage of its players. In 1913, however, a criollo team won the league for the first time, marking a turning point in Argentina's soccer narrative: after that year soccer passed out of its foreign phase to enter the national one. At the same time that soccer became more of a popular sport, the middle and lower classes were developing and finding new voices in the political arena: the 1912

Sáenz-Peña Law broadened the electorate by granting universal male suffrage, effectively breaking the power of the conservative elite and creating a new power dynamic in Argentine politics. As a result there was at once a sense of needing to defend "traditional" soccer on the part of the elite and a growing confidence on the part of the working-class youth that they could succeed at the English sport. The definition of Argentine style and the quintessential Argentine player, in other words, coincided with changes in Argentine society at large.

At first, however, cracks and pibes represented the immaturity and inefficiency of Argentine immigrants and Argentine soccer. When the archetypal figures first appeared in the Argentine press, they were considered lazy and irresponsible. As predominantly lower-class players they threatened the "established order" by challenging the dominance of the Argentine and expatriate elite.[5] Indeed, starting in 1913 a debate commenced about the relative values of the British and criollo "styles" of play. According to some, the criollo element "degenerated the game, bringing it to a very low moral level." The style, mostly played by sons of Italian and Spanish immigrants, reflected the players' social class. While the British and elite game was team-oriented and efficient, forceful and masculine, the criollo game highlighted individual play. The best criollo players acted like prima donnas, "pirouett[ing]," not passing the ball, and "occasionally scoring beautiful goals . . . by their own efforts." Foreign commentators also criticized the Argentine game as "excessively individualistic . . . [with] little style . . . and often inharmonic."[6] In other words, the benefits of the criollo game were hardly embraced by all. Criticisms came from those quarters most concerned about the impact that new immigrants would have on the nation.

By the 1920s, however, that fear was beginning to dissipate. The 1910s began and ended with promise. Although World War I created temporary privation, an economic boom in the immediate postwar years saw the Argentine economy expand at an impressive rate. Coupled with economic optimism, the 1912 expansion of suffrage led in 1916 to the first democratic elections in Argentine history. Workers and the middle-class voters successfully elected Hipólito Yrigoyen, who sought a middle ground between elite demands and those of the people who elected him. Political unrest culminated in the 1919 Tragic Week, but by the end of his term many in Argentina saw the need to find compromise.

In this period of economic and political optimism, when the nation seemed to be coalescing around similar political and economic goals, a positive spin on much of Argentine culture appeared. Historian Oscar Chamosa has shown that a new cultural nationalism developed, which suggested that the true Argentine—the criollo—was spiritually linked to the nation. As a result, national leaders and intellectuals began a renovation of rural folklore.[7] In a similar vein, positive writings about criollo soccer began to appear in the press. Indeed, like the tango, in the 1920s criollo soccer came to be seen as a legitimate representation of the Argentine people.

Much of this linking of soccer and the nation began in the magazine *El Gráfico*. A popular culture magazine founded in 1919, *El Gráfico* became increasingly sports oriented by the middle of the 1920s. In the magazine, according to prominent Argentine anthropologist Eduardo Archetti, authors crafted an image of the criollo style that came in part from the "Latin" traits supposedly carried in the blood of its progenitors. It was a "restless, individualistic" game "based on personal effort, agility, and skill." Since soccer styles were linked to innate traits, this style explicitly excluded players of British descent, even those born in Argentina. Anglo-Argentines played a soccer that was "phlegmatic . . . disciplined, method[ical] . . . collective," and based on "force and physical power." British soccer was "industrially perfect."[8] Innate "moral and physical" traits of the British race made players well suited for playing on a team that ran like a "well adjusted machine with gears." Players with British blood could not move with the flexibility, speed, or elegance of a bullfighter, alluding to Latin flexibility.[9] Since Argentines were Latin, Argentina's soccer had to reflect its heritage.

The Argentine game emerged not only from vague notions of "Latinness," however. In addition to the idea that Latin blood affected playing styles, commentators noted that poverty played a role in forming criollo players. For Borocotó, the pen name for *El Gráfico* journalist Ricardo Lorenzo Rodríguez, the criollo habit of dribbling "revealed the temperament" and background of a player. Dribbling, for example, reflected the nature of rioplatense players. In part, he wrote, this was because Argentine life was "made up of successive dribbling." Argentines dribbled to overcome "poverty with the smiles of eternal optimists" and to get around "loans that persecute us until death." Indeed, most Argentine players learned on the "field of life" instead of on the grounds of an elite athletic club. In the streets of Buenos Aires, the children of immigrants and poor Argentine youth could aspire to greatness and come to represent the country. But that was not the reason that they played the game. Rather, they played with improvised balls and makeshift goals in the streets, in small courtyards, in the paddocks on the city's margins, and in the pampas in order to "forget hunger" and bring joy into their "sad lives." These "shirtless" and "shoeless" players, who were "living incarnation[s]" of Argentine "folklore," took the English game and mixed it with Latin blood and poverty to create the criollo style: part art, part guile, all Argentine.[10] It was also a complete myth.

The invention of the national style struggled with inconsistencies. Although writers sought to highlight Latin racial characteristics and social background of the immigrant players, certain Anglo-Argentine players had criollo traits. Arnold Watson Hutton, the Argentine-born son of the Scottish teacher who had popularized the game at the elite English High School, was a "true juggler," while Harry Hayes was remembered for his rapid, precise passes along the ground—both supposedly traits of the "Latin" game. Others compared the Uruguayan style of play to that of the Scottish while noting that Argentina played more like the English. According to Uruguayan soccer player and league official Carlos Sturzenegger, both Uruguay and Argentina learned their styles from English touring teams. He described the "short, crisp passes" of Southampton Football Club on their club's 1904 tour of the Río de la Plata and noted that this was the base upon which Uruguay developed its game. Uruguayan star fullback Alfredo Foglino backed up this assertion, claiming that Uruguay's success came from "imitat[ing] the game of English teams."[11] The criollo style, in other words, had nothing to do with innate traits.

Diego Maradona, El Pibe, dribbles the ball in a 1986 World Cup match against Bulgaria. © DPA/ZUMAPress.com

Nevertheless, pride in criollo soccer and in the Argentine nation only grew across the 1920s as the country showed itself to be a power on soccer's world stage. At first writers tied the Argentine style to that of Uruguay, particularly after Uruguayan success in the 1924 Paris Olympics. Argentines vicariously enjoyed the power of the Celeste, a sentiment that was only amplified when Argentina defeated the Olympic champions shortly after its return from Paris in 1924. In 1928, when the two nations played each other in the finals of the

Lionel Messi

La Pulga (the flea)

Lionel Messi—like Diego Maradona, his compatriot and the player to whom he is most often compared—is one of the most written about soccer players in the world. However, unlike el Diez, as Maradona is sometimes called, Messi does not engender quite as much controversy. The only mark against Messi that critics can cling to is his long residence outside of Argentina, which, they say, impairs his ability to play *la nuestra*, the Argentine style. The outlines of Messi's tale are well known. A child prodigy from Rosario, by age ten his talents were already drawing comparisons to Maradona's. Argentine clubs expressed interest, but they balked at the price of medical treatments that he required for a growth hormone deficiency. He traveled to Barcelona for a lengthy trial with the club and eventually signed with the Catalan giant. He has played for Barcelona ever since.

Messi's rise has been meteoric. Since joining the Blaugrana senior squad in 2004, Messi scored 327 goals in 395 games between 2004 and 2013. He has led the team in scoring since 2008 and in the 2011–12 campaign scored 50 goals in league play and over 70 goals overall, both records for the Spanish league. He won four consecutive FIFA Ballon d'Or awards for player of the year and was a favorite to win a fifth in 2013 but lost out in the voting to Cristiano Ronaldo. With Barcelona Messi has won almost every championship imaginable: the Spanish League, the King's Cup, the Spanish Supercup, UEFA Champions League, UEFA Super Cup, and the FIFA Club World Cup.

Amsterdam Olympics, the Argentine game gained even further adherents at home. "The race," wrote *El Gráfico*, linking Argentina and Uruguay, "is one." The two countries "showed that the soccer of the Río de la Plata is the best in the world . . . in the tango and domination of the ball, Uruguayans and Argentines have no rivals." The criollo game, based on ideas of race that linked nation and blood with ethnicity and phenotype, allowed the Argentine magazine to claim a certain pride in Uruguayan victories. Moreover, Argentina took pride in the Celeste's success in Europe because Argentina regularly beat the world

Lionel Messi is known for many things, not just his scoring touch. He has legendary ball control and is able to steam through or around challenges at speed with the ball seemingly glued to his feet. His field vision makes him especially dangerous as a distributor, and he tends to give his passes just the right weight. The only thing that he cannot do—or that he has not done yet—is deliver the World Cup trophy to Argentina. Indeed, for all of his magisterial play with Barcelona, Messi has come under intense criticism in Argentina. The most prolific goal scorer in the world until 2012, with a seemingly otherworldly touch on the ball, Messi returned to earth when he played for the national team. At the senior level with the Albiceleste, by June 2013 he had scored "only" thirty-five goals.

But he has not led the team to the promised land. Argentina lost in the finals of the 2007 Copa América and in the quarterfinals in both the 2010 World Cup and the 2011 Copa América. In the last two tournaments Messi was held scoreless, leading to increased criticism of *la pulga*. Some commentators have suggested that living in Spain has sapped him of the criollo grit necessary for Argentine success. Then in 2012 Messi went on a tear with the national team, scoring six goals in World Cup qualifying and using his playmaking ability to lead the Albiceleste to the top of the qualification table. His run of form with the national team continued into 2013. Finally, many thought, Messi was bringing the improvisational flair that he always showed with Barcelona—the play of the quintessential Argentine pibe— to the national team.

champions. Between 1902 and 1930 the two nations played each other an astounding ninety-eight times, with honors evenly split: Argentina won thirty-eight and lost thirty-five, and twenty-five matches ended in draws.[12] As the stakes rose, however, the Argentine press began to differentiate between the two rioplatense powerhouses, and the good feelings of 1928 dissipated by the end of the first World Cup in 1930. There Argentina lost to Uruguay in the finals. And although Argentine pibes and Uruguayan pibes—criollo soccer—were the best in the world, Argentina did not want to play second fiddle to Uruguay.

Unraveling the Myth

Diego Maradona is the quintessential pibe. Raised in a glorified shantytown in Buenos Aires, he became an international soccer sensation before age seventeen. At eighteen he was the last person left off of the 1978 team that won the World Cup at home, and at twenty-six he captained the victorious 1986 squad. Maradona has lived his life out loud. Well-publicized drug addictions, suspension for a positive test during the 1994 World Cup, and struggles with obesity have done little to change people's opinions about him: they either love him or hate him.

He was also, in a single game, author of both the most infamous and one of the most famous goals in World Cup history. The first, early in the second half against archrival England, is known as the "hand of God" goal. Maradona leapt into the air to meet a cross, bringing his hand above his head to strike the ball into the net. Unseen by the officials, the goal stood despite the vigorous protests of the England team. For many, this represented soccer devoid of style and Argentine beauty. Unfortunately, the first goal tends to overshadow his next, scored only three minutes later. For this, Maradona used all the improvisation and guile of the supposed criollo style. Receiving a pass at midfield, Maradona wiggled his way out from between two England players. He then dribbled the ball down the right side of the field, feinting his way past four more English defenders on his way toward England's eighteen-yard box. Once there he made one more move to leave goalkeeper Peter Shilton on the ground and calmly placed the ball into the net. In the space of three minutes, Maradona exposed the Argentine style and the desire to win with style as a myth; Argentines just wanted to win.

Indeed, we only need to look at the contrasts between Argentina's 1978 and 1986 world championship teams to question the nature of a "national style." In 1978 César "el Flaco" Menotti's team won at home playing an "Argentine" style based on spectacular team play. The victory was seen as the triumph of the Argentine game over the pinnacle of European tactical acumen: the Dutch machine. Very precise and well trained, the Dutch game was based on the idea that any player

Diego Maradona (*front, center*) celebrates winning the World Cup with his teammates. © DPA/ZUMAPress.com

could play any position, throwing opposing defenses into disarray. The Argentine style, according to Menotti, was the "honest" way that Argentines played, with beauty and individual flair. Yet eight years later, with Diego Maradona's most controversial and the most spectacular of World Cup goals, Argentina won using—according to critics—Carlos Bilardo's disciplined and organized tactics. Was one less "Argentine" than the other? Hardly. Did Argentines complain that Bilardo's team played an ugly game? No, because they won the World Cup. Style comes not from bloodlines or connection to the soil but from mimicry of idols, practice, and tactical choices. It is only the constructed myth that surrounds a team that clouds our ability to sense the similarities between "national styles." Nevertheless, the idea of style still has a great deal of power, and losses are often blamed on the failure of coaches and players to play *la nuestra*.

Futebol arte?

To say that former Brazil international player and coach Carlos Caetano Bledorn Verri, better known as "Dunga," is unpopular would be an understatement. An excellent defensive midfielder known for his skilled tackling and conservative play, Dunga captained both the 1994 World Cup winning team and the 1998 runners-up. He then went on to coach the *Canarinha* from 2006 to 2010. For most Brazilians, the "era Dunga," as it is known, could not have ended soon enough. Although the team had exceptional success—winning the Copa América, the Confederations Cup and compiling a 40-6-11 record—his time as coach is remembered as a failure. Perhaps if he had coached a more free-flowing brand of the game he would still be coach today. Instead, Dunga met near-universal scorn in Brazil for the team's perceived lack of offensive panache. *Futebol força*, as the more closed, defensive style initiated in the 1970s and favored by Dunga is called, preferred results over flourish and seemed at odds with the free-flowing samba-style play of Brazilian myth.

Brazil's concept of a national playing style was introduced as early as 1919 and became popularized in the 1930s. But the hallmarks of Brazilian futebol—emphasis on individual brilliance and flamboyant play—caused considerable debate for two decades after. Much as the narrative of the criollo style in Argentina only became dominant in the 1920s, Brazilians debated the merits of futebol arte between Brazil's third-place World Cup finish in 1938 and its victory in 1958. Some commentators, like journalist Mario Rodrigues Filho and anthropologist Gilberto Freyre, thought the style reflected the positive effects of racial diversity in the nation. Others linked Brazilian style to the genetic decomposition of the country. For these commentators, the invention and improvisation that defined Brazilian soccer represented a failure of the nation to become modern and move beyond the limitations of its race. When Brazil won the 1958 World Cup in Sweden, however, futebol arte became the national badge of honor that it remains today.

Brazilian captain Dunga celebrates winning the World Cup with teammates. A young Ronaldo Lima is to Dunga's left. © DPA/ZUMAPress.com

Soccer's arrival in Brazil bears striking similarities to the sport's arrival in the rest of the region, coming in the late nineteenth century as the country underwent massive social and demographic changes. Along with the end of slavery in 1888, Brazil transitioned from a monarchy to a Republic in 1889 and experienced massive flows of investment, people, and ideas from Europe in the space of twenty years. Brazil, like other Latin American countries, experienced rapid population growth as a result of immigration, and cities burgeoned. With these currents came soccer. No one knows precisely when or where the first game was played in Brazil. Passing British sailors may have played it in the 1860s. Or it may have been played in Rio in 1878, or by the students of the Colégio São Luís de Itu in São Paulo, or by British railroad workers in 1875 in Paissandu, a section of Rio de Janeiro.

While there is no agreement on the first game, most people concur that an Anglo-Brazilian named Charles Miller did the most to promote the game when he returned to Brazil from England in 1894. Miller was born to a Scottish father and an Anglo-Brazilian mother whose family had been in Brazil for three generations. Although often called British, Miller likely spoke Portuguese before English: his mother spoke more comfortably in Portuguese, and the young Miller had Brazilian nurses and maids. After ten years at school in England, he returned to Brazil at age twenty, bringing with him a ball, a rulebook, a love for the game, and a desire to teach it to his elite friends. Shortly after his return, he formed a soccer team for the São Paulo Athletic Club, composed mostly of Anglo-Brazilians and British expatriates. Soon clubs began appearing all over São Paulo, supported by companies and neighborhoods. Over the course of two decades the sport diffused outward and downward: first to elite athletic clubs in São Paulo and Rio de Janeiro, supplanting rowing as the most popular elite sport, and then to the popular classes by way of neighborhood- or work-based teams.

Most histories of the game in Latin America argue that the sport had two births: the foreign and the national. The former marked the era of foreign dominance that began when soccer arrived; the latter, when "local" teams won the championship for the first time, representing both an assertion of "national" supremacy in the game and the origins of supposedly national styles. In Brazil a third birth story exists: when Afro-Brazilians entered the field in large numbers. According to Mario Filho, in his classic *O negro no futebol Brasileiro* (*Blacks in Brazilian Soccer*, 1947), this occurred when the game professionalized in 1933, but players of African descent had played for big clubs before. Joaquim Prado, for instance, briefly played for Fluminense. Arthur Friedenreich—son of a German immigrant and his Afro-Brazilian wife—became a star in the São Paulo league and the Brazilian national team and helped the team win the South American Championship in 1919 and 1922. By the 1938 World Cup, the star of Brazil and the tournament was a mixed-race player named Leônidas da Silva, known as the "Black Diamond." Leônidas came to represent not only the national soccer team but the nation as well. The leading scorer of the 1938 World Cup, he played with both speed and grace. Able to use his ball skills to dribble around opposing defenders, he was described as agile, musical, and above all exceptional.

It is no accident that Leônidas became a symbol of Brazil when he did. Beginning with the Revolution of 1930 and the rise of Getúlio

Vargas as president, the Brazilian state began searching for new symbols of the nation. Vargas, a populist who veered between Fascism and a leftist politics, ended a half-century of chaotic politics that had marked the period since the end of slavery and the birth of the Republic. He centralized the state by doing away with an informal agreement through which power alternated between north and south, and he sought to find popular avenues of "Brazilian-ness." He and other nationalist thinkers began to highlight homegrown expressions that set Brazil apart from other countries. So, for example, the Afro-Brazilian martial art capoeira went from being vilified and linked to supposed Afro-Brazilian criminality to being celebrated as an expression of a distinct Brazilian identity. Samba went from being the dance of poor and black Brazilians to official recognition as a national art. And soccer, already the king of sports in Brazil, received increased visibility as the idea of a national style was attached to the game.

Despite its popularity, soccer's development as the national sport had been stymied because of politics and interstate rivalries. Indeed, until the late 1930s soccer politics were as fractious as national politics. Championships were statewide rather than nationwide, and regionalism in both soccer and politics exacerbated interstate tensions. This phenomenon was visible most notably in the rivalry between São Paulo and Rio de Janeiro, which impeded the development of soccer on a national level. During the 1930 World Cup, for example, an Argentine walking down a crowded São Paulo street mistakenly thought that raucous crowds were cheering a Brazilian victory. No, he was corrected, the national team had lost and the crowd was celebrating: that year all but one member of the national team played in Rio de Janeiro—the Paulista league had refused to send their players.[13] In 1934 debates over the nascent professional leagues again kept many of Brazil's top players from being eligible to play, and the team lost in the first round of the World Cup. Things were different in 1938, however. Success that year altered the discussion about soccer in Brazil and marked the moment when the sport became more national.

The 1938 World Cup in France was a watershed for Brazilian soccer. Although Brazil had defeated touring European teams on Brazilian soil before, this was the first time that a Brazilian team won a game outside of the continent in a major tournament. Having finished second in the 1937 South American Championship, in 1938 the Brazilian team galvanized the country with the help of the Vargas government's publicity and radio and newspaper coverage. Trumpeted as a unifying force that would demonstrate Brazil's rise toward becoming a modern country, the team's third-place showing in 1938 World Cup was received across the nation with joy. Most, including the foreign press, agreed that Brazil would have made it to the finals if the leading scorer in the tournament, Leônidas da Silva, had not been kept out of the lineup for the semifinal clash against Italy.

Brazilian and foreign commentators noted that Brazil not only played well but also played a unique brand of soccer never seen before on the fields of Europe. It was, they said, a distinctly Brazilian style based largely on the play of Brazilians of African descent. According to one of Brazil's most important intellectuals of the twentieth century, Gilberto Freyre, the team played a mulatto football. "Brazilians," Freyre suggested, played soccer "as if it were a dance." This tendency, he continued, "probably" resulted from the "African blood" coursing through many Brazilian veins, which "tend[ed] to reduce everything to dance." According to academics Cesar Gordon and Ronaldo Helal, this ideology of Brazilian futebol developed as a part of the nationalizing efforts of the Vargas regime. During this era, they argue, words like "cunning, art, musicality, *ginga* (swing), and spontaneity" became attached to the Brazilian game as the foundation of an inherent national style.[14]

Freyre's analysis of the Brazilian style used the same logic as his history of Brazilian race relations, which continues to influence how people see race in the country. Freyre popularized the idea of Brazil as a racial democracy in his magnum opus, *The Masters and the Slaves*. All Brazilians, according to Freyre, carried blackness within them due to the social relations that developed under slavery. In an oft-quoted passage, Freyre stated that Brazilians' "affections . . . excessive mimicry . . . music . . . gait . . . speech . . . everything that is a sincere expression of our lives" came from "the female slave or 'mammy' who rocked us to sleep, who suckled us," or the "mulatto girl who . . . initiated us into physical love and, to the creaking of a cotton cot, gave us our first complete sensation of being a man." Because of these relations, he argued,

Brazil could not be a racist nation. Regardless of the paternalism and sexism in the comment, Freyre's concept was initially hailed as progressive, even radical, because it integrated Afro-Brazilians into the national narrative. But over time his mythical racial democracy was exposed as little more than a nationalist dream. Indeed, the veneer of progressivism in his attitudes peeled away to reveal essentially racialized ideas: blacks added the "music," "mimicry," and "gait" to Brazil while whites contributed their intellect and rationality.[15]

Thus, Freyre's definition of the Brazilian style, which would eventually underpin the dominant narrative of Brazilian soccer, linked sport and race. But the benefit of African blood was hardly universally accepted in 1930s and 1940s Brazil. Indeed, dominant ideologies about race had suggested precisely the opposite since Brazilian independence, arguing that blackness portended poorly for the future of the nation. The prominence of white supremacist ideology throughout Brazilian history crystallized in the late nineteenth century. Throughout Latin America social Darwinism and positivist philosophies held that societies functioned like biological organisms. From these ideas it followed that societies evolved from less developed to more developed, from less complex to more complex. Moreover, these attitudes combined with a racial ideology of the day that tied phenotype to social and cultural development, and that ascribed intellectual and emotional traits to each race. According to these ideas Europeans represented rationality, intellect, and potential for advancement, while nonwhite peoples impeded national development in different ways.

Adherents to these ideologies believed that Brazil could become a modern, developed nation only if it could rid itself of its internal racial impediments. Primary among the roadblocks to Brazilian evolution, according to national thinkers in the late nineteenth century, was its black and mixed-race population. Black, indigenous, and mixed-race Brazilians supposedly carried too many of the perceived negative traits of their ancestors and as such were considered inferior in a number of ways. They were, critics argued, lazy, irrational, passionate, impulsive, unintelligent, and backward. And, for those concerned about Brazil's racial heritage, overcoming these traits would be difficult, especially since according to the 1872 census more than 50 percent of the population was of African descent. So Brazilian intellectuals and national leaders sought to whiten the population through the importation of European immigrants in order to rid the nation of the "mark of Cain."

How did these racialized ideas translate into ideologies of soccer? On one hand, European players were considered rational and tactical, and much of European success was deemed based on training and practice rather than innate skill. Here was European civilization in soccer terms: calculated and ordered. Yet the rationality of European players could also be their downfall, a box outside of which they could not play. For the Brazilian journalist Tómas Mazzoni, writing in 1938, Europeans were trapped by tactics and overthought the game. European players were "intoxicated with theories" and "mechanized" by their coaches and the strategies that they learned. By contrast, Latin Americans, and Brazilians more specifically, benefited from "improvisation." Brazilian soccer at its best was "spontaneous," "elegant," and "inspired." While Mazzoni's language was not inherently racialized, others were quite clear about the racial character of Brazilian soccer. Gilberto Freyre, writing for the *Correio da Manha* in June 1938, proudly highlighted the "courage" of Brazil to send a "clearly Afro-Brazilian team" to the World Cup. The "mulattoism" of Brazilian soccer came down to "a set of characteristics, such as surprise, craftiness, shrewdness . . . which is related to dance, to capoeira."[16] Because of Brazil's success in 1938, by the end of the World Cup the Brazilian style had been inextricably linked to race.

To defeat Europeans at "their" game, Brazil developed an antirational style based on intuition, trickery, and spectacle—all traits that supposedly came from Brazil's African and mixed-race heritage. Nevertheless, Brazilian soccer nationalists still highlighted European rationality, noting how the sport tamed many of society's excesses. Soccer suppressed Brazilians' pernicious influences, channeling them into a positive creative force. Brazilian society, in Freyre's words, was dominated by its "primitive elements" that would have "likely taken on violent forms of expression" had it not been for the rationalizing influence of soccer. Like the mixed-race nature of the nation itself, Brazilian soccer benefited from the antimodern, irrational nature of Africans combined with European rationality and civilizing influence.[17]

While few today take Freyre's ideas about racial democracy seriously, his influence can still be seen in discussions of Brazilian soccer. By linking the style of Brazilian soccer to genetic traits, Freyre and Mario Filho took learned skills such as ball control, pace, and a particular type of passing and made them seem innate. To be Brazilian meant to have a certain racial mixture that brought with it not only a national character but also a national way of playing soccer. Thus, Brazilian player Robson de Souza—Robinho—could say without a trace of irony that "all Brazilians" know how "to play football," even if not all have the opportunity to take advantage of that knowledge. More logical reasons for Brazilian style to have developed a certain way—lack of coaching, scant access to field space leading to a more improvisational appearance and more "raw talent"—were ignored in favor of racial explanations.[18]

But these definitions of Brazilian style did not reject racialized thinking or racist stereotypes. Instead they just viewed African contributions to Brazilian soccer as beneficial. That is, rather than interpreting the perceived African predilection for play and spontaneity as a negative, Brazilian intellectuals began to see them as positive attributes that contributed to Brazil's superiority. Nevertheless, they were still stereotypes. By the same token, European rationality became a weakness; without innate skill, European players were, in the words of Tómas Mazzoni, little more than "robots on the field."[19] However, if success in 1938 helped turn blackness from a national stain to a mark of pride, failure in the 1950 World Cup would show how little racial attitudes had actually changed. Once again racialized traits would be used to show how black players and the African influence on Brazilian soccer was the country's downfall.

The Maracanazo, 1950

Nineteen fifty was destined to be the year that Brazil won the World Cup for the first time. Instead, that year marked Brazil's most devastating

Edson Arantes do Nascimento

Pelé

If Leônidas da Silva first showed the supposed traits of futebol arte to the world, then Pelé and Garrincha perfected them. By the age of fifteen Pelé debuted on the São Paulo club Santos' senior squad, and by seventeen he was a worldwide sensation. Skilled with both feet, in the air, and with an infectious smile, Pelé has been an icon of world soccer since he set foot on the field in Sweden in 1958. Then a seventeen-year-old prodigy, he would go on to play in three more World Cups, winning in 1962 and 1970 (although in 1962 an injury kept him out of most of the tournament).

Born to an oft-injured soccer player in extreme poverty in Três Corações, Pelé displayed a precociousness with the ball from an early age. While his mother did not want him to play soccer, fearing that he would end up injured like his father, he eventually had his way and made it onto Bauru's youth team at age fourteen. Signed by Santos at fifteen, in 1956, Pelé would play with the São Paulo giant until 1974, though not wholly by choice: a 1962 law declared him a national treasure and banned his transfer outside of Brazil.

When he finally left Santos at age thirty-five, he spent three years with the New York Cosmos of the North American Soccer League. He is the leading goal scorer of all time, with nearly 1,300 goals—though many of these were scored in exhibition matches—and trails only Mia Hamm in international goals, having scored 77 as a member of the Verde-Amarela. In international play after the 1958 World Cup, teams often resorted to physical play

defeat, the blame for which was placed squarely at the feet of Brazil's style and supposed racial inferiority. In hosting the first World Cup since 1938, Brazilian leaders sought to highlight both the country's soccer prowess and the development of a new, modern Brazil. The centerpiece of the tournament was the Maracaná Stadium, designed to hold two hundred thousand people. Though not actually finished in time for the final match, it still hosted the final, which should have been the crowning glory of the tournament both for the country and the soccer team.

and hard fouls to keep him off the ball. As a result, he missed much of the 1962 World Cup to injury, and continued rough play against him in 1966 caused Pelé to retire—albeit temporarily—from international play. His return to the national team set-up in 1970 inspired Brazil to their third Cup win and displayed not only his personal dominance of the game but Brazil's as well.

But the 1970 World Cup victory exposed another side to Pelé: his naivete. Upon his return from Mexico, Pelé—and the entire team—was feted by the Brazilian military government and used as propaganda by the regime. In fact, Pelé played into the military's hands twice, once in 1972 by suggesting that Brazilians were not ready for democracy, and again in 1979 when he suggested that soccer was a way to make people happy in the face of their hardships. Given Pelé's association with futebol arte, there was some irony to his relationship with the military: the junta government actively sought to take the "arte" out of Brazilian soccer and replace it with futebol força.

Pelé had as active a life off the field as on it. He lent his name to numerous business ventures (some of which have failed miserably) and remained linked to soccer, working as a scout and acting as an ambassador for FIFA. Nevertheless, Pelé managed to remain controversial. In 2012, for example, he argued that racism was not a problem in soccer, a comment that drew criticism from around the soccer world. Regardless of his political missteps, however, Pelé remains the most well-known soccer player in the world, the very definition of "futebol arte."

Going into the final match, Brazil was nearly assured of victory because of the unique format designed for the 1950 World Cup. For the first and only time, there was no knockout phase to decide the winner. Instead, after the group stage the top four teams played a round robin, with each team playing each other once. The team with the most points at the end of the championship round would be the world champion. And entering the final match against Uruguay, Brazil needed only a tie to clinch the Jules Rimet Trophy. But someone forgot to give Uruguay the script.

Garrincha

The Mr. Hyde to Pelé's Dr. Jekyll was Manuel Francisco dos Santos, more commonly called Mané Garrincha or Garrincha (a Portuguese word for "wren"). He played a crucial a role in Brazil's successes in 1958 and 1962 that cemented futebol arte as *the* Brazilian style.

Garrincha was born in 1933 in Pau Grande, a small town in Rio de Janeiro state. One of his legs was shorter than the other and bowed outward, which some say contributed to his supernatural dribbling ability. Videos of Garrincha show him dribbling past opponents and then waiting for them to catch up, so that he could dribble past them again.

For most of his professional career Garrincha played for the Rio club Botafogo, with which he signed when he was eighteen. In his career at Botafogo, according to his official club biography, Garrincha played in over 600 matches, scored 243 goals, and had countless assists. His teams won the Brazilian Championship, the Rio-São Paulo Tournament, and the State Championship, among others. He left the Rio club after injuries and alcohol had taken their toll and played out his career with a series of other teams, including Flamengo and Corinthians.

Impressive as his professional career was, Garrincha truly shone with Brazil. He played a key role in the 1958 team that won the World Cup for the first time. In 1962 Garrincha single-handedly led Brazil to its second World Cup title after Pelé was injured in the second game. In the tournament Garrincha scored four goals: two in the quarterfinals against England and two more in the semifinal match with Chile. More importantly, he directed play on the field, opening up space for his teammates with his dribbling skills. He received the Golden Boot and was named Player of the Tournament. In twelve years he played at least fifty matches with the Verde-Amarela, losing only once and never when teamed alongside Pelé.

Considered by many to be Brazil's second-best player ever, Garrincha is known as the joy of the people. Unlike his internationally better-known peers, Garrincha remained firmly attached to his hometown and never considered himself a star. Indeed, a part of people's attachment to him was his fallibility. A womanizer and an alcoholic, his lifestyle contributed to the brevity of his international career and ultimately to his death in 1983 at age forty-nine. Tens of thousands lined the streets to watch his funeral procession in a final honor to a man who epitomized the Brazilian style.

The story of Brazil's defeat in the final of the 1950 World Cup, known as the Maracanazo, tends to focus on three key points in the game: the party atmosphere in the streets prior to the match, with Brazilians supremely confident of their victory; Brazil's goal, which sent the crowd into a frenzy; and the final twenty-five minutes, during which Uruguay tied the game and then took the lead. The second Uruguayan goal, with eleven minutes left, is said to have silenced everyone in attendance. What is left out of the story is the fact that, by most accounts, Uruguay dominated play for much of the match and refused to back down against a supposedly stronger Brazilian squad. Ignoring this final point placed undue blame for Brazil's loss on the shoulders of two players rather than on the whole team and called into question the very essence of the Brazilian style.

The failure of Brazil to win the World Cup at home caused a major reassessment not only of Brazilian soccer but also of Brazilian society. By 1950 soccer had become one of the principal ways for Brazil to express its nationality with confidence. For many, international respect on the soccer field was an indicator of Brazilian social advancement. As a result, the loss in 1950 indicated that Brazil still lagged behind other countries in terms of national development. That the Brazilian team had been so close to victory only made the sting of the Maracanazo worse and prompted a national soul-searching. Something had let the Brazilian team and Brazilians themselves down at their moment of victory.

Almost instantly the discourse on race switched again. The spontaneous love of the game, the trickery and cunning of Brazilian players—those traits seen as deriving from Brazil's African past and celebrated as athletic assets a decade earlier—once again became hallmarks of Brazil's failure. Brazilians of color on the 1950 team were shunned. Most blamed the goalkeeper, Afro-Brazilian Moacir Barbosa, for the loss. Fans and commentators suggested he had misplayed the fateful shot in the seventy-ninth minute that sealed Brazil's loss. Barbosa was ostracized. Although he played professionally for another twelve years, he had played his last game with the national team. He would also be barred from commentating on Brazil national team matches and from national team practices for the rest of his life. João Ferreira, better known as Bigode, also suffered from the loss in 1950. Also a Brazilian of African descent, Bigode had the primary duty of marking Uruguayan winger Alcides Ghiggia during the final. Twice Ghiggia passed him easily to the outside, the first time slotting a pass to Juan Schiaffino for the tying goal and the second time dribbling into the eighteen-yard box and scoring himself. Accused of being too easily intimidated—an accusation that extended to all black Brazilians—Bigode too would never play in a Brazilian uniform again. With the loss in 1950, then, the African base of Brazil's style became the subject of intense debate.

More than affecting the lives of individual players, however, 1950 marked a change in attitude toward soccer in Brazil. According to historian José Leite Lopes, the "supposed inferiority of the Brazilian people" became the official answer for the loss. A completely revamped team cruised through group play in Switzerland in 1954 only to be defeated by Hungary in the quarterfinals. Brazilians again chalked up their loss to the "mongrel" nature of their nation. For José Lyra Filho, the head of the Brazilian delegation to the 1954 World Cup, failure resulted from the "state of the Brazilian people." He compared the "physiognomy" of the "mostly . . . black and mulatto" national team unfavorably to teams from largely "white" nations. According to journalist Manuel Bandeira, it was not only Brazilians who thought of their black players as responsible for their failure. Bandeira recalled an English commentator who had called the 1954 team a "mob of hysterical negroids."[20] From being the pride of Brazilian soccer in 1938, black Brazilians had become pariahs. In 1958 they would become heroes again.

Redemption, 1958

The year 1958 marked the coming-out party for futebol arte for soccer fans around the world. The Brazilian team, captained by Bellini but known as the team of Pelé and Garrincha, Didi and Nilton Santos, emerged from Sweden with the Jules Rimet Trophy. It played with apparent abandon and a free-flowing style that looked effortless. Yet, prior to the team's departure for Europe, Brazilians openly doubted their chances after having failed in 1950 and 1954 with teams that, on paper, were among the best in the world. In the end these earlier squads reinforced the idea, current among some intellectuals, that Brazil's "racial cocktail" made players crumble in the face of pressure. João Saldanha, journalist and coach of the national team in 1970, argued that as preparation for 1958 began, "conservatism persisted" as national team selectors sought to choose the "whitest team possible." In fact, the 1958 squad contained more Brazilians of African descent than any team preceding it, even if there was debate among the coaching staff about whether these players had the maturity to play in the high-pressure environment of the World Cup.[21]

The failures of 1950 and 1954 convinced Brazil's soccer establishment to prepare for the 1958 World Cup as no team in history had. No longer could soccer be just a game, nor could the national team rely solely on bringing the best players together and expect victory. Instead the Brazilian soccer federation began to plan every detail of the team in advance using the latest scientific knowledge to prepare the team better. The combination of science and skill made the Brazilian team unstoppable.

One year prior to the 1958 World Cup, the Brazilian Confederation of Sports sent a team representative to Sweden to scout the best hotels for training purposes. They asked the team hotel in Sweden to replace the women on its staff with men for the duration of Brazil's stay because they wanted as few "distractions" as possible. Indeed, the discipline imposed by the coaching staff marked this Brazilian team as different: a dress code and regulations about shaving and smoking suggested that this team wanted to put forward a professional air. The federation had sent a scout to all of the European World Cup qualifying matches to get advance information on potential opponents and then attended training sessions and matches of the three teams that Brazil would face in the first round. Three separate plane reservations were made so they would not have to scramble for flights home in case Brazil made it to the finals. Brazil employed a staff dietician and dentist, which was the first time this had been done in the world of sports. Trainers maintained meticulous records on all players' training regimens. A team psychologist performed tests on all of the players to gauge their ability to deal with stress although, fortunately for Brazil,

The Brazilian team that defined *futebol arte* poses with the Jules Rimet Trophy after defeating Sweden in the 1958 World Cup finals. Garrincha is in the front row to the left. Pelé is in the middle of the front row. Brazil never lost a game in which the two played together. © DPA/ZUMAPress.com

the coaches chose to ignore his advice (his tests suggested that neither Garrincha nor Pelé would perform well). In other words, this was hardly a squad based solely on exuberance or passion. The players were drilled and practiced, technically skilled, in peak physical shape, and ready to play. Moreover, the Brazilian team employed a relatively new 4-2-4 scheme to give more flexibility to the team. Perhaps Brazil was not a "machine," but neither was it focused solely around individual skills.

While Brazil's futebol arte got credit for the win, it was all of the advance planning, training, and tactical work put in by coaches and players that made the victory look effortless. The Brazilian team, especially once the coaching staff inserted Garrincha and Pelé in the third game, seemed graced with players whose skills far outmatched those of their rivals. And the victory solidified the idea that the wide-open, free-flowing style appeared based on individual prowess known as futebol arte was *the* Brazilian style. But what if the team had lost in the finals? What if Brazil had finished second to Sweden, or lost in the semifinals to the Just Fontaine–led French team? Would the loss have prompted soul-searching on the part of the Brazilian soccer federation and recognition of the need to alter the way that the team played? Perhaps a reduction in the number of Afro-Brazilians on the team? This had, after all, been the response to the Maracanazo. Would a loss in 1958 have occasioned the same type of response?

The answer, of course, is that we will never know. Having secured the World Cup in 1958, Brazil repeated the feat with a Garrincha-led team in 1962 (Pelé was injured in the second match) and again in 1970. Most commentators only discussed the racial composition of the Brazilian team to note how much black Brazilians had brought to the game. João Saldanha attributed a large measure of the team's success in a thinly veiled euphemism to "the varied ethnic composition" of the team.[22] By 1970, then, the narrative first suggested in the 1930s and 1940s by Gilberto Freyre and Mario Filho had become *the* story of Brazilian soccer. Forgetting the meticulous preparation and planning that made the squad so successful, the narrative suggested that in order to play the Brazilian way, teams needed to be open and attacking, displaying the supposed racial characteristics of the nation.

The promotion of one particular style of play and one particular narrative of style over another was developed at a particular moment and coincided with conscious efforts on the part of the Brazilian state and intellectuals to craft a new vision of the nation. That vision was more inclusive and attempted to reconcile Brazil's racial and ethnic heritage but nevertheless hinged on earlier pseudoscientific notions of race. If Freyre and others felt pride in the racial composition of the national team in 1938, they nevertheless based that pride on racialized stereotypes that characterized Brazilians of African descent as creative yet irrational.

Yet, if Freyre's notion of racial democracy has been shown to be little more than rhetorical flourish and a romantic vision that has delayed recognition of ongoing racial problems in Brazilian society, Brazilian attitudes toward the national game have not changed. Players and fans alike still expect the team to play the Brazilian style, where the players

Neymar da Silva Santos Júnior

Neymar

Brazilian soccer is in something of a rut. By many accounts, true futebol arte has not been seen since the 1980s. In 2014 the Canarinha won't have lifted the trophy in fourteen years, the second-longest gap between victories since 1958. Brazilians are pinning their hope on Neymar da Silva Santos Júnior, aka Neymar, who promises to bring futebol arte back to Brazilian soccer after the long *era Dunga*. And indeed, Neymar's play in Brazil's 2013 Confederations Cup championship seemed to justify those hopes.

Neymar has some major backers. In 2012 Pelé called Neymar the best player on the planet. Diego Maradona retorted that this was true "only if you say that Messi is from a different planet." Nevertheless, the argument may turn out to be an interesting one. Neymar has been an icon almost since the day he stepped onto the field, anointed as the next Pelé—or at least the next Ronaldinho. But comparisons with Pelé are natural. Like the Brazilian great, Neymar began his playing career with Santos, making his senior squad debut a little later than Pelé, at age seventeen. In eighty-five games with Santos between 2009 and 2012, Neymar scored forty goals. The prolific start to his professional career also drew a great deal of interest from European clubs—notably Barcelona and Real Madrid—who competed through much of 2012 for the right to transfer him. At that time Santos' president said that he would not transfer Neymar overseas for any price. In 2013 Santos relented and Neymar signed with Barcelona for a $74.7 million transfer fee. Before leaving the São Paulo giant, he led Santos to three titles in his short career: Brazilian Cup, the São Paulo Championship, and the Copa Libertadores.

On the international stage, by the end of 2013 Neymar had played in forty-six matches with the Brazilian senior team, scoring twenty-seven goals. As a junior player on Brazil's under-twenty (U20) and under-seventeen teams, Neymar proved that he could play with the best. He scored nine goals in seven matches for the U20 team in the South American Youth Championship in 2011, leading the team to the championship.

But it is not only Neymar's goal scoring that draws people to him. Like Pelé before him, he has tremendous ball control and an infectious smile. More importantly, from a Brazilian standpoint, he plays the free-flowing style that the country favors and supposedly invented—futebol arte. For many in Brazil, he will bring them not only the World Cup, but he will be the redeemer of the national style that Brazil has been trying to recapture since the 1980s.

Neymar, Brazil's hope for reviving *futebol arte*, celebrates after scoring against Honduras in the quarterfinals of the 2012 Olympic Games. © Juanjo. Martin/EFE/ZUMAPress.com

dance with the ball. Furthermore, many in Brazil still believe that the Brazilian style is innate. For example, Vincentinho, a junior coach with Flamengo, argues that Brazilians are "born with innate talents . . . [and] football is one of these talents," but not all have a chance to draw them out. For author John Lancaster, "no country plays beautiful football as naturally and consistently as Brazil." While the racial narrative of Brazil's style of play may now be submerged below the surface, the vein connecting the samba-dancing stars of today to the racialized attitudes of the late nineteenth and early twentieth centuries is just below the surface. What had been perceived as Brazil's "racial" weakness—the supposed traits of its African-descended population—had not been discredited; it had only been turned into a strength.[23]

Brazil has won the World Cup a record five times. It is also the only nation to have qualified for every World Cup. Brazil, in other words, produces excellent soccer players and lots of them. Its fans are passionate about the game, eager to win and to do so with panache. And it cannot be denied that Brazilians are perceived to play a different style of soccer than much of the world does: more open and more attacking, apparently relying less on tactics or coaching and more on skill. For many Brazilians the beautiful game represented—and continues to represent—something innate in the national makeup, as though the experience of being Brazilian fosters a tendency to play soccer a certain way. It is, of course, not just Brazilians who believe this. If one were to conduct a survey of soccer fans worldwide, likely Brazil would be most people's second-favorite team. The narrative of the fun-loving Brazilian not only belies Brazil's immense drive to win but it too easily becomes a surfeit for racialized definitions of the past: that Brazilians seek to "turn everything into play" as a result of their African roots. But, while the style that Dunga played—and coached—may have been less fluid than Brazilians like, few would trade the 1994 World Cup he captained for a beautiful loss.

Conclusion

The narratives of la nuestra and futebol arte developed at particular moments in the national histories of Argentina and Brazil. They were designed to create idealized images of the countries rather than to describe actual differences in playing styles. For Argentina, the elevation of cultural forms such as tango and soccer helped to integrate masses of new immigrants and the working classes into the nation. Soccer provided an avenue to bring people together and to express pride in themselves and their country. The myth of the pibe and la nuestra helped to make these new citizens feel not only that they belonged but that they were essential parts of the body politic. Brazil also needed to incorporate new immigrants but had perhaps more pressing concerns with how to allay fears about as well as how to integrate its black population. The narrative of futebol arte, contested as it was between 1938 and 1958, nevertheless dovetailed with the myth of racial democracy. In this narrative the mixed-race heritage of the country represented Brazil's strength in soccer and beyond. For both countries, then, a great deal was at stake in the early twentieth century. And by crafting national soccer identities that included marginalized populations, both constructed versions of the sport that retain their hold today. Long after Brazil's racial democracy was exposed as a myth, futebol arte—with its racial underpinnings—is still held up as the innate style of the nation. Similarly, Argentina's invented criollo version of the game—the supposed guile, individuality, and spontaneity that comes from the land—retains its hold on Argentine fans.

Interlude 1

Symbiosis: The Media and Soccer

It is difficult to imagine, in our world of smart phones, tablets, and wireless hotspots, how revolutionary telegraph wires could have been. And yet they were. Whereas news could take weeks to reach its destination prior to the telegraph, with the advent of the new technology in the 1800s information traveled across continents within hours. When soccer arrived in Latin America at the end of the nineteenth century, telegraph lines were just reaching many of the major cities in the region, yet within less than fifty years the entire world was connected by wire. Newspapers, which proliferated at the end of the nineteenth and beginning of the twentieth centuries as more and more people learned to read, also helped link people across nations and regions. And the development of mass media would play a major role in the growth and popularity of soccer in Latin America and around the world.

Newspapers helped spread the popularity of the sport as the print media began to cover sports more regularly in the first decade of the twentieth century. By the middle of the 1910s sports journalists and sports-only newspapers appeared throughout the region. In Argentina the Buenos Aires daily *El País* began printing sports scores in 1901, and in 1903 *La Nación* created a stand-alone sports section. Soon thereafter separate sports magazines appeared as well. The *Mexican Sportsman*, a bilingual sports-only magazine, appeared in Mexico City in 1896. By 1933 eight sports papers could be purchased on the streets of the capital. In the Brazilian media landscape, five sports newspapers circulated in 1912, and by 1930 the number of sports-only papers reached nearly sixty. Similar trends occurred throughout the region as the increased popularity of sports helped expand daily newspapers' circulation.

But newspapers did not just report on sporting events. After around 1908 sports and the *meaning* of sports became major topics of discussion. Print media and soccer formed a symbiotic relationship, and sports journalism became a profession in its own right. Early sportswriters played a crucial role in spreading soccer's popularity by, among other things, creating a link between soccer and the nation: by promoting it as healthy and modern, they linked soccer to the development of good citizens and a strong nation. Moreover, sports journalists crafted heroic stories about sports personalities and connected these heroes to nationalist narratives.

Newspapers and magazines formed only one part of the link between the growth of sport and mass media. Indeed, the telegraph, the radio, and eventually television and the Internet went hand-in-hand with soccer. Expectant fans filled the streets of Montevideo and Buenos Aires to get news via telegraph of the Celeste's performance in the 1924 Olympics, eventually breaking into rapturous celebration when the news arrived that Uruguay had won the gold medal. Then it was radio's turn. In fact, the first game aired "live" on the radio in Argentina occurred only a few months after the Paris games, when Uruguay played Argentina in Buenos Aires. The radio announcer in Montevideo received a cable every few minutes that he would relay over the air. That match, on October 2, 1924, set in motion major changes in both the media and sports landscape. It highlighted the capacity of radio to bring games live into homes around the nation, thereby creating a national community of listeners.

But radio did not provide regular coverage of games in Latin America until the 1930s, coinciding with the development of professional soccer. In Brazil the availability of cheap, locally produced radios led to their proliferation around the country. And radio stations, in search of revenue sources, found that soccer had a ready audience to help bring in valuable advertisement dollars. By the time that the 1938 World Cup came around, the games were broadcast across the country, making Leônidas da Silva a national hero.

With the arrival of television, soccer's relationship with media would become tighter still. Televised broadcasts of professional and national team games began in the 1950s. Again, TV's need for ad revenue and soccer's ready audience made for a perfect symbiosis. Television expanded soccer coverage, which grew audiences, which helped expand coverage more. But TV would not truly capture viewers' imaginations until the 1970 World Cup in Mexico. That year new technologies brought the games to life with full color instead of black and white. Moreover, broadcasters used slow-motion technology in the World Cup for the first time. Now Latin Americans could feel closer to their national teams as they fought for glory on the soccer field.

Soccer's links to the media have only deepened over the last fifty years. The twenty-four/seven sports news cycle of ESPN has been exported to Latin America. Almost every country in the region has daily shows devoted to soccer. With pay-per-view or live streaming (both legitimate and on pirate networks such as rojadirecta.me, ustream.tv and justin.tv), Latin Americans can watch their soccer heroes play professionally overseas. Indeed, the Internet was among the best ways to watch the Copa América in 2011: YouTube broadcast the entire event to over fifty countries.

At the same time that soccer has become more accessible online, however, television stations have attempted to restrict access to the sport. Many professional league games in Latin America are carried on cable or pay-per-view only, meaning that a portion of the population cannot watch. Knowing the importance of soccer to the country, in 2009 the Argentine government committed $1.6 billion over ten years to broadcast soccer on state television. In so doing, it seized the opportunity to give the vast majority of Argentines the ability to watch soccer every weekend, and it gave itself a public relations boost. Increasing access to soccer, President Cristina Fernández de Kirchner said, would bring about "a more just and democratic society."

3

Paraguay

Caudillos, Corruption, and Soccer

When Juan Carlos Galaverna went to watch a regional league match in his hometown of Ypacaraí in September 2006, he likely did not think it would embroil him in an international incident. Galaverna, a political leader from Paraguay's traditionally dominant Colorado party, had recently left his post as president of the Paraguayan Senate, though he remained a senator. He attended the game between El Triunfo and El Porvenir to see his son, goalkeeper for El Triunfo, play. On a normal day, a match in the regional leagues would be of interest only to local fans: the teams in the league cannot be promoted to the first division. But this was not a normal day.

In the eighty-fifth minute, referee Carlos Amarillo awarded a penalty kick to El Porvenir. The ensuing goal tied the game, which El Porvenir would go on to win on penalty kicks. An enraged Galaverna called a local radio station alleging a conspiracy that went to the heart of international soccer. He first blamed the "homosexual" referee for awarding the phantom penalty, but then Galaverna went higher up. The Paraguayan senator accused Nicolás Leoz, the longtime president of the Confederation of South American Football (known by its un-wieldy acronym, CONMEBOL), of influencing the referee to affect the outcome. Galaverna suggested that Leoz's motivations went well be-yond soccer. A member of the ruling Conservative Party, he believed that Leoz fixed the match in order to show his support for the opposi-tion Liberal Party in upcoming elections.[1]

Three days later Galaverna expanded his accusations on the floor of the Senate. He implicated none other than Sepp Blatter, the head of soccer's worldwide governing body, FIFA, in the incident. Blatter and other FIFA representatives were in Paraguay at the time celebrating the one hundredth anniversary of the Paraguayan Football Associa-tion. In his speech on the floor, Galaverna compared Blatter to a mafia don and criticized the Paraguayan president and vice president for at-tending a gala in Blatter's honor. It would be, Galaverna said, like "the *Godfather*" with all of the mafia heads together in one party.

Galaverna never succeeded in tying Leoz to fixing his son's soccer match, and his accusations seemed nonsensical. Nothing more than political spectacle came of the controversy, but it highlights how sports and politics mix at an intensely personal level in Paraguay. Since both Leoz and Galaverna were so powerful, it would seem foolish for them to meddle in a local match. Yet precisely because corruption and personal influence seem to infiltrate every level of Paraguayan society, Galaverna's claims did not seem so far-fetched. Indeed, in soccer as in politics, Paraguay's history is riddled with leaders who sought control through the exercise of outsized personal power.

Paraguayan history has been dominated by strong leaders sometimes called *karai guasu* in the native language Guaraní. In Spanish, these men might be called caudillos. Caudillos were strong, charismatic, of-ten corrupt leaders who had little use for the rule of law, and who dominated the Latin American landscape for much of the middle of the nineteenth century. For example, in the early- to mid-1800s, men like Juan Manuel de Rosas of Argentina, Rafael Carrera of Guatemala, José Antonio Páez of Venezuela, and Antonio López de Santa Anna of Mexico all led their nations as heroes on horseback. They ruled through a combination of personal appeal, patronage, and fear. Most had been military leaders who showed both bravery and skill on the battlefield, which earned them the respect of their subordinates and the wrath of their enemies. And they had lots of enemies—many who were would-be caudillos with their own loyal followers, biding time until they came into power. Internecine competition between caudillo bands led to intense instability throughout the nineteenth century and did little to benefit nations or the majority of their citizens. Instead these squabbles erupted over personal gain and the ability to distribute the spoils of power. Though caudillos-as-rulers generally left the historical scene in the late nineteenth century, they still exist today in a variety of guises. Some even suggest that they can exist outside of politics, as the establishment of personal fiefdoms can extend to other arenas, such as business and sport.

In Latin American history caudillos have become shorthand for describing leaders more concerned about extending their own power than about the people over whom they rule. And though the historical narrative of caudillos has them exiting the stage in the late 1800s, some say that they have appeared in different forms in the twentieth century as well: in populist cloaks, like Juan Perón in Argentina and Hugo Chávez in Venezuela; in revolutionary garb, like Fidel Castro in Cuba; or in the form of military dictators, like Augusto Pinochet in Chile. These men do not really fit the caudillo mold. They may exhibit some traits of caudillos—populism, charisma, and intimidation are all elements of a good caudillo—but in other ways they fail to measure up. Nevertheless, the fact that the term is used to describe them speaks to the continuing power of the concept. And strong personalistic leaders—from José Gaspar Rodríguez de Francia immediately after independence to Alfredo Stroessner in the mid- to late-twentieth century—litter Paraguayan history.

Paraguay, according to political scientist Peter Lambert, is a nation "characterized by division: rural and urban, rich and poor, Spanish and Guaraní." Yet, he notes, certain things bind Paraguayans together beyond the "national football shirt . . . the national flag . . . or populist rhetoric." For Lambert, Paraguayan identity rests on five pillars: "isolation, war, land, immigration, and language."[2] All of these can be seen as a by-product of strongman rule in the country. The questions of isolation, land, and migration appear to be directly related to caudillos and the corruption that tends to go along with their rule.

Indeed, a major impact of strongman rule in Paraguay has been a stunting of economic development, in part due to corruption and favoritism that exacerbated social inequalities inherent in the system. In order to keep supporters happy, rulers often allowed allies to acquire land illegally and to act with impunity, which disenfranchised the majority of the population. This in turn played a role in the continued poverty of the country and started migratory flows from the country to the city and out of the country. Soccer players, like others in the country, suffered the same conditions as their compatriots. As such, soccer offers a window through which to examine the impact of caudillos: from underdevelopment to corruption and migration.

Paraguayan Exceptionalism, Soccer or Otherwise?

Paraguay often gets left out of discussions about Latin American history and regional soccer history. Many historians—and Paraguayans themselves—consider the country to be an outlier—something that does not fit the general model. After independence, Paraguay did not suffer through the seemingly interminable battles for power between competing caudillos that plagued the majority of the region. As the rest of the region experienced three decades of stability in the late-1800s led by leaders who sought to modernize their countries and increase ties to Europe, Paraguay experienced thirty years of intense political infighting. And from the turn of the century through the two world wars, populist leaders brought modest levels of industrialization to much of South America, but Paraguay descended further into political chaos. In 1954 Alfredo Stroessner came to power, and for the next thirty-five years Paraguay returned to the caudillo era, with brutal, apolitical, personal rule. The *stronato*, as it is called, occurred just as many other nations in the region began to experience more openly democratic governments. Finally, the transition to democracy that began in 1989 put Paraguay on course with the rest of the region.

Yet up close the country experienced many of the same trends as its neighbors. While there were no caudillo wars, nevertheless from 1814–70 a series of strong leaders ruled according to whim rather than national interest. The late nineteenth century, for all its political instability, still brought export-led growth based on agricultural crops. And while foreign influence was limited, it nevertheless had a major impact on the country, especially after 1840. As with elsewhere in the region, European attitudes toward modern living and inclusionary ideals made their way to Paraguay. Youth in the early 1900s were caught in the thrall of liberal ideas just like their neighbors in Uruguay, Argentina, and Brazil. They would help bring the Liberal Party to power shortly after the turn of the century. From 1904 to 1939 Liberals also ruled Paraguay, even if their rule was chaotic. In other words, from a closer view, Paraguay was not as much of an outlier as might be imagined.

The same holds true for soccer. Paraguayans tend to think that their soccer, like their nation, developed differently from the rest of the region. The relative lack of economic and social development in Paraguay led, some say, to a different brand of soccer in the country. This was a soccer learned in the wide-open spaces of the Paraguayan countryside instead of in the urban spaces of Argentina, Brazil, or Uruguay. Indeed, Paraguayan soccer historian Miguel Angel Bestard sums up this view most clearly in *Paraguay: Un siglo de fútbol*, noting that Paraguayan soccer developed idiosyncratically, with little influence from its neighbors. The Guaraníes, as the Paraguayan soccer team is sometimes called, evinced little of the "rioplatense style" of Argentina and Uruguay, and even less of Brazil's supposed "futebol arte." Instead, the Albirroja—so called since 1921 for the white-and-red stripes on the uniform—played a more direct aerial game, bred in the open spaces of rural Paraguay.[3] Yet while Paraguayans often like to highlight their distinctiveness in the region, in soccer history the truth may show that the national sport shares the same trajectory as other Latin American countries. In closer focus, soccer's development is not so different from the rest of the region: soccer arrived in Asunción with expatriates and spread from there. From elite to poor, from city to countryside, the sport's development in Paraguay parallels that of the rest of the region.

Soccer came to Paraguay as the country emerged from nearly a century of despotic rule that stunted national development. As the rest of the region experienced the instability and infighting that exemplified the mid-nineteenth century caudillo era, two rulers kept Paraguay stable—if poor and isolated. José Gaspar Rodríguez de Francia (1814–40) and Carlos Antonio López (1841–62) ensured a cowed and peaceful Paraguay over their combined forty-six years of rule. Francia shut the country off from foreign influence, making it, in the words of Paraguayan intellectual Augusto Roa Bastos, "an island surrounded by land." Francia's policies created a nearly self-sufficient Paraguay but at a high cost. Estimated illiteracy ranged as high as 90 percent at the time of his death, while Francia neglected infrastructure development and completely curtailed political freedom. He summarily executed his enemies, had secret police watch all foreigners who entered the country, and allowed his allies to exploit the mostly indigenous peasants and make the economy work to their benefit.

López changed tack considerably. While he retained a tight grip on power and discouraged political freedoms, he encouraged foreign experts to come to Paraguay to help develop a national infrastructure and supported public education. Under López, railroads, port facilities, telegraph lines, an iron foundry, and a shipyard all portended well for Paraguayan development. Still, development should not be overstated: in the 1840s Paraguay's capital, Asunción, was home to just over twelve thousand people. Moreover, López extended his own power and wealth at the expense of much of the country. By the time of his death, the López family was the largest landowner in the country. Nevertheless, López appeared to put Paraguay on track to catch up to its neighbors in terms of development. But it was not to be.

The War of the Triple Alliance undid all of the gains of Carlos Antonio López in a haze of gun smoke and left a country broken by war. Between 1864 and 1870, Carlos' son Francisco Solano López waged a suicidal war against Argentina, Brazil, and Uruguay. Although no accurate count of the prewar population exists, an estimated one-half of the population, and roughly 60 percent of men aged fourteen to sixty, died as a result of the fighting. The war not only decimated the population but also destroyed Paraguay's infrastructure and stalled the economic development of the country. As the rest of the region sprang into a period of export-led growth leading to unequal but nevertheless noticeable economic development, Paraguay struggled to regain its footing. Among the things that helped Paraguay recover from the trauma of war was soccer.

There are two stories about soccer's beginnings in Paraguay, neither of which is mutually exclusive. One version claims that British railroad workers played the first games in 1886 and thus planted the seeds of soccer. The other says that students at the national teacher training school played the first game at some point in the 1890s. Either version fits nicely with the narrative of how the game arrived in Latin America as a whole: in the bags of expatriates or as part of a modernizing curriculum. Stories of these first games lack the kind of detail that historians use in efforts to establish accuracy (one was played in Borja, the other on school grounds). Most agree, however, that the "father of Paraguayan soccer," Dutchman William Paats, taught at the teacher training school.

Paats arrived in Paraguay from Holland at age eighteen, in 1894. When he became a teacher at the Normal School, he introduced the game to students. The first clubs began forming as offshoots of the school, and in November 1901 the first "official" match took place on the Plaza de Armas in downtown Asunción. Although the capital city, Asunción was little more than a large town, with a population hovering near fifty thousand. As with other countries in the region, support for the game developed early among expatriates and wealthy Paraguayans: the first teams comprised foreign businessmen and the local economic elite. Political support for the game soon followed. President Emilio Aceval, for example, offered a prize to the winner of the November 1901 match. Teams proliferated among the elite after the first game. Club Olimpia formed in 1902, and a group of that team splintered off to form Club Guaraní a year later. Club Nacional—named after Colegio Nacional, an elite high school—appeared in 1904. By 1920 more than fifty teams played in Asunción and around the country.

As elsewhere, the wealthy patrons of the sport initially sought to restrict participation to their own social class. When the Liga Paraguaya de Football (Paraguayan Soccer League) formed in 1906, it opened membership only to the most affluent clubs, all of which were based in Asunción. Nevertheless, soccer spread quickly outward from the capital, where the rural fields of Paraguay provided plenty of opportunity for the majority of the population to learn the game. Moreover, semiregular political upheaval in Asunción made it easier to play soccer in the countryside than in the city. With fewer political machinations and more open space, teams developed outside of Asunción quickly, suggesting a rapid nationalization and popularization of the sport. Thus, 1906 saw not only the birth of the Paraguayan League but also the creation of the first clubs in the interior of the country. El Porvenir and El Triunfo formed in Tacuaral (now Ypacaraí), as did Concepción Football Club in Concepción. A year later, in 1907, the club 10 de Agosto began playing in San Lorenzo del Campo Grande. So too the development of the Liga Salesiana, comprising teams from the poor neighborhoods of Asunción, seemed to confirm the sport's rapid popularization. Eventually poor youth would come to dominate the Paraguayan League and, by extension, the national team.

The importance of soccer's rapid spread out of Asunción lay not only in the development of supposedly distinctive style of play. While rural and poor teams had to wait before gaining admittance to the Liga Paraguaya, their creation marked a major shift for Paraguay. With the birth of regional teams, soccer truly became the national sport; the "salt and sugar" of Paraguay's patriotism, to quote Paraguayan poet Jesus Amado Recalde.[4] In a country rife with political divisions and where the route to power came through violence, soccer was one element capable of uniting the nation. When playing soccer, political affiliations mattered little, and in stadiums everyone—even rival factions and rival teams—wanted the same thing: victory for their team. Soccer provided a common denominator for much of the country to coalesce around.

The expansion of soccer outside of Asunción was partly caused by the political realities of the capital city in the early twentieth century. Political life in Asunción was one of almost constant uproar. Revolts, military coups, and deep political mistrust ruled the country—whose politics played out almost entirely in the capital. The first two decades of the twentieth century saw a rotating cast of presidential characters; fifteen men sat in the presidential chair between 1902 and 1920.

At first the young members of the urban elite saw soccer as a way to differentiate themselves from the politics of the old guard. Soccer offered a different way to think about political and social interactions. Tired of the individualistic, caudillo-style leadership of traditional Paraguayan politics, young leaders sought out more inclusive models of society. Soccer provided a form of training ground for these youth as it focused on teamwork over individuality, collective rather than personal good, and skill over class connections. Indeed, young elite soccer players in the early twentieth century believed that the sport could lead to a different future for the nation, uniting political factions and helping to establish stable government. And they expressed the desire for change in the names of teams: "Libertad," for example, formed in 1905 after Liberals came to power and Paraguay began a short-lived turn toward more open government. Yet this hopefulness faded as political infighting between Liberal Party factions burst through the surface in the Revolution of 1908. Cancellation of the Paraguayan League that year made Paraguayan soccer players' youthful optimism appear to be nothing more than naïveté. If at first soccer had the power to unite the country, in other words, it too succumbed quickly to politics. Teams began to align themselves with either the Liberals or the Colorados, with club names reflecting the political passions of the day.

Still, soccer leagues and the national federation sought to keep politics to the side as much as possible, and soccer continued to offer hope for reconciliation. Soccer players and officials tried to keep play going even when tensions between the two political camps erupted into open conflict. During the Revolution of 1922, for example, two Paraguayan teams left the country when the league suspended play due to the conflict. Both acted to bring relief to Paraguay, either materially or psychologically. One traveled around the region raising money for the

Salvador Cabañas

The Shot Heard 'Round Paraguay

It was, perhaps, the most important shot in Paraguayan soccer history. Unfortunately, it took place nowhere near a field but in a Mexico City bar. Paraguay had finished an impressive World Cup–qualifying campaign four months earlier, when the Albirroja entered the final game of qualifying in position to win CONMEBOL. As it was, Paraguay finished tied for second place with Chile, only one point behind Brazil. This was a team with promise: it had the offensive flair to match the supposed Guaraní fighting spirit. Ultimately, the team was forced to play without its most potent offensive weapon and lost in the World Cup quarterfinals. What could have been may forever be the ghost that haunts the 2010 team.

That an actual ghost did not cast a pall over the team is something of a miracle. That shot. At the time, Salvador Cabañas Ortega was a typical soccer migrant. As one of Paraguay's best players, his best professional opportunities lay outside the country. He first moved to Chile before striking it rich with Club América in Mexico's Primera División (also known as the Liga MX), the wealthiest professional league in the Americas. In the early morning of January 25, 2010, Cabañas, Paraguay's leading scorer and among the best strikers in Mexico's professional league, walked into the bathroom of BarBar, a popular nightspot in Mexico City. He never walked out. In security camera footage, José Balderas Garza—a Mexican drug dealer—and his bodyguard can be seen entering the bathroom. A short while later Cabañas enters, and shortly after that two men leave. Cabañas was left on the bathroom floor, a .38 caliber bullet in his brain. Somehow he not only survived the attack but was conscious when emergency personnel wheeled him to an ambulance. After hours of intensive surgery to control bleeding and swelling, Cabañas survived. On April 14, 2012, Cabañas took the field again for the Paraguayan third division team where his career started, Club 12 de Octubre de Itauguá, with a bullet still lodged in the left side of his brain. He played forty-one minutes in front of a crowd of fewer than one thousand. It was a far cry from where he could have been.

Salvador Caba-
ñas, Paraguay's
leading scorer in
the 2010 World
Cup qualifying
matches, playing
for his profes-
sional team,
Club América.
Cabañas was
shot in the head
at a Mexican
nightclub in
January 2010.
© Alejandro
Godinez Ayala/
ZUMAPress.com

Over the course of his professional career, Cabañas scored 174 goals, winning both the Chilean and Mexican league scoring titles in different years. With the Paraguayan national team, he scored ten goals in forty-four matches. Cabañas would serve as motivation for the Paraguayan team as it prepared to play Italy to start the 2010 World Cup. The Guaraníes received a letter from Paraguayan president Fernando Lugo, which urged them to "remember our beloved, stupendous example of gritty Paraguay spirit."

Red Cross to help those injured in the fighting. The other traveled to the South American Championship in Brazil where they almost won the tournament. They finished tied on points with Brazil and lost the gold medal in a hard-fought tie-breaking match. The performance of the Guaraníes acted to unite all Paraguayans, regardless of political affiliation. Although revolution wracked Paraguay, in other words, soccer provided an avenue to see the country as united, at least on the soccer field.

Indeed, one way to help unite the politically fractured nation was through international soccer. Paraguay was relatively late in developing a national team, squaring off against Argentina for its first international match in 1919. Soon regular cup competitions pit the Albirroja against Argentina (Copa Rosa Chevallier Boutell), Brazil (the Copa Oswaldo Cruz), Uruguay (Copa Artigas), and later Bolivia (Copa Paz del Chaco). Though a late starter, Paraguay often played the role of giant killer. On Argentina's second visit, in 1921, the Guaraníes defeated the Albiceleste. The same year, Paraguay played its first Copa América and beat Uruguay 2–1. Indeed, in the early twentieth century when the Celeste dominated world play, only Argentina and Paraguay could regularly defeat Uruguay. Although Paraguay has always fared less well against Brazil and Argentina, it nevertheless regularly ranks as the next-best team in the region. Paraguay has won more Copa Américas and has been to more World Cups than any nation other than the big three, and its ability to compete with its regional rivals remains a source of pride.

International matches, in fact, continued to play a uniting role in Paraguay throughout the first half of the twentieth century. As the national team's appearance in the South American Championship and the Red Cross tour showed that soccer could help the nation both materially and spiritually in 1922, so too during the Chaco War (1932–35) and its aftermath the sport aided the national healing process. Fought against Bolivia over the barren desert in the east of the country, the Chaco War cost between thirty thousand and forty thousand Paraguayan lives (and caused an estimated one hundred thousand total deaths) and destabilized the country. Once again, in the middle of the war, the Paraguayan Soccer League and the Red Cross organized a benefit tour of neighboring countries to raise money for wounded soldiers and war widows. During the chaotic two decades that followed the war, soccer remained a constant in the country's daily life. Indeed, the sport expanded domestically during these years while internationally the Guaraníes continued to compete against its regional rivals and qualified for the World Cup in 1950. And the team won the 1953 South American Championship, one year before Alfredo Stroessner's coup, which brought a new caudillo to power and submitted the country to his brutal rule for decades.

The Caudillo of CONMEBOL

As mentioned earlier, caudillos can exist outside of politics as personalistic leaders who access and retain power through a combination of corruption, patronage, and intimidation. Indeed, they exist throughout the world of soccer. Some might say that Sepp Blatter is a caudillo. So, too, Nicolás Leoz, the former head of the regional governing body of soccer, ruled the Confederation of South American Football for almost thirty years as something of a personal fiefdom. CONMEBOL oversees every facet of the sport in the region, from player transfer rules to drug testing. It also organizes regional club championships, the Copa América, and the World Cup qualifiers for South America, similar to other regional bodies such as the Union of European Football Associations (or UEFA, in Europe) or the Confederation of North, Central American and Caribbean Association Football (or CONCACAF, in North America, Central America, and the Caribbean).

Nicolás Leoz was born in the Paraguayan Chaco, the desert region in the west of the country, in 1928. As a result of his work in law and sports (in both the Paraguayan basketball and soccer leagues), Leoz became involved in the South American Soccer Confederation. He became president of the organization in 1986, and Paraguay quickly gained a place of central importance within CONMEBOL. Since its founding in 1916 until 2013, CONMEBOL had only nine presidents. Until Leoz took over the organization, CONMEBOL's offices had traditionally moved to the president's country, bringing with it a few jobs and favors to be doled out to friends and loyal followers. However, none of the previous

Former CON-
MEBOL President
Nicolás Leoz talks
during a press con-
ference at CONME-
BOL headquarters
in Luque. © Andrés
Cristaldo/EFE/ZU-
MAPress.com
. . . .

presidents did so with the skill of Nicolás Leoz. To be fair, none had the opportunity to either: after Leoz took over CONMEBOL, soccer underwent unforeseen changes as a result of globalization and technology, giving the office a great deal more power and visibility than it ever had before.

Like a good caudillo, Leoz used his influence to bring CONMEBOL to Paraguay. Instead of moving the headquarters temporarily, however, as his predecessors had done, in 1992 Leoz began making plans for a permanent headquarters for the organization. A close friend of then-FIFA president João Havelange and then-secretary-general Sepp Blatter, Leoz brought the power and money of FIFA to bear on the project. Although technically FIFA had no input over the headquarters' location, FIFA's support helped Leoz convince the national federations to vote in favor of Paraguay. Leoz brought money and jobs to

Paraguay in exchange for unquestioned support for the project from government officials in a classic case of caudillo-style patronage. In 1998 CONMBEOL headquarters opened in Luque, a suburb of Paraguay's capital, Asunción. The project cost $3.5 million, and the municipal government in Luque granted CONMEBOL the land—some say for a "symbolic amount," while Leoz insisted that the land was donated. In 2012 a world-class convention center and hotel opened attached to the headquarters, as did the Museum of South American Soccer. Paraguay, for its part, took the extraordinary step of giving the confederation inviolable rights in its headquarters, effectively giving CONMEBOL diplomatic status.[5] In short, Leoz successfully leveraged the power of international soccer to bring money and jobs to Paraguay order to consolidate his own authority.

Paraguay was hardly the logical choice as a permanent base for CONMEBOL headquarters. The country was in the midst of an economic downturn in 1992, when the decision to build the confederation offices was made. Black market commerce nearly equaled legitimate trade, and Paraguay remained an underdeveloped country with a

Nicolás Leoz and FIFA president Joseph "Sepp" Blatter at the 2011 Copa América. © Marcelo Sayao/EFE/ZUMAPress.com

rurally based economy. Moreover, Paraguay had barely emerged from thirty-five years of Alfredo Stroessner's despotic rule, and as a result its infrastructure was extremely poor. It had few functioning telephone lines, and electricity, hotels, and transportation (both internal and international) were barely adequate. In short, there was little reason to suggest that Paraguay was a good choice for the headquarters of the international organization. Yet Leoz made it happen, and CONMEBOL now has a permanent headquarters in one of the most difficult countries to reach in South America.

Without doubt, until 2013 Leoz was one of the most powerful men in world soccer. In Latin America only Sepp Blatter—head of FIFA—surpassed him, but other caudillos existed in Latin American soccer as well. Indeed, Leoz's resignation from both CONMEBOL and the FIFA executive committee in April 2013 left Julio Grondona, head of the Argentine Football Association since 1979 and senior vice president of FIFA, as the last remaining soccer caudillo in the region. Not only is Grondona immensely powerful but—like a good caudillo—his detractors accuse him of all manner of corruption, from taking bribes to nepotism. Likewise, Ricardo Teixeira—ex-president of the Brazilian Football Confederation, ex-head of the 2014 World Cup organizing committee, and son-in-law of ex-FIFA president João Havelange—until recently stood as another example of caudillo rule in Latin American soccer. However, Teixeira resigned his posts in March 2012 amid clouds of scandal.

Accusations of corruption plagued Leoz for years. Indeed, as FIFA reeled in crisis over allegations of malfeasance in the bidding process for the 2018 and 2022 World Cups, Leoz's name surfaced again and again. He reportedly requested to be knighted in exchange for voting in favor of England's failed 2018 World Cup bid. Given that he has received national honors in at least ten countries—including (according to his staff) the French Legion of Honor and the Spanish Order of Isabella the Catholic—a knighthood might not have seemed too farfetched. Members of the Football Association were told that a title would "weigh heavily" on his decision. Other claims suggested that Leoz had requested that a championship in England be named for him.[6] Older allegations dogged the caudillo of Latin American soccer as well. Leoz was accused of receiving more than $700,000 in payments from International Sport and Leisure (ISL), a marketing company that owned exclusive rights to FIFA events from 1989 to 1999. After ISL's bankruptcy in 2001, FIFA worked diligently to keep ISL documents that implicated members from being released to the public. In late 2011, however, FIFA reversed course and asked that the documents be released in the interest of transparency. The documents helped bring down Ricardo Teixeira, but Leoz seemed to weather the storm: in May 2012 he was named CONMEBOL president for life, at age eighty-three.[7] Yet the ISL scandal would eventually bring Leoz down as well. In April 2013, days before the publication of the findings of an internal investigation into corruption at FIFA, and citing health reasons—not implausible for a then-eighty-four-year-old man—he stepped down from both FIFA and CONMEBOL. Still, many would argue that Leoz, following a hallmark of caudillos, had clung to power for too long. It is a story that Paraguay has known all too well throughout its national history.

The Stronato, Rural Migration, and Soccer

When Paraguay qualified for the 2010 World Cup in South Africa, the team had two clear offensive leaders: Salvador Cabañas and Nelson Haedo Valdez. Between them they scored eleven of Paraguay's twenty-three goals in the tournament, which saw Paraguay finish second behind Brazil—a disappointing finish for the Albirroja, which had its sights on winning the qualification marathon outright. And while Paraguay played well at the World Cup, losing to eventual champion Spain in the quarterfinals, it was without one of its two most potent weapons. Cabañas was unable to play after a vicious attack in a Mexican bar earlier in the year. He had a bullet lodged in his brain.

After the assault on Cabañas, a large part of the team's offensive leadership fell onto the shoulders of Valdez. Nelson Haedo Valdez hails from the wide-open spaces of eastern Paraguay, and odds suggest that he should not be playing professional soccer, let alone playing in some of Europe's best professional leagues. Instead, had he been an average Paraguayan from the rural east, he would have been with his family

Nelson Haedo Valdez celebrates a goal during Paraguay's Copa América soccer match against Brazil, 2011. © Guillermo Arias/Xinhua/ZUMAPress.com

in San Joaquín, a poor town in an impoverished region, working in the fields for little pay. Or perhaps he would have been one of the new migrants to the capital city, Asunción, which has seen its population explode from little over one hundred thousand in 1953 to over 2 million today. Like many others, Valdez migrated outside the country in search of work. The difference is that unlike his compatriots who work in unskilled positions in Argentina, Brazil, Spain, and the United States, Valdez earns enough to send Christmas gifts to fifteen hundred children each year.

Valdez's story starts as a common one in modern Paraguay. As one of seven children from a peasant family, he spent his youth playing soccer with an orange or stuffed socks. At age six he began practicing before school and acquired a drive to succeed that is often associated with stereotypes of the Guaraní spirit. By fifteen Valdez's story begins to diverge from that of the typical Paraguayan farmer. Valdez convinced his parents to let him play professional soccer and left home for the outskirts of Asunción to play with the Paraguayan second-division team Atlético Tembetary. Unable to afford housing, Valdez lived under the stadium stands in a makeshift bed and worked to supplement his soccer earnings. Eventually a German banker saw Haedo Valdez play and gave him a ticket to try out with Werder Bremen, where he earned a spot on the team. This country boy, barely able to speak Spanish let alone German, was suddenly playing in the Bundesliga.[8]

⚽

The poverty of Valdez's home in eastern Paraguay reflects persistent challenges—many based on the trickle-down effects of corruption and cronyism—that face rural Paraguayans. Much of the population in the east is landless laborers: peasants who raise crops on other people's land for little pay. For much of twentieth century, they lived surrounded by thousands of hectares of unused land, the majority of it owned by government ministers, generals, or foreigners who had never been to Paraguay. Indeed, according to Peter Lambert and Andrew Nickson, access to land has traditionally been "synonymous with" access to power and wealth. As a result, land reform has been seen both as critical for improving the plight of the rural poor and as a threat to the status quo.[9] And throughout the century presidents proposed land reform programs, but instability and corruption stopped most plans from having any impact. In the late 1930s the governments of Rafael Franco and José Félix Estigarribia, for example, had some success in distributing land to impoverished peasants and enshrined rural and urban workers rights into law. Yet underlying political instability made these plans difficult to carry out: both presidents' terms lasted less than eighteen months. Only with Alfredo Stroessner's rise to power in 1954 did real reform appear possible.

Stroessner came to power in a military coup that ended a chaotic period of seven governments in seven years. His opponents thought he would be easy to overthrow. Instead, utilizing the secret police, extrajudicial killings, exile, and arbitrary arrest, Stroessner consolidated his power. And using a combination of fear and patronage, he ruled—in true caudillo style—until 1989. After generations of political instability, many applauded the arrival of normalcy in the country. Members of the Colorado party saw immediate benefits as Stroessner doled out jobs to loyal followers. Indeed, by the end of his term Colorado party membership was almost a requirement for any job—government or not—in the country.

Stability under Stroessner supported economic development. From the 1950s until the 1970s international donors and bilateral aid helped to launch major development projects. For instance, the construction of the Itaipú Dam, a joint Paraguayan–Brazilian project, created thousands of jobs and provided electricity to much of the country. And in the 1970s the Paraguayan economy began to hum: dam construction and a boom in cotton and soy production created sustained economic growth in the country for the first time in decades. Not surprisingly, economic growth won Stroessner a great deal of support among the rural poor. Nevertheless, corruption—which some Paraguayan historians claim reached new heights under Stroessner—diminished the impact of development and land reform efforts. Indeed, much of the land and wealth ended up in the pockets of Stroessner's cronies instead of going to the people for whom it was intended. As a result, impoverished Paraguayans saw little benefit from the country's development.

Agrarian reform under Stroessner, crucial for the impoverished, predominantly rural country, began in 1963. Problems arose almost instantly, and the reform ended up being a way to distribute lands to followers as a way to retain their loyalty. Military officers acquired vast tracts of land and inequality actually rose during the land distribution efforts. Often, large landowners quickly turned the land over at inflated prices to Brazilians—who came to be known as *brasiguayos*. This practice, though technically illegal, was commonplace. Some peasants who owned land took advantage of the high price their land could fetch and moved to the burgeoning cities. Those peasants who remained found themselves in a more and more precarious position.

Other factors combined to make the situation faced by poor Paraguayans worse. Corruption insinuated itself to such an extent that few opportunities for mobility existed and social spending under Stroessner was almost nil. Indeed, throughout the stronato, poverty and inequality worsened: as much as 52 percent of the population lived in poverty after thirty years of his rule in 1985. Moreover, in comparison to its neighbors, Paraguay fared poorly in terms of both poverty levels and income inequality. Land inequality highlights a starker reality: in 2012, 1 percent of landowners owned 77 percent of all fertile land while 40 percent of landowners owned just 5 percent of all land in the country.[10] The land reform project, then, forced more Paraguayans into poverty.

In addition to extending inequality in the countryside, however, corruption in the land reform project added to the flow of migrants leaving rural areas for political reasons or for opportunities in the city and overseas. Migration has been an essential part of Latin American history since the arrival of Europeans in the 1500s. Europeans in turn brought over African slaves, who would be the major immigrant group until the late nineteenth century. Then, between 1870s and 1930, a flood of European immigrants arrived. In the post–World War II era the migratory flows reversed: the largest movements have been either outward migration or from rural zones to the cities. Indeed, while much of this flow of people leaves the region—for the United States and Europe—the majority of it has been intraregional. For Paraguayans, economic displacement forced many residents of rural areas to leave the countryside.

Starting in the nineteenth century Paraguayans have migrated to other Latin American countries both to escape political persecution and to find better jobs. During the López reign, Paraguayans in Argentina formed the Foreign Legion, which supported Argentine troops in the War of the Triple Alliance. Legionnaires claimed to be loyal to Paraguay but not to the despotic Francisco Solano López. Many settled in Argentina and Brazil—working either in the agricultural sector near

Lucas Barrios

Lucas Barrios represents an alternate type of Paraguayan soccer migrant: one who moves to Paraguay in order to play. Barrios was born and raised in Virreyes, Argentina, to an Argentine father and a Paraguayan mother. He developed his game playing in Argentina and Chile but burst on the scene with Colo-Colo in 2008 after playing for a variety of teams in both Argentina and Chile. In fifty-eight games with Colo-Colo in the 2008 and 2009 seasons, he scored fifty-three goals. Although he was a rising star, Barrios was also a realist. He spoke of his desire to play for the Albiceleste, but he also knew that Lionel Messi, Sergio Agüero, Carlos Tévez, and Gonzalo Higuaín all ranked above him in the Argentine pecking order.

In March 2010 Barrios "migrated" back to Paraguay in order to play international soccer, and he immediately began to speak of his pride in wearing the Paraguayan jersey. Barrios would go on to play for the national team in South Africa and again in the Copa América squad that finished second to Uruguay. He was not alone as a naturalized citizen: Jonathan Santana and Néstor Ortigoza both grew up in Argentina and, like Barrios, do not speak Guaraní.

FIFA regulations allow players to switch national allegiance provided that they do so before they turn twenty-one and before they have played an official senior national team match. However, FIFA also retains the right to deny any request for a nationality change. And soccer migrants move all over the world. Brazilians play for Togo and Qatar, French-born players represent many West African nations, and British-born represent

the border or settling in the capital cities. Outmigration continued in the twentieth century, picking up pace during the Stroessner years as a result of "repression combined with a lack of access to land."[11] During the stronato, political migrants left Paraguay in a steady stream. Estimates of Paraguayans who fled Stroessner's brutality range as high as 1.5 million.[12] Most went to Argentina and Brazil while smaller numbers went to the United States and Spain. Even after his fall, migration continued: as of 2010 the International Organization for Migration estimated that roughly 770,000 Paraguayans, approximately 12 percent of the population, live outside the country. This percentage is down

Jamaica and other former colonies. Ecuador's former captain and goal-keeper Marcelo Elizaga was eligible to play for Argentina, as was Uruguayan goalie Fernando Muslera. David Trezeguet, the former French international, and Italian international Mauro Camoranesi both could have played for Argentina as well.

Indeed, players switching nationality to play for a national team is nothing new in international soccer, especially in Latin America. The 1934 Italian squad that won the World Cup boasted four Argentine-born players, Raimundo Orsi, Attilio Demaría, Enrique Guaita, and Luis Monti. Argentine players also went to represent Spain, Uruguay, the United States, Mexico, and France in the World Cup. Alfredo di Stéfano, famously, played for Argentina, Colombia, and Spain. Likewise, Brazilian players have represented other countries at the highest level, with one winning the 1934 World Cup with Italy. Uruguayan players have also opted for the national team jersey of another country.

The trend to claim a second citizenship in order to play international soccer raises questions about nationality and identity. Some players move to countries where they have no roots. Others, like Lucas Barrios, return to play for the country of one of their parents. As Barrios himself made clear, the decision was not based on a sense of Paraguayan identity but rather on a desire to play soccer at the highest level. For fans, this hardly seems to matter. Although Barrios' Argentine-birth is mentioned in Paraguay, few question his loyalty to the Paraguayan jersey.

sharply from the 1970s, when as much as 25 percent of the population lived abroad.[13]

For almost a century Paraguayan soccer players have been among the streams of migrants leaving the country. Starting in the 1920s Paraguayan soccer stars left to earn money or to escape the constantly unstable political situation. Soccer historian José Maria Troche noted the lack of continuity in the national team, suggesting that the team was in "constant transformation due to emigration." Prior to the 1970s players could only represent a country if they lived there, meaning that the decision to sign with a foreign team carried a great deal of weight. For generations Paraguay's best players opted to go abroad: Manuel Fleitas Solich, Delfín Benítez Cáceres, Arsenio Erico, and Gerardo Rivas all left Paraguay after a short spell on the national team in order to seek stability elsewhere. Though they did not necessarily leave for political reasons, in at least one case Paraguayan soccer players helped out their countrymen: Arsenio Erico's house in Buenos Aires became, in the words of his biographers, "a refuge for many of his compatriots."[14]

More recently, players such as Nelson Haedo Valdez have continued the migratory flow of soccer players leaving the country for work. Sixteen of the twenty-five-man squad that made up Paraguay's national team in qualifiers for the 2014 World Cup played outside of Paraguay. Valdez, for example, played in Germany, Spain, Russia, and the United Arab Emirates after leaving Paraguay in 2001. His teammate Lucas Barrios never played professionally in Paraguay, spending his playing career in Argentina, Chile, Mexico, Germany, and China. Soccer players migrate for better salaries and greater visibility, but the need to migrate highlights trends of migrants everywhere: they move to improve their lives. Soccer migrants have more opportunity and choice than their poorer compatriots who leave in search of a better life, but, as in the case of Haedo Valdez, often the line between the two types of migrants is quite thin. Historically, of those who migrate for soccer, many remain abroad when their playing days are done. Some, however, return to Paraguay.

A Once and Future Caudillo?

José Luis Chilavert is one of those who returned. After playing most of his professional career in Europe and Argentina, Chilavert came back with purpose. Standing a little over six feet tall and weighing well over two hundred pounds, he does not cut a small figure. Chilavert's personality has always outsized even his outsized body, and though he has put on a good deal of weight since his playing days, even at the peak of fitness Chilavert seemed larger than life—a sort of soccer caudillo. On the field he commanded unflagging loyalty from his teammates, spurring them to consistent heights: he won league titles with four of the

Paraguayan goalkeeper José Luis Chilavert in action against Germany in the 2002 World Cup. © Alain Mounic/Fep/Panoramic/ZUMAPress.com

seven teams he played for, and Paraguay reached two World Cups with him as netminder. He boasted that he was the best goalie at the 1998 World Cup and backed up his claim, being named both a tournament all-star and World Goalkeeper of the Year.

Chila, as he is often called, was also known for his flamboyance and his quick temper. He scored eight goals for the Albirroja and added another fifty-four professional tallies over the course of his career but was suspended for high-profile incidents such as spitting at Brazilian star Roberto Carlos and fighting with Colombian star Faustino Asprilla. Chila's oversized persona extends beyond the soccer pitch.

Over the course of his career he clashed frequently with soccer's governing bodies and with club ownership (he once sued the French soccer club Strasbourg for back wages), fans, other players, and politicians. In 2011 Chilavert attacked Argentine soccer agent Pablo Martín Seijas in an airport because Seijas had insulted both Chilavert and Paraguay, calling Chila a "starving Paraguayan."[15] For all of these actions, Chilavert can be labeled a caudillo, but to do so would be to misunderstand the man. While in some ways he seems to represent the archetypal modern caudillo—charismatic, strong, and fearless—in other ways he does not. For example, he takes strong political positions that would benefit the country rather than himself.

Even granting Chilavert his eccentricities, the Paraguayan soccer community was shocked in 1999 when he boycotted the Copa América. The decision was even more stunning considering the tournament was being hosted for the first time in Paraguay. The reason Chilavert would not play? Ten years after the end of Stroessner's traumatic rule, Paraguay's poor still lacked access to basic services. Not enough had been done to raise the country out of the depths of the dictatorship. The country's roads, airports, hotels, and other tourist infrastructure were in the midst of development but still lagged well behind that of other South American nations. Poverty remained at unacceptable levels, with more than 50 percent of Paraguayans living under the poverty line. Fewer than half the population had more than a sixth-grade education, and land reform had actually taken land away from small farmers. In Chilavert's opinion, the millions of dollars spent on hosting the tournament would have been better spent redressing some of Paraguay's social inequalities—especially education.[16] Chilavert may have boycotted the tournament, but the rest of the country did not. Paraguay was not going to miss another chance to host the Copa América at home, even if its best goalie and team leader was not going to play.

Although it would be the first Copa América hosted *in* Paraguay, it was not the first to be hosted *by* Paraguay. Twice before, in 1923 and 1953, the national federation was forced to organize the championship in another country. In 1923 the country was just emerging from the throes of a bloody civil war that had begun a year earlier, so the federation was in no state to organize the tournament. Instead the Paraguayan federation organized the 1923 tournament in Uruguay. Paraguay was still in no shape to host the South American Championship in 1953, so the Paraguayan soccer officials organized the Copa in Lima, Peru. Years of instability and corruption in the early twentieth century left the country vastly underdeveloped. For example, though Asunción's population hovered around one hundred thousand, the mostly dirt roads had a tendency to become impassable mud pits in the rain, and there was only one hotel to speak of in the capital. The second-biggest city in the country, Villa Rica, was little more than a town of fifteen thousand and could be reached only by an uncomfortable train trip of many hours. Moreover, the largest stadium in the country could hold fewer than twenty thousand people, hardly large enough for the crowds expected to see both the reigning world champion and runner-up, Uruguay and Brazil.

Hence, the 1953 championship in Peru may be the only one where the "host" nation won while facing hostile crowds throughout much of the tournament. With one game to go in the tournament, Paraguay and Brazil were tied atop the table. The final match pit Peru against Uruguay; with a win, Peru would be South American champion. Playing in Lima against the already eliminated Celeste, most assumed a Peruvian win to be a foregone conclusion, meaning that Paraguay would finish in a tie for second. The Albirroja coach, Manuel Fleitas Solich, felt so sure of this outcome that he left for Buenos Aires. When he heard that Uruguay had defeated Peru, Fleitas Solich rushed back to Lima, arriving only hours before the championship game. Two hours later, Paraguay had won its first South American Championship.

Yet, while celebrated as a national victory, Paraguay's failure to host the tournament at home exposed major problems in Paraguay. After more than a century of independence, the country had little to show. Without resources, neither an adequate stadium nor other infrastructure could be assembled to run the tournament. A little more than a year later, Alfredo Stroessner came to power via military coup. And forty-six years later, Paraguay would finally host its first Copa América.

José Luis Chilavert stands with Juan Afra (*left*) and Horacio Cartes (*right*), Colorado Party candidate for president, 2013. © [E]Jose Villaba/Xinhua/ZU-MAPress.com

As host country in 1999, though, Paraguay fared poorly: after winning its group, the Albirroja lost in the quarterfinals. No doubt the Guaraníes would have fared much better had Chilavert played. But he chose the moment of the 1999 Copa to make a political statement through soccer. And, perhaps surprisingly, Paraguayans loved him more for it. With his personal boycott, Chilavert's appeal moved beyond the soccer field.

So what do we make of Chilavert? In refusing to play in the Copa América, Chilavert placed the nation over nationalism, calling attention to Paraguay's ongoing economic, social, and political woes, particularly in the countryside. His actions, though perhaps costing Paraguay in the tournament, won him further loyalty from the Paraguayan population. Risking his international career to stand up for the underrepresented poor of the country marked Chilavert as a man of the people. And his fiery eccentricity and fierce nationalism cast him as a sort of modern day caudillo. Having been a soccer star—leading the team to higher heights than thought imaginable—with his outsized charisma and populist rhetoric, some say he is the next karai guasu of Paraguayan politics.

While there is a tendency to place the caudillo tag on popular politicians in Latin America, to do so with Chilavert would be unwise. He is hardly the only soccer player to use his position to make social commentary during his playing days. Sócrates, the captain of Brazil's 1982 World Cup squad, led a prodemocracy movement on his professional team. Rómario, the star of Brazil's 1994 world championship team, now represents Rio de Janeiro in the Brazilian Chamber of Deputies for the Socialist Party. And notwithstanding his fiery personality, penchant for conflict, and the loyalty he inspires in players and fans alike, to caudill-ize Chilavert would reduce him to two dimensions. In fact Chilavert has displayed strong political tendencies, which traditional strongmen who sought personal rather than national goals generally lacked. Moreover, he has won immense popularity in Paraguay not through favors or fear but through taking sometimes unpopular positions on key issues. Nevertheless, it will be interesting to see what the future holds: Chilavert promised that he would run for president when he turns fifty, in 2015.

Whether perceived as outliers or not, both Paraguayan history and Paraguayan soccer have been greatly affected by caudillos and corruption. Strong leaders with little interest in the greater good of the country and its people dot Paraguayan history. From Francia through the López years and the stronato, leaders have done more to enrich themselves and their followers than to develop Paraguay. In part as a result of this corruption, nearly 35 percent of Paraguayans lived below the poverty line in 2010. In turn, migration became a common path for the poor. Many moved to Asunción while others moved abroad in order to make a living. But Paraguay's endemic corruption affected soccer as well. Lack of infrastructure in 1953 led to the soccer federation hosting the Copa América in Lima while in 1999 it caused a boycott by the Guaraníes' most valuable player. Even the arrival of CONMEBOL headquarters to Paraguay resulted from the strong and corrupt leadership of Nicolás Leoz, the caudillo of Latin American soccer. Indeed, the narratives of Paraguayan history and soccer rest, in many ways, on the twin pillars of caudillos and corruption.

"Y va a caer"

Soccer and Politics in Chile

In mid-September 1973, lines of people stood outside the entrance to Chile's National Stadium in Santiago and strained to see inside. Security guards diligently kept the throngs from the gates, eager to ensure that stadium security was not breached. But those outside did not want to get in. They were not trying to glimpse a soccer game or any other sporting event. Rather, they sought information about loved ones who might have been inside, or tried to pass food and clothes to friends and relatives. The guards held machine guns and other heavy weapons. Mostly young conscripts, they had been tasked with policing over twelve thousand people arrested earlier that month.

After the violent overthrow of democratically elected president Salvador Allende on September 11, 1973, the Chilean military rounded up his supporters and brought them to the national soccer stadium. Built thirty-five years earlier, the stadium that had hosted the finals of the 1962 World Cup transformed overnight into a makeshift concentration camp: locker rooms became torture chambers, bathrooms execution centers. A little more than two months later, the Soviet Union

A Chilean soldier takes a prisoner for questioning at the National Stadium.
© RIA-Novosti / The Image Works

boycotted a World Cup qualifying match scheduled to take place at the stadium in protest of the military regime. In so doing, the USSR forfeited an opportunity to play in the 1974 world championship in West Germany, giving the spot to Chile. It is an ignominious distinction that four of the five Latin American countries that played in West Germany in 1974—Brazil, Chile, Haiti, and Uruguay—were under dictatorships, while the fifth (Argentina) had just emerged from military rule and would soon succumb to the armed forces again.

There is no shortage of literature that suggests sports serve the interests of politicians and others who seek to control populations. This argument proposes that governments use sports to distract the population from the mundane and sometimes vicious nature of modern life.[1] Nazi Germany and fascist Italy are often cited as early examples of regimes mobilizing sports—and sporting venues—to manipulate the masses and promote a particular vision of the nation. In the Latin

American context, Argentine sociologist Juan José Sebreli argued that soccer did nothing but make the population more violent and prone to manipulation by the government. Looked at from this light, the co-optation of the National Stadium and other stadiums around Chile highlights the pernicious potential of sporting venues and sport itself. Indeed, this is one of the dominant narratives of soccer and politics in Latin America: that the military dictatorships of the 1970s effectively used soccer to keep the masses docile.

Just as easily, however, narratives of soccer in Chile could interpret the use of the National Stadium to tell the opposite story. Rather than recounting its use as a symbol of totalitarianism and political oppression, it can be interpreted as a site of hope and rebirth. There, on the night of March 12, 1990, seventy thousand people witnessed the reinauguration of Chilean democracy after seventeen years of military rule. This act was a conscious reclamation of the National Stadium: as new president Patricio Aylwin addressed the crowd, the names of those who had disappeared during the Pinochet years lit the scoreboard behind him.

In Chile as elsewhere in Latin America, soccer and politics have long had a tense relationship. Soccer represented, and continues to represent, a space without rival for political mobilization. Because at both the professional and international levels the sport is followed so intensely by the Chilean public, it offers politicians and social groups alike fertile ground for conveying political messages. So too soccer stadiums retain symbolic power: national leaders use the spaces where soccer is played for political rallies and displays of authority.

This is not a new relationship. In Chile, soccer and politics have been tied together closely since the arrival of the sport. From the outset, the sport marked political and social terrain in the country. On one hand, politicians used the sport to promote themselves and their political platforms. On the other hand, it formed the base from which Chilean workers and the poor stood up to be counted in the political process of the nation. Soccer clubs came to represent neighborhoods and formed an integral part of barrio identities. They also became a place where community leaders got their starts. These leaders, both players and administrators, then felt empowered to stand up for their political and economic interests. Chilean citizens gave the sport meaning in their own ways, even as politicians attempted to co-opt soccer to their own ends. In other words, both politicians and broader social groups used soccer matches, soccer players, and soccer stadiums as avenues for political co-optation and mobilization. From the moment that soccer arrived in Chile, it was put to political use. Not only did politicians use sport to reinforce the status quo but political opposition also employed it as an effective venue of protest.

Backdrop: Chilean Development

In stark contrast to the rest of Latin America, Chile gained political stability shortly after independence. By 1830 the internecine wars that plagued the rest of the region during the caudillo period came to an end and Chile established a form of representative democracy. Voting rights were limited to a small economic elite, but power rotated peacefully between parties and presidents. While other countries in the region relied heavily on one or two export crops, Chile constructed its economy on both agricultural and mining exports. Grain production in the valleys to the south of Santiago supplied the country with much of its food needs and allowed for the export of surplus. Copper mining accounted for over 50 percent of Chile's government revenues by the late 1850s, and overall export earnings quadrupled between 1845 and 1875. Moreover, Chile's location on the west coast of the continent gave it easy access to the western United States, and the California Gold Rush fostered an agricultural export boom in Chile.

To support the export economy, the Chilean government gave concessions for railroad construction. Between 1849 and 1875 Chile's copper-producing north was linked with the southern port of Talcahuano. Thirty years later the national rail network reached the far southern city of Puerto Montt. Railroad development accelerated economic exploitation, played a role in unifying the country, and helped speed the spread of soccer. The extension of telegraph lines performed the same task. By 1877 telegraph lines linked Santiago to more than forty-five towns and cities throughout the country. Linking the country together by rail and telegraph made communication between regions easier and more regular, facilitating the construction of the idea of a common Chile. Along with creating a greater sense of Chileanness, railroads and telegraph lines helped modernize the rapidly industrializing country as the end of the century approached.

Chile's modernizing and nationalizing efforts included education as a key component. Political leaders, inspired by European ideas about the modern nation-state, sought to inculcate civic values through a public school system. As a result, Chile founded its first public university, built schools and libraries throughout the country, and began to train teachers in modern pedagogical methods. During the 1850s the government built hundreds of public schools, and by the early 1860s more than forty-five thousand Chilean children attended primary school.

Inculcating civic and national values became increasingly important as Chile's population grew and urbanized at the end of the nineteenth century. From a population of less than 1 million in 1830, Chile contained 2.75 million people by 1895. Santiago, the nation's capital, grew from roughly 115,000 people in 1863 to over 500,000 by 1920. Valparaíso also experienced rapid growth, its population doubling between 1863 and 1900. Cities at this time began to grow not only because of the rapidly expanding export sector but also due to industrialization. In the late nineteenth and early twentieth century Chile began to develop a textile industry, mainly in Santiago, that drew workers from rural areas and abroad.

All of these factors—from stable politics, a strong economy, and a nationalist education curriculum, to a rapidly growing public education system, immigration, and urbanization—played a role in the development of soccer in the country. In addition to these phenomena, the coastal city of Valparaíso, the economic center of the nation for much of the nineteenth century, was home to a powerful group of British expatriate businessmen who imported, along with consumer goods, a love for the sport.

The Politics of Soccer

According to Chile's dominant soccer narrative, expatriate and elite youth first played soccer in the late 1880s. Teams rapidly formed in social clubs, and interest in the game grew to such a point that a group of British expatriates and Chileans of British heritage met in a bar to create the first official tournament in 1894. These youth explicitly tied the sport to ideas about modernizing the country. For example, in the preface of a soccer rulebook published in Chile in 1901, José A. Alfonso commented that soccer raised the "physical virility" of young men and also improved their "moral values."[2] Playing soccer, in other words, not only kept one physically fit but improved individuals and the nation. Nationalist leaders agreed. For them, soccer offered a way to inculcate the population with modern values and to distract them from the dislocation of urbanization and industrialization. But while the state and the wealthy supported soccer to help retain the social status quo, it also grew from the bottom as a grassroots sport. For the working classes, soccer represented both a release from the daily grind and alternate avenues for political and social organizing.

Like in other Latin American countries, many of the founders of Chilean soccer were educators. As such they were tied to the state's efforts to "modernize" and "improve" the population. For example, the first president of the Football Association of Santiago, Joaquin Cabeza, taught at the government-run pedagogical institute. He had become convinced of soccer's capacity for carrying messages of modernity during a year's study in Germany. David Arellano, the founder of Colo-Colo—one of Chile's most popular clubs—was also a teacher. And schools, both private English-language *colegios* and public institutions, became the seedbeds for soccer in Chile. The Instituto Nacional, Chile's venerable public school, and the national teaching school both formed teams in 1897. Soccer became a part of school curricula across the nation as newly trained teachers brought the game to all corners of the country. For educators and national leaders alike, soccer taught teamwork, self-sacrifice, and commitment, all of which helped to create healthy, productive, and responsible citizens.[3]

Due to its link with national educational institutions, and the spread of schools due to the Chilean state's commitment to funding education, soccer diffused throughout the country quickly. Records suggest that club teams developed in the Chilean interior rapidly. By 1894 soccer was being played in the northern mining region of Antofagasta, where British merchants and financiers lived in the copper mining communities. The fact that two working-class Chilean clubs, Antofagasta Juniors and Union Bellavista Sporting Club, formed in 1896 highlights how quickly the sport spread from British communities to Chilean ones. Expanding along with railroad construction, by 1897 the sport had moved south to Concepción, and extended farther to the north into Iquique. By 1903 Chillán was home to nine teams that represented a broad swath of Chilean society, from the elite to workers. Indeed, by the early 1900s Chileans of all social classes and political orientations used soccer for both recreational and educational activities.

Soccer influenced the development of Chilean politics in different ways. Perhaps it offered a form of escape from the increasingly complex daily life for many Chileans. But more than that, before the expansion of voting rights and the beginning of mass participation in politics in the late nineteenth and early twentieth centuries, soccer provided an avenue for political expression. By the mid-1920s, as Chile's economy and society became more "modern" and politics more inclusive, soccer brought new voters into the political and social milieu, acting as a sort of training ground for democracy and democratic attitudes in the region. How? Among other things, participation in soccer clubs promoted teamwork and necessitated negotiation between club members. Likewise, clubs themselves were often democratic institutions, holding elections for offices and voting on important issues.[4]

While soccer supported the development of democratic institutions, the Chilean elite sought to use soccer as way to control the working classes. Through the sponsorship of teams and tournaments, factory owners and landowners gave their workers a healthy outlet for their leisure time. Company owners and managers hoped that, rather than attend bars and brothels on their days off, workers would watch (or play in) soccer matches. In so doing they would become more physically and mentally sound, ultimately becoming better workers and citizens. The temperance movement also believed that workers would be less likely to fall into vice if they played soccer in their leisure time instead of going to bars. The state, for its part, considered soccer to be a tool for mobilization and cooptation. These relationships have often been seen as one-way streets: companies sponsored clubs and the workers responded; political actors manipulated the masses through sports and made them docile workers.

But it rarely worked as neatly as this. Workers, immigrants, and the popular classes in general saw the sport as a way to organize alternate avenues of political expression just as politicians, reformers, and industrialists used soccer in efforts to reinforce the status quo. While businessmen might have hoped that they could create a "more pliable workforce" through sponsorship of a team, "participation in company teams often strengthened workers' identification with one another."[5] Soccer, then, became a tool for class and ethnic consciousness, and enabled alternate forms of political training. Indeed, workers' clubs formed rapidly, both in particular factories and around specific trades, and by 1906 the Workers' Football Association (WFA) had formed. The WFA was part of a proliferation of soccer-related institutions in Santiago. Its formation suggests that, try as it might, the elite could control neither the growth nor the meaning of the sport. By the early 1900s hundreds of soccer teams, from elite social clubs to humble neighborhood clubs, provided opportunities to play soccer and to create affinities based on class, profession, and political leaning.[6]

Playing soccer or cheering on one's favorite team, then, carried with it political meanings. But it also created a common language that cut across political and class lines. Soccer operated—and continues to operate—on two levels at the same time: the micro level and the macro level. On one hand, these levels mark division. On the other, however, they bring people together. The micro level, which deals with individual experience, helped soccer cement class, ethnic, or regional identity. It also acted against the wishes and hopes of the elite, who wanted to use sport as a method to control workers and the poor. Players in the WFA found an outlet for expressing or consolidating class consciousness instead of being disciplined into docile workers by soccer. On the

macro level, which addressed larger national context, people of all social classes and political loyalties united behind the national team, regardless of what internal disagreements there might be. Why? Because
soccer seemed innocuous. It was recreation and leisure. Although support for a particular team suggested a certain place in the social, political, or economic hierarchy, it also presupposed an acceptance of that
hierarchy as legitimate. Even the most heated rivalries, in other words,
still underpinned the foundations of Chile as a nation.

In Chile the most intense early rivalry was that between Santiago
and Valparaíso, which played out in competitions known as intercities.
This rivalry played on geographical and "ethnic" difference and, while
it stoked passions and called attention to distinctions between the cities, it nevertheless helped to knit the country together. As pioneers of
soccer in Chile, Valparaísians considered theirs to be an "English" city
as a result of the influence of British merchants not only in the city's
economic life but also its sporting life. They thought themselves more
cosmopolitan than their rivals from the capital, going so far as to insult
santiaguinos by calling them "mestizo," a term meaning mixed race.
In response, Santiago clubs turned the mestizo epithets into badges
of pride. Those from Santiago argued that they represented the true
heart of the nation. For santiaguinos, the "English" from Valparaíso
represented a foreign invasion that only they, as "authentic" Chileans,
could defend against. Nevertheless, intercity matches simultaneously
pit Chilean against Chilean and united opposing fans. Players and
their fans sought to show that their city, region, or barrio was the best
in Chile, so pride in the neighborhood or town intertwined with pride
in the nation. Thus, from very early on in soccer's existence in Chile,
the sport played a crucial role in the formation of a modern nation,
acting as a conduit between politics and society. From workers' organizations to business owners and politicians, Chileans and other Latin
Americans recognized the political potential of the sport.

Soccer Coups

Chilean players remember the trip to the Soviet Union for a number of reasons. Some recall the chilling cold—twenty-three degrees

Fahrenheit—during the game, others a trip (that may or may not have happened) to the Bolshoi Ballet. Still others simply enjoyed walking around Moscow in the crisp fall air as they attempted to acclimate to Russian food and hospitality. The game itself was an ugly affair, a rough encounter played at night with the winner one step closer to the 1974 World Cup. Without doubt, the star of the game was Chile's captain and central defender, Elías Figueroa, who seemed to win every ball and effectively shut down any attempted Soviet attack. He played, it was said, like a man possessed. The rest of the Chilean team, led by forward Carlos Caszely, gamely tried to penetrate the solid Soviet defense, but with no luck. The game ended in a 0–0 draw, and the return leg was scheduled in November. That the game in Moscow happened at all, however, was just short of miraculous.

After their final training session before traveling to the Soviet Union, the Chilean national team—really Colo-Colo in national uniforms with a smattering of players from other teams—were sent home and told to reconvene the following morning at Juan Pinto Durán Sports Complex, the national team's training facility. Those from cities other than Santiago went back to their hotels to rest while other players went home to see their families. The next day players woke up and started working their way toward the training center. The trip took much longer than normal: military roadblocks impeded progress and trucks full of soldiers clogged roads all over the city. Those who reached the facility found few coaches and support staff, and fewer teammates. By 11:30 it became clear that they would not be leaving Chile that day: It was September 11, 1973. Throughout that morning as players tried to get to their rendezvous point, Chilean Air Force jets strafed the National Palace and tanks rolled through the streets to encircle the building. By 2 p.m., Salvador Allende had been overthrown in a military coup. After a week of intense negotiations, on September 17, the military government granted the national team permission to begin its trip to Moscow. Theirs was the first civilian flight to leave Santiago after the coup.[7]

Star Chilean striker Carlos Caszely meets with President Salvador Allende.

Among the players on the Chilean national team in 1973 was Carlos Caszely Garrido. Short and stout, Caszely's stocky legs propelled him forward surprisingly fast. Said to possess one of the best first touches of his generation, Caszely was also a lightning rod. He would be the first player ever to receive a straight red card at a World Cup, in 1974. In 1982 Caszely missed a penalty that might have propelled Chile into the second round of the World Cup. In the immediate aftermath of the coup, more importantly, Caszely was a Communist. Although he spent months at a time traveling with Colo-Colo and la Roja (as the national team is called), he still found time to campaign for leftist Unidad Popular candidates in that year's parliamentary elections.

Caszely was not the only Chilean player who opposed the military takeover that brought Augusto Pinochet in power. Leonardo "Pollo" Véliz, star left wing of Union Española, Colo-Colo, and the national team from 1970 to 1974, also remained firm in his leftist politics. At the urging of Allende, Véliz had been collaborating on a music project with Chilean folk legend Victor Jara, mixing social commentary and soccer. On the national team's return from the USSR, Véliz carried out what he called a "minor protest": he wore a Soviet hammer and sickle flag pin under his lapel when the new military government welcomed the team home from Moscow. Small as it might have been, this act carried a great deal of risk. Véliz had been intimately tied to the government of Salvador Allende, many of whose supporters were imprisoned and murdered in the days and weeks following the military putsch.[8] Jara, his musical collaborator, was murdered in the Santiago Stadium on September 16. Chilean soccer players, in other words, were no strangers to politics.

Ultimately, the 0–0 tie in the Soviet Union saw Chile qualify for the World Cup. A FIFA inspection team arrived in Santiago on October 24 to examine the National Stadium and gauge the atmosphere in Chile after the coup. With the seven thousand or so remaining prisoners shoved into locker rooms, the inspectors toured the stadium. Nothing seemed amiss; they were told that the locker rooms were closed

Elías Figueroa, captain of the Chilean national team, wins a header against West German player Gerd Mueller during the 1974 World Cup. © ullstein bild—Berlin-Bild / The Image Works

Elías Figueroa

Don Elías

Not all members of the Chilean national soccer team supported the opposition to Augusto Pinochet. Most players likely remained neutral while others supported the military government. Elías Ricardo Figueroa sided with the military. He also led la Roja in the most difficult of times. Captain of the 1974 World Cup squad, he was credited by teammates as being almost single-handedly responsible for the 0–0 draw with the Soviet Union in 1973. A defensive anchor for the team, he commanded the center of the field with speed, size, confidence, and tactical ability. After representing Chile in 1966 in England and earning the nickname "the red wall," by 1974 Elias was at the peak of his game. Although Chile failed to make it out of the first round in West Germany, Figueroa was voted the best defenseman of the tournament. In all, Figueroa represented Chile in three World Cups: 1966, 1974, and 1982.

Born in Valparaíso in 1946, Figueroa was diagnosed with polio at age eleven and essentially had to learn to walk again. After doing so, nothing seemed beyond his capacity. His professional career began with the youth squad of Santiago Wanderers in 1962. That year, Chile hosted the World Cup and Figueroa found himself playing a warm-up game against the Brazilian

for painting and repair. Noting that the field appeared in good condition and that the country was completely calm, FIFA's inspectors gave the green light for the match. With the positive report in his hands, FIFA president Stanley Rous announced that the game would go on as scheduled, on November 21. It was not to be. The Soviet Union, citing the ongoing humanitarian and political crisis in Chile, refused to travel to play in a concentration camp. Instead, the fans that went to the stadium that day saw the national team kickoff against a nonexistent opponent and walk the ball into the net. Officially, the match ended as a forfeit. It was the first time that a nation boycotted a FIFA event for political reasons.

national team. He impressed Brazil's star players, who found it difficult to maneuver around the fifteen-year-old amateur. Figueroa's professional career spanned nearly twenty years, during which he played professionally in Chile, Brazil, Uruguay, and the United States; after 1967 every professional team that he represented won at least one championship. Individually, Figueroa was named South American Footballer of the Year for three straight years, 1974–76. He is widely considered the best player ever to play for Chile and one of the best defensemen ever. Franz Beckenbauer, the German great, once called himself "the European Figueroa."

Though beloved for his soccer, Figueroa did not escape controversy off the field. Shortly after the military coup in 1973, Figueroa allied himself with Augusto Pinochet's government and is generally remembered for his support of the regime. He publicly supported Pinochet in 1980 and 1988 in referenda on the dictator's rule. During the final years of the military government Figueroa became a television and radio commentator for the state-run network, a post that he gave up after Pinochet's fall. After the return of democracy, Figueroa remained outside of Chilean politics and started a winery, Don Elías vineyards. In 2011 he was nominated as an alternative candidate to Sepp Blatter by the organization ChangeFIFA in response to corruption in the sport's governing body. He turned down the nomination.

Chile's transformation into a repressive dictatorship surprised observers. For the better part of the twentieth century it had been a poster child for stable democracies in the region. While every other South American country underwent massive upheavals and seemed destined for permanent revolution, Chile had a remarkably stable political system. With the exception of one short civil war in the 1890s and a brief military foray into politics in the 1920s, Chileans exhibited an uncanny ability to resolve national problems at the ballot box. From 1932 until 1970 every president served his term peacefully and turned power over to an elected successor. Moreover, power almost always rotated from party to party, suggesting that Chile's multiparty system worked. Indeed, Communist and Socialist parties regularly participated in elections, won seats in Congress, and formed working coalitions with parties of all political stripes, including the far right. Yet by the middle of the twentieth century the apparently strong fabric of Chile's multiparty democracy began to fray. The growing strength of right- and left-wing politics, coupled with an ideologically driven centrist party, revealed a huge political divide among the electorate.[9] Perhaps paradoxically, the long-term stability of the democratic system in Chile served to blind citizens to the potential for military intervention and autocratic rule.

Compounding matters for Chile, the growth of left-wing political strength at home coincided with rising concern in the United States over the potential for the spread of leftist ideologies in the Americas. In 1954 the United States funded the overthrow of Jacobo Arbenz, the democratically elected reformist president of Guatemala, and the Cuban Revolution caused panic in U.S. government circles. As a result, the United States committed increasing amounts of money to Chilean political parties to stop the left-wing Unidad Popular coalition from coming to power. Starting with the Chilean presidential election in 1958, the CIA funneled money into the campaigns of both right-wing and centrist political politicians. In 1958 rightist Jorge Alessandri came to power with a slim plurality, winning just over 31 percent of the vote. By 1964, with greater investment from the United States, opposition centrist Eduardo Frei won over 55 percent of the vote (marking only the second time that a Chilean politician won an outright majority in a presidential election). Leftist Salvador Allende finished second with over 38 percent. The combination of worsening relations between political parties and increased U.S. intervention in Chilean electoral politics spelled trouble for the nation.

Elections in 1970 revealed a country further polarized by the events of the prior six years. Worker mobilization, both in the cities and in the agricultural sector, increased markedly. More than that, however, the presidential campaign took on uncommonly vicious tones. Both the right-wing National Party and the centrist Christian Democrats received assistance from the United States. Nevertheless, the Unidad Popular coalition and Salvador Allende won the presidency on the promise of leading Chile down a democratic road to Socialism. The right mobilized immediately to stop Allende from coming to power:

Chilean military leaders, with U.S. assistance, organized the "kidnapping" of the head of the Armed Forces, René Schneider, with the intent of blaming leftist revolutionaries. The plot backfired when Schneider died resisting the attack. The leaders of the plan were arrested, Schneider was buried as a martyr of democracy, and Allende's passage to the presidency was ensured.

Allende's stay in the presidential palace, however, would be the shortest of any Chilean president since the 1930s. Less than three years after his inauguration, he died in office during Pinochet's coup.[10] Many Chileans would agree that Allende's time as president was one of increasing tension and conflict in the country. Still, few would have imagined the ferocity with which the military attempted to uproot Chile's democratic traditions. The U.S. Embassy estimated that the military killed between 2,000 and 10,000 people in the first days after the coup, although the official number of deaths related to the seventeen-year military regime has been recorded as 3,100. Tens of thousands of Chileans were rounded up and herded into the National Stadium where many were tortured, raped, and killed. In fact, throughout the country soccer stadiums served as convenient locations to hold, question, and in many cases kill opposition leaders and supporters.

More than the immediate repression of the left wing, the military junta that came under the increasing control of Augusto Pinochet began to close down all mediums of expression in the country. The Communist and Socialist parties were outlawed, while those of the center and right were declared "in recess." Press censorship became the norm while unions and student and professional organizations had their leadership removed and replaced by government appointees. This held true for the soccer federations as well.

Narratives of State Control

The Pinochet government quickly set about dismantling the democracy that had differentiated Chile from most of its neighbors, and then turned its sights to other aspects of Chilean society, including soccer. Professional soccer in Chile had long-standing economic problems that dated back beyond the 1960s. Clubs overextended their budgets by signing players to contracts that they knew they could not pay, and by the early 1970s many teams were on the verge of bankruptcy. Pinochet saw the failing clubs as an opportunity: if he could bring clubs back to solvency, he could win popular support for his regime. But Pinochet considered soccer to be more than just a way to distract the population. Indeed, the military government saw the sport as a crucial way to "help the social development of the country."[11]

Pinochet's most obvious efforts to control soccer came in the form of the leadership of the national governing bodies of the sport: the Asociación Central de Fútbol (ACF), the Asociación Nacional de Fútbol (ANF), and the Federación de Fútbol de Chile (FFC). The ACF, which oversaw the professional league, and the amateur ANF both had new directors within a year of the coup. The junta banned all forms of elections in the country, so club presidents and military appointees effectively chose members of the soccer governing bodies. Pinochet saw sports as a way to create structure out of the "chaos" of the Allende years, and a way to "strengthen national unity." In Pinochet's eyes, the "physical, intellectual, and moral" development of Chile had regressed during the Unidad Popular government. His goal was to use soccer to strengthen national unity and renovate the country.[12]

One avenue for using soccer relied on improving and expanding the Chilean professional league by raising revenue for the sport. To this end, the government tasked the General Direction of Sports (DIGEDER), Chile's umbrella organization for sport, with developing a system for strengthening soccer. DIGEDER itself had been formed in the 1940s as a part of the country's efforts to promote healthy bodies and patriotic citizens. Perhaps it should come as no surprise, then, that the precursor to DIGEDER, the Department of Sports, was a unit of the Ministry of Defense. In 1975, with Pinochet's blessing, DIGEDER introduced Polla Gol, officially known as the System of Sports Predictions, a betting system designed to defray the rising cost of soccer, keep ticket prices low, and redistribute revenue among teams. In a kind of lottery, each week Chileans could buy a ticket and bet on the outcomes of weekly games. Anyone who predicted over a certain number of games correctly received a cash prize. Each week Polla Gol paid out a percentage to winners, a percentage to teams in order to help pay operating costs, and a percentage to DIGEDER for the development of sports.

If DIGEDER itself was uncontroversial, Polla Gol caused concern from the moment Pinochet created it and remained a subject for accusations of corruption throughout his regime. Not only did it make Chilean soccer dependent on the government for much-needed funds but soccer clubs themselves waffled about support for the betting system. Ultimately, clubs received little of the benefits: clubs split between 4 and 15 percent of Polla Gol profits. Regardless of criticism, however, the government made clear its commitment to the betting system in 1987, calling it a crucial support for DIGEDER and, hence, for the nation. Soccer, according to the government, helped to train people to live in society, as it "possess[es] moral and ethical, biological and psychological values." It was a "socializing agent that contributes to the adaptation of the individual to his environment," and also gave fans the opportunity to be in the "presence of a community and [a] shared belief in a common cause." Without Polla Gol the Chilean soccer league would collapse and with it—according to Pinochet's appointees in DIGEDER—Chilean society.[13]

Polla Gol was only one way that Pinochet sought to create legitimacy and popular base through soccer. Many of his other efforts focused on Colo-Colo, one of Chile's oldest and most popular clubs. In 1976, in part as a result of the team failing to make payroll, he had the ACF intervene in club management, effectively handing operations of the club to his political allies. In 1978, while still being operated by Pinochet associates, Colo-Colo reached an agreement with star striker Carlos Caszely to return to the team—and Chile—after five years of playing overseas. His return was met with a great deal of fanfare by the Chilean press, which chose to gloss over Caszely's outspoken anti-Pinochet politics. Ten years later Pinochet sought to use Colo-Colo again. In a move clearly aimed at gaining support before the 1988 referendum on his rule, he offered Colo-Colo $300,000 to complete construction on a new stadium. As this offer made clear, the true aim of Pinochet's interventions in soccer had little to do with the sport and more to do with politics. But these moves failed to have the desired effect. Colo-Colo, and soccer in general, continued to struggle.

Attendance at stadiums dropped, the quality of play faltered, clubs continued to miss payroll, and stadiums fell into disrepair. As soccer went, so went the nation.

Although an extreme case, Pinochet's takeover of Colo-Colo was hardly the first time that politicians worked to bail out soccer clubs. The inability of clubs to pay players' salaries had been a concern in Chilean soccer since it professionalized in 1933, putting the sport in a near constant state of economic crisis. Teams from lower leagues could not compete with the promises of higher salaries from larger clubs, so they often signed contracts that they knew they would be unable to pay without political intercession. Prior to the coup, local politicians had a variety of ways to funnel resources to clubs. They facilitated land transfers for stadium construction, provided "cultural funds" to sponsor club activities, and supported efforts to attain bank loans or government grants. Politicians saw support for soccer as a way to tap into popular fervor and influence voters. By being seen as supporting a club, politicians sought to curry favor among voters. For the clubs the benefits were clear: they could spend above their means without much concern.

Among the early efforts to hitch politics to soccer were those of Arturo Alessandri. Chilean president from 1920 to 1924 and again from 1932 to 1938, Alessandri looked to the sport as a way to build political power for his party. A constant increase in soccer attendance in the 1930s spelled out clearly the sport's popularity: from fewer than 100,000 fans in 1933 to nearly 830,000 (the equivalent of 16 percent of Chile's population) in 1940.[14] Yet the country had little soccer infrastructure to speak of: there were few stadiums, no national stadium, and many major clubs had to rent out rivals' fields for home games. Alessandri saw the growth of soccer as a spectator sport as a potential opportunity.

Alessandri announced in 1936 that the government would fund a national soccer stadium to fit the modern image of the nation. Construction began in 1937 amid much fanfare and was completed in late 1938. At the outset the conservative Alessandri seemed to have tapped into the populist appeal of the sport. But during the time that it took to construct the stadium, Chile experienced both an economic downturn and a rise in political opposition, and any goodwill generated by the stadium evaporated. Elections in 1938 swept Alessandri's party from office. Later that year at the opening ceremony for the stadium, just two weeks before the end of his term, the assembled crowd booed throughout his speech. Alessandri had attempted to use the power of sports to paper over economic hardship and to bolster political support for his party. Thinking that building a national stadium would perform both of these tasks, Alessandri gambled on his ability to manipulate soccer to his own ends. He lost. Nevertheless, others would try their hands at using soccer for political goals.

Soccer Dreams (1962)

Chile's hosting of the 1962 World Cup came out of the blue. The head of Chile's World Cup bid committee, Carlos Dittborn, inspired little confidence when he closed his argument in front of the FIFA meeting in Lisbon in 1956: "Because we have nothing," he said, "we want to do everything." This was hardly an assurance that FIFA would accept today, when it demands state-of-the-art stadiums, hotels, and communications networks. In fact, very few in Chile believed that they had a chance to win the bid. After all, Argentina, the other finalist, had a well-established soccer infrastructure to highlight its readiness to host the Cup. Chile, on the other hand, had no venues other than the National Stadium large enough to hold World Cup crowds. Roads and communication systems languished in disrepair. But Chile won the bid as the result, according to some, of Cold War politics: the entire Soviet bloc voted in favor of Chile in order to prevent Argentina from hosting the World Cup.[15] In 1958, with little work complete on the necessary infrastructure, Arturo Alessandri's son Jorge was elected president. He inherited a World Cup project that he did not want. Perhaps the younger Alessandri had learned the lessons of his father. He initially saw little value in mixing the World Cup and politics and balked at the cost of tournament preparations. Nevertheless, he quietly approved the monies set aside for construction and infrastructure improvement.

Alessandri became even less interested in hosting the 1962 World Cup after a devastating earthquake hit Chile in May 1960, killing thousands and causing tens of millions of dollars in damage. At first he suggested that the money earmarked for the World Cup committee should be diverted to reconstruction efforts. But the outpouring of international support for Chile and the organizing committee's insistence convinced the president to see the potential benefits of hosting the event. He began to believe not only that the World Cup would provide a much-needed psychological lift to the population after the earthquake but that it would also provide the opportunity to develop the country. As a result he ultimately committed to the World Cup project. The country strengthened its transportation and communication infrastructure, beautified host cities, and repaired and built stadiums in preparation for the Cup. By the time the tournament arrived, Alessandri seemed to understand soccer's political potential, posing for photographs with workers and making self-congratulatory speeches. He was not, however, the only politician to use hosting the World Cup as a political tool. In 1962 Salvador Allende, then a senator, promised to introduce a law that would give houses to the Chilean national team if they beat the Soviet Union in the World Cup quarterfinals. The law passed, and Chile won.

The World Cup in 1962 was Chile's biggest success on the world soccer stage. Playing in front of home crowds in Santiago throughout the opening round, la Roja defeated Italy and Switzerland before winning its quarterfinal matchup with the Soviet Union. Although Chile lost to eventual champions Brazil in the semifinals, it beat Yugoslavia to win third place. If, from the standpoint of Chilean soccer, the tournament was a complete success, from an organizational perspective it was not. The World Cup in Chile ranks among the worst in terms of attendance. It was too difficult to get to Chile from much of the world, and internal transportation networks to games in secondary cities were poor. As a result many games were played in half-full stadiums, and tens of thousands of expected tourists never arrived. Yet Chileans still remember 1962 as a crucial moment in the nation's history, when it overcame political, geological, and sporting obstacles.

Building off of Chile's sporting success in the World Cup, in 1963 Alessandri sought to foster support for the government by controlling the price of soccer tickets. His government invoked a seldom-used thirty-year-old law that permitted the government to cap prices for items of "primary necessity." Soccer, apparently, entered the same class as bread, heating oil, and gasoline. Again the following year Alessandri ruled that ticket prices could not be raised, which many interpreted as a thinly veiled election year ploy to garner more support for his National Party. Just as his father's project of building the National Stadium failed to sway the electorate, the younger Alessandri's efforts failed as well. Yet he can hardly be blamed for trying. In a country of about 8 million people in 1965, more than 3 million tickets were sold for soccer matches. In other words, politicians saw that soccer *could* be a powerful mobilizing force in politics, but they did not yet know how to harness it.

Chilean politicians were not alone in attempting to manipulate soccer for political purposes. In 1970 the Brazilian military dictatorship used the World Cup victory in Mexico along with its star, Pelé, to project itself as a government of the people. The government highlighted the Verde-Amarela victory as a sign of the nation's progress and flew the team directly from Mexico City to Brasilia to meet with the president. In 1978 Argentina hosted and won the World Cup in the midst of a violently repressive military government. For the most part, hosting the Cup was a boon to the military dictatorship of Jorge Videla. The junta assumed that a month of soccer would temporarily distract Argentines from dire political and human rights problems. And they were partly right: although around the world an anti–World Cup solidarity movement formed, much of the international press ignored or downplayed the political situation, and winning the Cup created a euphoric atmosphere. But the World Cup in Argentina was not without its glitches. Some reporters visited the Mothers of the Plaza de Mayo, a group of women who met in one of Buenos Aires' main plazas every day asking the whereabouts of their children. Others printed stories about political repression. In other words, governments around the region sought to use soccer to their advantage, but they could not always control the message in the way that they wanted.

Just as politicians in Chile and around the region sought to use the sport to promote their image of the nation and their political agendas, so too opposition groups used soccer to promote their positions. Perhaps the most well-known Latin American example of the counter-politics of soccer is the Brazilian team Corinthians. In the late 1970s and early 1980s, in the midst of a military dictatorship, the club Corinthians became the focal point for democratization efforts. Led by the charismatic, chain-smoking medical-doctor-cum-soccer-star Sócrates, Corinthians' players openly supported a slate of candidates in club elections who had close ties to the democracy movement. Players vowed not to play if the slate linked to the military won. The prodemocracy slate won, and Corinthians Democracy expanded outside of soccer to push for more representative government in Brazil. But Corinthians Democracy was not the only prodemocracy soccer movement in the decades full of military rule in Latin America. Indeed, soccer

For the 1974 World Cup, the Chilean team received heavy security. Here the police guard the Chilean national team on arrival to their hotel. © ullstein bild—Mathias Krohn / The Image Works

Workers erect barbed wire to protect the Chilean national team hotel. Concern over the team's security prompted exceptional measures. © ullstein bild—Kasperski / The Image Works

became an immediate vehicle for protesting the overthrow of Chile's democratically elected government.

The 1974 World Cup in West Germany took place nine months after the Pinochet coup and in a country undergoing deep political upheavals of its own. It had been the site of terrorist attacks two years earlier during the Munich Olympic Games, and as the World Cup approached the West German government planned for heightened security around the matches. Tensions reached the boiling point the day before the tournament opened, when a bomb attack damaged the Chilean consulate in West Berlin. Newspaper reports noted that helicopters and two thousand extra police guarded the Brazil–Yugoslavia match on the tournament's first day, making it "one of the best guarded pieces of real estate on the earth."[16] The Chilean team also found itself under intense security, staying in hotels and training on fields surrounded by barbed wire and armed guards.

While all of the protective measures succeeded in forestalling violence during the tournament, they failed to keep protesters from conveying their message. Knowing that the World Cup would draw an estimated 600 million viewers from around the world, exile and solidarity groups sought to publicize the violence of the Pinochet regime by protesting during Chile's matches. West German police sought to restrict access to the fields for protesters, searching for banners, signs, and other protest material, but they failed to intercept everyone.

During Chile's match against hosts West Germany, protesters attempted to drown out the Chilean national anthem by chanting "Chile Sí, Junta No!" At least six large banners could be seen around the stadium with messages ranging from "Chile Socialista" and "Facismo No" to "Pinochet." Increased security for the following game against East Germany reduced protest but failed to stop it completely. Once again, chants of "Chile Sí, Junta No!" rang across the stadium and were

Police arrest demonstrators who raised banners protesting the Pinochet regime during Chile's first match in the 1974 World Cup. © ullstein bild— Schirner X / The Image Works

Police arrest protesters who ran onto the pitch with a large Chilean flag to protest the military government during Chile's 0–0 draw with Australia. © ullstein bild—Dannenbaum / The Image Works

audible to the television audience during the 1–1 draw. And during Chile's 0–0 tie with Australia, which effectively knocked Chile out of the tournament, a torrential rainstorm allowed a group of protesters to run onto the field with a large Chilean flag, disrupting the game for a few minutes. This protest caught Chilean national television unaware, and for a few moments the antigovernment action aired live throughout the country.[17] It was a moment that few in Chile would forget, and it showed that soccer stadiums could be ideal venues for airing political grievances. Chilean protesters would return to the soccer field ten years later as national protests against the regime erupted onto the streets.

Roots of Protest

Historians have a tendency, almost an occupational hazard, to paint with a broad brush when constructing narratives. And the generalizations that we make typically obscure a good deal of lived experience.

So, for example, the Pinochet dictatorship is often portrayed as unchanging over its seventeen years. Yet this is hardly the truth. Over the course of the regime certain things held constant: the threat of arbitrary arrest, torture, and death, for example, or the favoring of free-market economic policies. However, there was also variation within the regime over time. Subtle policy changes and small political openings marked a government adapting to stay in power. The *mano dura* (iron fist) of Pinochet's early years softened slightly with the *apertura* (opening) of 1983 only to harden again later that year.

While Pinochet's political project attempted to limit opposition through repression, his economic policies favored intense free-market capitalism. Chile's economic gurus, known as the Chicago Boys (because most had studied at the University of Chicago), promoted privatization of key state sectors including social security and health care. At first, the "Chilean miracle" appeared to be working. Inflation came down from a peak of 700 percent in the final year of the Allende government and the economy grew, albeit slowly. Under the surface, however, poverty mushroomed. Income disparity widened, and both underemployment and unemployment soared. Pinochet froze wages in 1981, meaning that real wages (the rate of pay when inflation is taken into account) dropped. By 1982 unemployment in Chile reached 19 percent with a further 13 percent of the population employed by the government-sponsored minimum employment program (MEP). A year later, unemployment stood at 26.4 percent; fully one-third of the Chilean working age population was out of work or employed by the MEP. That year Chile's gross domestic product *fell* by 14.5 percent.[18]

Chileans had had enough. Workers in Chile's all-important copper sector called for a work stoppage. To everyone's surprise, the strike spread from the poor to the middle classes, which had played a major role in bringing down Salvador Allende's government. Truckers, middle-class housewives, and other former supporters of the military coup came out actively in opposition to Pinochet. Pinochet responded with the apertura: a limited opening designed to allay opposition concerns without doing anything about them. As part of the opening, the government permitted the Democratic Alliance—a combination of center and moderately left-wing political parties—to hold a rally in May 1983.

Three hundred thousand people attended. Pinochet responded with increased government repression, but students, professionals, and workers continued the protest. A spiral of violence ensued.

But Pinochet responded not only with force. His regime also tried to deflect attention from the gathering economic crisis with soccer. Working through the soccer federation, the military government sought to increase its popularity by placing first-division teams in every corner of the country. So the ACF increased the number of teams in Chile's first division and lengthened the season. From sixteen teams in 1982, the league expanded to twenty-two in 1983 and twenty-six in 1984. A forty-two week professional soccer schedule, the government hoped, would keep some Chileans' minds from their daily struggle. Pinochet's plans did not work. Attendance spiraled down. Instead of uniting the nation and strengthening professional soccer, expanding the league had the opposite effect. The quality of play dropped. Officials, from referees to linesmen, came under more pressure for their game calling. The league continued to lose money and teams continued to have trouble making payroll.

In fact, Pinochet's efforts to politicize the national game backfired. The economic crisis of the 1980s gave opposition groups the support that they needed to edge back out of the shadows. And among the first places that they reappeared was in the soccer stadiums. Illegal unions held impromptu organizational meetings and planned actions against the government in the locker rooms and stands of stadiums around the country.[19] The rabid fans of the Universidad de Chile football team are often credited with being among the first to publicly disavow the regime: the chant of "y va a caer, y va a caer" (and he will fall and he will fall) rang out from the student section on September 11, 1983, during a Copa América game against Uruguay at the National Stadium.[20] Even as la Roja defeated Celeste for one of the only times in Chile's history, the newsworthy event was the eruption of protest at the match.

Antigovernment protests soon became a regular part of Chilean soccer matches. At first only Universidad de Chile supporters took part, but protests soon spread to stadiums across the country. Fans used the sheer number of spectators at games as a shield; there was no way that regime forces could arrest entire sections of the stadium.

Alexis Sánchez

El niño maravilloso

Alexis Alejandro Sánchez Sánchez has been compared to Cristiano Ronaldo and Lionel Messi for his speed with the ball and ability to make defenders look bad. After debuting with the club team Cobreola at age sixteen, within a year he moved to Chilean giant Colo-Colo before being signed by the Italian side Udinese. There, between 2008 and 2011, Sánchez began to show his true ability, scoring twenty goals in ninety-five games. He was named player of the year in the Serie A for 2010–11.

Even before his transfer to the Italy's top-flight league, he was on the radar of the Chilean national team administration. He featured in Chile's surprise third-place finish at the Youth World Cup in 2007 and became a regular on the senior national team in 2009. Sánchez is the youngest player to earn a cap for Chile, earning his first at age seventeen. After a successful qualifying campaign, the 2010 World Cup (Chile lost to Brazil in the Round of Sixteen), and the 2011 Copa América, Sánchez transferred to Barcelona for €26 million and quickly showed that he fit with the best in the world. Sánchez started thirty games across all competitions with the Blaugrana in his first season, scoring fourteen goals and serving up thirty assists.

Born in Tocopilla, a coastal city in the north of the country, Sánchez was raised by his mother, who cleaned fish and worked as a housekeeper. At age eight, his uncle moved with him to Rancagua so that he could attend the soccer school of a Chilean professional team. Homesick, he returned to Tocopilla after two years and continued playing there before being signed by Cobreola.

Though not involved in politics, Sánchez became the ambassador for Chile's "Choose to Live Healthy" campaign in 2011. Selected by Chile's first lady, his image is used by the government to promote physical activity and fight against child labor. Assuming Chile qualifies for Brazil, Sánchez will no longer be a *niño* at the 2014 World Cup. At twenty-five he will likely be the main strike target. As it is, by the end of 2013 he was already ninth on la Roja's all-time scoring list with twenty-two goals in sixty-two appearances with the national team.

Chilean striker Alexis Sánchez celebrates a goal against Uruguay, 2010. © EFE/ZUMApress.com

Furthermore, it was not always clear whether fan protest centered on the poor play on the field, the actions of the referee, or the government. Stones and bottles thrown at players and officials brought a response from the elite paramilitary police known as Carabineros, blurring the lines between "hooliganism" and political action. Either way, the crescendo of violence at soccer games remained a weekly reminder of people's displeasure with the economy and the government. In other words, just as soccer served as a vessel for right-wing leaders of Latin America to promote their vision of nationalism, so too it could be used as vehicle for protest. It could even help to overthrow the government.

End Game

It was part of one of many campaign spots televised for the "No" vote in the 1988 plebiscite on continuing Augusto Pinochet's rule. Every night for roughly one month prior to the vote, the prodemocracy Concertación por el No (Coalition for the No) received fifteen minutes of free airtime. Along with the song "Alegría ya viene," the campaign interspersed testimonials explaining people's personal reasons for opposition to eight more years of military rule. Among the testimonials, that of Olga Garrido stands out as among the most powerful. By 1988 it was understood that state-sponsored terror was not only directed at leftist activists but that it could happen to anyone. And Garrido in many ways represented the everywoman: petite and composed, and a mother of two, this simple woman was still a victim of the regime's violence. In the advertisement she spoke directly into the camera, telling of her arrest and torture by Pinochet's military apparatus. Garrido explained that she could forget her physical torture, but that she would not easily forget the "moral" torture, which she carried in her mind and her heart. Because of this, she said, she would vote against Pinochet. The camera slowly panned away to show a Colo-Colo pennant on the wall and a man standing next to Garrido: Carlos Caszely. As the former star striker for the Chilean national team came into focus, he said that he too would vote no, as he took his mother's hand in his own.[21]

From the early twentieth century, political leaders in Chile and around the region recognized that soccer held an important key to their societies. They could use it in efforts to win popularity or to quiet a restive population. Whether they sought to mobilize or pacify the population, soccer seemed to offer a way. However, national leaders failed to recognize their inability to control the meaning of the sport. While they could try to convey a message using soccer, in other words, they could not guarantee its impact. Nor could they keep the opposition from attempting to use soccer for their ends. Just as politicians used the sport in efforts to build legitimacy, protesters exploited soccer to question authority and help bring down the regime. Especially in Chile, where early adoption of the sport by all social classes helped the development a pluralistic mindset, the meaning of soccer was difficult to control.

Interlude 2

Professionalization

Perhaps nothing had a greater impact on Latin American soccer than the advent of the professional game, which began in the early 1930s. In the narrative of Latin American soccer history, professionalization is often considered the third phase of soccer's development, crucial to its expansion. Although resisted at first, professionalism ultimately expanded soccer's popularity in the region for both players and spectators, and cemented soccer's place as the national sport.

Professionalism came late to Latin American soccer. Unlike in England and the United States, where players took money for play by the early 1900s, Latin America officially adhered to the amateur ideal—a supposedly British notion that sport should be played only out of love—until the 1930s. Being paid to play a sport was considered demeaning both to the player and to the game as a whole, and critics feared that paying players would reduce fan loyalty and diminish the level of play. Thus, the struggle against professionalism in the region, which began in the 1920s, had the nature of a moralizing fight for the heart of the sport.

Many early Latin American players, who generally came from the economic and social elite, saw amateurism as a way to limit the ability of the working classes to play. Since workers, recent immigrants (from the countryside or overseas), and other non-elites could not afford to take time off from work to practice, amateurism ensured that few men without means could take the pitch. Yet it would be a mistake to think that only the elite favored amateurism. Among the working classes, too, many opposed paying players. In Chile, for example, many workers took a nativist stand against professionalism, worried that it would bring foreigners into Chile to play.

Although resisted by both the elite and the poor, professional soccer eventually arrived in Latin America. It first appeared in the form of "disguised professionalism." This ill-kept secret developed in the 1920s, when team sponsors—whether social clubs or factories—hired star players to "work" in factories or offices. Players' work schedules were made to never interfere with practice time or games. A less veiled form of play-for-pay existed as well: players for many clubs received "gifts" for winning matches and some form of remuneration for traveling to play. In fact, disguised professionalism was so widespread that one of the arguments made in the 1930s in favor of paying players was that they were accustomed to it: many had been receiving money for over ten years.

By the 1930s teams and national associations worried that a failure to compensate players would cause them to move out of the country to play. And they were right. Brazil, Argentina, and Uruguay lost players of Italian and Spanish heritage who received generous offers to play in their ancestral homelands. Many of these players would go on to play in Olympic and World Cup competition for the Italian or Spanish national teams.

In 1932 FIFA stopped resisting professionalization and announced that each national federation could decide whether to permit professional leagues. Shortly thereafter, in 1933, Brazil professionalized, causing a schism in Brazilian soccer. The same occurred in Argentina. There, the payment of players in 1931 splintered the Argentine Amateur Football Association as the largest clubs broke away to form the professional Argentine Football League. The two leagues came back together in 1935. Chile professionalized in 1933 when the largest clubs in Santiago formed a renegade league. The Liga Profesional, as it was known, received almost immediate recognition from the national federation, which saw that soccer's survival in the country required the acceptance of professional teams. Mexico and Honduras professionalized somewhat later, Mexico in 1943 and Honduras in 1951, but the effect was the same.

In the end the advent of professional soccer in Latin America did little to diminish the importance of the game. To the contrary, it brought about a higher quality of play, with a more regularized schedule and more revenue for team owners. Perhaps more importantly, it further opened the playing field; in Brazil professionalization allowed Afro-Brazilians to enter the game in increasing numbers while elsewhere it fostered growth among the working classes. And though it would eventually begin to erode the bonds between player and club, players did not become truly mercenary for a long time. At the same time, professionalism did not stop Latin American players from leaving their countries to play elsewhere in the region and in Europe, where many of the top players had been emigrating since the 1920s. Indeed, that trend continues to this day, as many Latin American players use local clubs as stepping-stones to more lucrative contracts in Europe.

5

Dark, Expressive Sportsmen
of a Distant Continent?

Race and Soccer in Honduras

October 14, 2009, dawned tense in the Honduran capital, Tegucigalpa. Four months earlier the elected president, José Manuel Zelaya, was ousted by a military coup and forced into exile. The governmental crisis that brought Roberto Micheletti to power came as a surprise in Honduras, which has historically had less upheaval than its neighbors. In late September, Zelaya returned secretly to the country and was sequestered in the Brazilian embassy, further ratcheting up pressure in the capital. Violence and protests increased daily, and no solution to the impasse seemed on the horizon.

Yet for many Hondurans tension that day focused not on politics but on apparently more trivial concerns: a soccer match. It was the final day of qualifying for the 2010 World Cup, and the Honduran national team, known as Los Catrachos, La H, or La Bicolor, had a chance to qualify for the first time since 1982. To do so, however, two things needed to happen. First, the Bicolor had to defeat El Salvador in El

Salvador, which was itself no easy task. But victory at Estadio Cuscat-lán would mean nothing if Costa Rica won its game against the United States. So Honduras needed the U.S. team to tie or defeat the Ticos. Complicating matters for Honduras, the United States had nothing to play for: it had already qualified for South Africa and so did not play its strongest squad.

FIFA arranges qualifying games so that they start at roughly the same time in efforts to cut down the potential for match fixing. At 6:05 p.m. in San Salvador (8:05 p.m. in Washington, D.C.), the two games began. Things appeared to be going against Honduras after twenty-five minutes. Costa Rica's dynamic striker Bryan Ruiz had scored twice in a three-minute span to put Costa Rica on top. Carlos Pavón's goal for Los Catrachos in the sixty-fourth minute raised Honduran spirits, but they would still need a miracle: by the seventieth minute, the United States had yet to score, and when the final whistle blew for La H, Costa Rica still led 2–1.

On the field in San Salvador after their match ended, Hondu-ran players whispered silent prayers and waited to hear their fates. Throughout Honduras, from the capital to the north coast, from the mountains to the Pacific Ocean, people remained glued to their TVs and radios. Televicentro had switched to the final minutes of the U.S.–Costa Rica game, which had extended well into extra time. And then it came: around 9:10 p.m. an ecstatic and spontaneous scream echoed throughout Honduras, sending the nation into the streets, bringing players and fans alike to their knees in tears, and unifying the frac-tious politics of a small, impoverished Central American nation for a moment. Honduras would be represented, for the whole world to see, in the most important global sports event.

But what picture would the world see? The dominant narrative of Honduran history suggests a mestizo country in which the population is mostly a mixture of Spanish and indigenous blood. Yet viewing the Honduran national team that night, one was reminded of a description of the Brazilian team in the London *Times* on June 30, 1958: "dark, expressive sportsmen of a different continent." In other words, a lot of the players looked black. Indeed, people watching who knew nothing of the country except its soccer team would think most Hondurans

The Honduran national soccer team celebrates in El Salvador's Estadio Cuscatlán, after the United States defeated Costa Rica to put Honduras through to the 2010 World Cup. October 14, 2009. © EFE/ZUMAPress.com

had African blood. More than half the players on national team at the 2010 World Cup in South Africa were of African descent. The presence of so many black players when officially Afro-Hondurans make up around 2 percent of the population raises many questions about race in Honduras. It could suggest that, since the national team is multiethnic, Honduras has few problems with race. But at a more fundamental level, the racial makeup of the Catrachos calls the Honduran narrative of race into question.

Race, Latin America, and Honduras

For much of the twentieth century most Latin American countries have downplayed the existence of their African-descended populations, choosing instead to highlight their mestizo heritage. In the early twentieth century, nationalist elites in Honduras and elsewhere created a narrative of race that foregrounded their European and indigenous background at the expense of their countries' African roots.

"Mestizo," a term that loosely means mixed race, actually very specifically connotes the combination of two broad backgrounds: European
and indigenous. In reality, however, Latin American peoples formed
from the combination of indigenous, Africans, and Europeans from
the first contact between Europe and the Americas. As this mixture
occurred, Europeans sought to ensure that only those of pure European blood remained on the top of the social pyramid. They thus
created racial hierarchies based on the interplay of phenotype (skin
color, hair texture, etc.), heritage, and social class. Three "pure" categories—European, black, and indigenous—existed alongside dozens of
intermediate categories that came to be known as *castas*. These castas
included the more common mestizo (one-half each European and indigenous), mulatto (one-half each African and European), and *zambo*
(one-half each indigenous and African). Some of the categories had
strange names, like coyote, *salta atrás* (jump backward), and *tente en
el aire* (up in the air), but all of them were intended to keep people in
their place, with laws regulating the behavior of different castas. Yet
while the Spanish and Portuguese established this racial hierarchy in
which whiter was better, the boundaries between categories were always fluid and shifting. More importantly, however, due to a flawed
understanding of genetics, Latin American elites believed all of these
mixtures would eventually lead toward a whitened population.

In the late nineteenth century nationalist elites in Latin America argued that generations of intermixing and waves of European immigration would "whiten" and "civilize" their populations. Racial ideologies
of the era, now loosely grouped together and called "scientific racism,"
valorized light skin and European heritage. Thinkers such as Herbert
Spencer, Gustave Le Bon, and Auguste Comte argued that human societies evolved just as biological organisms did, and that a nation was
higher on the evolutionary chain as it became more developed, modern, "civilized," and white. Along with these ideologies came the now
debunked theory called polygenism, which suggested that different
races came from different roots and each had social traits attached to
them. The African branch of the family tree was generally minimized
or denied. Thus, racial narratives began to define Latin American nations as mestizo, or made up only of the combination of Europeans

and indigenous people. In some places, such as Brazil, ignoring the African past was a little more difficult and whitening took on increased importance.

Indeed, the easy choice for discussing race and soccer in Latin America is Brazil. It has the second-largest African-descended population in the world, with just fewer than 97 million of its 190 million people claiming African heritage. Samba, capoeira, and soccer have been national symbols since the early twentieth century. In 1938 Leônidas da Silva, nicknamed the Black Diamond, represented Brazil and its "style" of soccer to the world, and the representation of futebol arte by a black face would reach new heights with the emergence of Pelé in 1958. But discussion of race and soccer in Brazil tends to marginalize the question of Latin America's African roots. Why? Because Brazil (along with Cuba) is already accepted as an Afro–Latin American country. To study Brazil would allow us to continue to ignore the African presence in other locations. That is, too much focus on Brazil as the center of Afro–Latin America allows us to pretend that blackness only exists there and permits the continuation the myth of mestizo or white nations everywhere else.

So too this chapter could focus on Uruguay. Though not often thought of as a nation heavily influenced by Africa (it is in fact considered the "whitest" country in the region), the descendants of enslaved Africans and free blacks have a visible role in Uruguayan society and culture, with *candombe* (an Afro-Uruguayan drum ritual) standing as a symbol of the nation. In soccer, the Celeste has always represented the nation as a mixed-race country. The presence of two black Uruguayans on the national team caused the Chilean soccer federation to protest the use of "Africans" by the Celeste in the 1916 South American championships. José Andrade became a celebrity in Europe during the 1924 and 1928 Olympics, and the captain of the 1950 World Cup champions, Obdulio Varela, was also of African descent. Looking at blacks in Uruguay would certainly call into question notions of race in the region but would not pose challenges to the dominant narrative of *mestizaje* as Uruguay has never claimed to be a racially mixed country.

Honduras, however, is a different story. Like most Latin Americans, most Hondurans would tell you that theirs is a mestizo nation.

Hondurans recognize the presence of blacks in the north of the country and acknowledge that they come from one of three ethnic groups that arrived after the late 1700s: the Garifuna, the *negros ingleses* or creoles, the Miskito. Yet this version of history only tells a part of the story. It is not exactly a half truth, but neither does it offer an accurate picture of Honduras.

Race (ism) and Soccer

Black Hondurans have remained barely visible in representations of the country over the past century, largely as a result of conscious decisions made by national political and intellectual leaders. The active suppression of blackness and the elevation of mestizo heritage left the Afro-Honduran population on the sidelines of the country's economic and political activity. Yet in certain facets of Honduran life, particularly sports and the arts, black Hondurans are prevalent. Indeed, perhaps nowhere else have black Hondurans had as big an impact as on professional and international soccer. Over the last thirty years or so Honduras has been something of a Central American soccer powerhouse, generally vying with Costa Rica for the title of best team in the region. Since 1982 Honduras has qualified for two World Cups; has made the quarterfinals of the 2012 Olympics; has won the Confederation of North, Central American and Caribbean Association Football (CONCACAF) championship once; has finished second at CONCACAF twice; and has been Central American champion four times. Afro-Hondurans played an integral role in its development from the moment that soccer first developed in the country.

In fact, the national sport is often held up as proof positive that racism does not exist in Honduras. Since black players proliferate in the ranks of professional teams and the *selección* (national team), the argument goes, race cannot be an issue. But this portrayal belies reality. Until recently educational levels for the three main groups of Afro-Hondurans—the Garifuna, *negros ingleses*, and Miskito—lagged well behind that of their mestizo compatriots. The government banned the Garifuna language until the 2000s, which stunted access to adequate schooling and professional opportunities for much of the black population. And plans to increase Garifuna language education were cancelled after the 2009 coup.[1] So while soccer may portray a racially harmonious nation, political and economic realities tell a different story.

Most male symbols of Afro-Honduran excellence are sports stars. They are the muscle and workers behind the nation while the mestizo population provides its brain. Indeed, there is a popular saying in Honduras that sums up its racial attitudes by pulling on racial stereotypes associated with the country's three main cities: the capital city (Tegucigalpa), the economic center (San Pedro Sula), and the main port (La Ceiba). The saying goes like this: Tegucigalpa thinks, San Pedro Sula works, and La Ceiba parties.[2] Because Afro-Hondurans make up a large part of the population in both San Pedro Sula and La Ceiba, the popular phrase reflects the perception that Afro-Hondurans are workers and partyers, but not thinkers or political leaders. Moreover, there is a continued belief that somehow black Hondurans are not "pure" Hondurans. This is seen in political speeches, school textbooks, and media representations, which all present the country as mestizo. In 1995, for instance, Honduran president Carlos Roberto Reina drew on stereotypes of African characteristics when he noted that the Garifuna had added their "happiness and extroverted character" to the nation.[3] Thus, Reina recognized a certain contribution the Garifuna brought to the nation but did so in a way that kept them distinct from and outside the majority mestizo community. This exclusionary attitude can also be seen and heard on soccer fields around the country.

Johnny Palacios did something uncommon in October 2011. In a postgame press conference, instead of apologizing for receiving a red card in a match in the Honduran Liga Nacional, he swore at the referee. In an interview with a Tegucigalpa newspaper after the event, Palacios clarified that he had merely retaliated for racist abuse leveled at him by the referee, Mario Moncada. Asserting that Moncada had used racial epithets in the past, Palacios explained that he had grown tired of the taunts and was defending himself. According to Palacios, who plays for Olimpia and the Honduran national team, the referee called him a "black homosexual" (negro culero).[4] Moncada denied the charges, claiming that since he had a black grandchild he could not be racist and certainly would not use racist language.

True or not, the allegations opened up a nagging question not only for Honduran soccer but for the sport in general. Within the space of three weeks after Palacios' accusation, Uruguayan striker Luís Suárez and England captain John Terry were both accused of using racist taunts during English Premier League games. In response, Sepp Blatter, the head of FIFA, said that racism did not exist in soccer. Anything said on the field, he suggested, could be settled with a handshake at the end of the game. Blatter faced intense criticism for his comments, including calls for him to step down. Suárez received an eight-match ban as a result of his taunts while Terry was stripped of the England captaincy and ultimately resigned from international play as a result of the fallout from the incident.[5] Racism in soccer, in other words, is hardly a phenomenon restricted to Honduras.

Palacios is of African descent, like roughly half of the national team players over the past decade. While his was only the most recent—and perhaps the most public—case of racism faced by Honduran players, others had alleged racial abuse in the past. Among the first to do so publicly was Milton "Tyson" Nuñez, a leading player on Honduran national teams from the mid-1990s until 2008. In 2009 he complained of racial taunts that he suffered as a soccer player. According to Nuñez, in stadiums and on the street people hurled racial slurs at him. Rodolfo Richardson Smith also remembered hearing racist chants during games in the Honduran professional league. More surprising, he said, was that even when playing for the national team, Hondurans insulted him based on his race. Smith noted that when he played well he had no problems, but if made a mistake on the field fans used racial epithets and threw rocks at his house.[6]

At a certain point Afro-Honduran players had enough. In May 2011 Osman Chávez, central defender for the national squad, began discussions with other Afro-Honduran players. They had grown tired of hearing racist taunts during games and seeing comments to articles posted on the Web that denigrated them based on their race. As a result, the players—Chávez, David Suazo, Maynor Figueroa, Hendry Thomas, and Wilson Palacios—along with nonblack members of the national team agreed to boycott national media until the Honduran newspapers' online versions filtered out Web comments that disparaged their race. While the long-term effects of the campaign remain unknown, it generated a good deal of immediate interest. All of the Honduran newspapers picked up the story and one, *Deportivo Diez*, created an antiracism Facebook page. Indeed, Chávez has begun to speak out whenever he can against racism. To hear "hatred and contempt" from his own countrymen, he said, "humiliates" him.[7]

Fans and referees are not the only ones accused of racism. Coaches and team directors have discussed the "problems" of having "too many blacks" on the national team. Indeed, many coaches refuse to play black players in midfield, which is considered to be one of the more cerebral positions. Instead, they prefer to play them in more "athletic" roles in defense, as strikers, or as wingers. According to some politicians, who have a surprising desire to affect the selection to the national team, black players "are not intelligent" and so bring down the play of the squad.[8] Apparently the national team management does not agree with these assessments: by and large the opponents of Afro-Hondurans on the national team have been unsuccessful in their attempts to reduce the number of blacks on the team.

Others think that racism does not exist in Honduran soccer and accuse black players of imagining the problem. Former national team psychologist Mauro Rosales suggested that Chávez and his colleagues overreacted to the situation, claiming that "blacks, by nature, have low self-esteem and therefore look for ways to call attention to themselves." Still others affiliated with Honduran soccer dismiss charges of racism entirely. In an interview for the newspaper *Proceso Digital*, Rafael Leonardo Callejas, president of the Honduran Soccer Federation and ex-president of the country, not only denied claims of racism in Honduran soccer but suggested that the word "racism" be "completely erased from the language" because Hondurans were not racist people. Soccer, he maintained, provided the opportunity for all Hondurans to prosper regardless of race.[9]

On this score, perhaps Callejas was correct: the preponderance of Afro-Hondurans in soccer reflects the reality that they have fewer opportunities for economic advancement than their mestizo compatriots. Garifuna and negro inglés unemployment rates run nearly double that of the rest of the population, and what jobs they do have tend to be low skill and low wage. Afro-Honduran men work predominantly in subsistence fishing or agriculture or in construction, or else they find jobs in the burgeoning tourism industry. Afro-Honduran women work as market vendors or as maquiladoras in the export processing zones that have developed over recent decades.[10] For the most part, it is rare to see black Hondurans in professional positions—teachers, lawyers, and doctors—outside of historically black sections of the country. The majority of the Afro-Honduran population faces both poverty and continued racism on a personal and institutional level.

Even those who praise the community do so using racial stereotypes. It is common, for instance, to note the beauty of Afro-Honduran bodies while extolling mestizo intellect. "We are at a disadvantage," commented Luis Green, secretary of state for the rights of indigenous people and Afro-descendants, noting that lack of economic opportunity was one reason why so many Afro-Hondurans turned to soccer.[11] The sport, in other words, provides a way out of poverty, slim though the probability of becoming a professional player may be. Although most do not make it professionally, however, even reserve players earn three to four times the monthly minimum wage. To be sure, not all players come from poor backgrounds. Some, like Carlo Costly, Carlos Pavón, and David Suazo, are second-generation national team players whose fathers played professional soccer. But for the overwhelming majority of Afro-Hondurans, soccer represents a better life. Soccer then, rather than showing Honduran racial tolerance, highlights the vexing challenges faced by black Hondurans. While some of those problems stem from issues within the black community, others derive from a misunderstanding of Afro-Hondurans' place in national history.

Afro-Honduran Roots

Of the three Afro-Honduran groups included in the Honduran historical narrative, the Garifuna are by far the largest. Also known as the Black Carib, the Garifuna came to Honduras via the Caribbean. A mixture of runaway and shipwrecked slaves and indigenous Caribs, they lost a protracted war defending their communities against the British and French on the Caribbean island of St. Vincent. In 1797 the British deported the survivors to islands off the Central American coast, from whence they moved to the mainland of what would become Honduras. While the dominant Honduran historical narrative claims that the Garifuna remained on the north coast and isolated themselves from the rest of the country, in fact this was not the case. To the contrary, they actively engaged in the defense of the Spanish colony in the 1820s and participated in the political intrigues that wracked Central America and Honduras after independence.[12] The arrival of U.S. fruit companies in the late nineteenth and early twentieth centuries placed new pressures on Honduran resources and increased tensions between the dominant "mestizo" population and the Garifuna, leading to repression of the black population by the Honduran government in the 1920s and 1930s. Today the vast majority of the Garifuna population remains in three northern coastal states, including the business capital, San Pedro Sula.

The second black population in Honduras arrived in the early nineteenth century. The so-called *negros ingleses* (black English or creoles) formed as an amalgam of free blacks who left the British Caribbean islands, primarily Jamaica and the Cayman Islands, and settled primarily on the Bay Islands off the Caribbean coast. Their numbers were augmented by Anglophone blacks imported from the Caribbean by U.S. fruit companies to work on their plantations. They too experienced racism and repression from their compatriots and the Honduran government. Numbering about twenty thousand according to the 2001 census, they remain on the Bay Islands where they comprise roughly half of the state's population.

The Honduran narrative of the African arrival becomes more complicated when we look to the third of the Afro-Honduran populations, the Miskito. The Miskito Coast, made famous in the United States by the Harrison Ford movie *The Mosquito Coast*, stretches from northeastern Honduras into Nicaragua. As early as the mid-1500s indigenous groups mixed with runaway slaves to form a mixed indigenous-African population that became known as the Miskito. The Miskito helped British pirates and privateers in raids against colonial Honduras, which in part shaped the Honduran narrative of race: Africans and people of African descent were neither to be trusted nor to be considered truly Honduran because they had assisted attacks on the territory.

What the Miskito highlight is the presence of African-descended populations in Honduras well before the arrival of the Garifuna in 1797 or the negros ingleses in the 1800s. Indeed, it suggests that Africans came to the region with the Spanish conquistadores. Spanish explorers fanned out into Central America after the conquest of the Aztec empire in 1521, establishing footholds in what would become Honduras in 1523. Although the accounts of the conquest of Central America rarely mention the racial background of the conquistadors, there is evidence that free and enslaved blacks supported the European takeover of the region, including at least one enslaved African who took part in the Spanish conquest of Honduras.

The black population in Honduras grew significantly from then on. Though often misperceived as a colonial backwater, Honduras provided Spain with much needed resources early in the colonial period. Substantial gold mines near Trujillo on the northern coast and silver in the mountains around Tegucigalpa and Comayagua meant that Honduras was an important part of the Spanish colonial economic world for its first two hundred years. Honduran ores never accounted for more than 5 percent of Spanish revenue from the colonial world, but they nevertheless brought both free and enslaved people to the territory. More than indigenous laborers were necessary in order to produce the estimated 2 million pesos worth of gold from the area around Olancho. Yet only scattered references to enslaved Africans exist, which perhaps explains their relative absence from historical accounts of later periods in Honduran history.

Around two thousand slaves worked in Honduras and composed perhaps 10 percent of the workforce in the 1540s. Many of these slaves were sold elsewhere as new mines were discovered in other parts of Latin America. This officially left fewer than one hundred working in gold panning by the end of the sixteenth century. Unofficially, however, many more slaves worked in Honduran mines and had to be imported from Africa. When production shifted to silver in the late 1500s, African slaves continued to perform most of the work. Honduran colonists made regular requests to the crown to import slaves to the colony due to the shortage of indigenous labor and prohibitions against their use, but scant records exist of shipments actually being received. Two hundred Africans arrived in 1581, and smaller numbers continued to land sporadically.

If we cannot ascertain the number of African slaves brought to Honduras, however, we can tell that the Afro-Honduran population was large. In the colonial era, entire towns were considered black or mulatto. Comayagua, a major mining center throughout the colonial period, had at least four hundred enslaved Africans working in the mines. By the late 1600s the town of Yoro comprised 3 Spaniards and 167 *pardos* (blacks). One century later, the population of the same town appeared as 48 Spaniards, 2,446 *ladinos* (a generic term for mixed race), and 267 *indios*. Later censuses would confirm the ladino majority in Yoro. So too Olanchito comprised predominantly people of African descent. In 1801, according to Mario Felipe Martínez Castillo, a Honduran historian, the 7,910 people who lived in the towns of Yoro and Olanchito were "all mulattos."[13]

In other words, when we scratch at the surface of race in Honduras, it becomes clear that the dominant narrative obscures more about Afro-Honduras than it shows. Many more people of African descent lived in Honduras in the early colonial period than is commonly thought. This oversight led many to conclude that Honduras has always been a mestizo nation, and it would help in the construction of Honduran mestizo identity in the twentieth century. However, on one point the narrative is relatively accurate: the majority of black Hondurans tended to live in the northern third of the country, near mines, ports, and plantations. That is, Afro-Hondurans lived in precisely those areas that became most open to foreigners and foreign influence in the late 1800s. And along with the people who came to develop banana plantations in the 1890s came soccer.

Honduran Soccer

The arrival of the banana industry in the late nineteenth and early twentieth centuries is crucial to understanding the development of soccer in Honduras. In the late 1900s U.S.-based banana companies arrived to places like La Ceiba, San Pedro Sula, Tela, Trujillo, and the Bay Islands on the north coast of Honduras. They began carving out huge plantations and importing laborers and other staff from around the world. There, along with baseball, soccer spread among the banana workers and their children.

This was the beginning of the era of the so-called Banana Republics. The U.S. fruit companies that controlled the coastal regions extended their influence to presidential palaces in Central America so that they effectively influenced national politics. Minor Keith, for example, railroad entrepreneur and cofounder of the United Fruit Company, married the niece of Costa Rica's president. Samuel Zemurray, founder of Cuyamel Banana Company and later president of United Fruit, hired mercenaries to place his friend Manuel Bonilla in the Honduran presidency. And when direct influence with Central American and Caribbean politicians failed, connections to the U.S. government ensured the defense of U.S. companies' interests. In the first decades of the twentieth century, U.S. troops entered Nicaragua, Cuba, Haiti, the Dominican Republic, Panama, and Mexico while customs receiverships—U.S. control over customs revenues—effectively ensured U.S. political hegemony over much of the region.

The development of banana exports caused massive migration to the coast from the Anglophone Caribbean and the interior of Honduras. It also brought ships laden with goods and expatriate businessmen, engineers, and sailors to the north coast. On one of these boats, arriving to the port of La Ceiba in 1896, came the seeds of soccer to the country. Arriving on a French ship, the young Julio Luis Ustariz brought the first soccer ball to the country. Although few records exist, Honduran historians suggest that soccer became popular in northern coastal cities around the turn of the twentieth century. The sport gained official support in 1906, when the Honduran government hired Guatemalan Miguel Saravia to teach physical education at the normal school in Tegucigalpa; soccer was one of the games that he taught. From there the game developed and—because it was being taught to future teachers—spread throughout the country.[14]

Honduran embrace of soccer poses a vexing question for sports historians. Generally speaking, sports experts suggest that those areas that came under British economic influence adopted soccer while those falling under the shadow of the United States became aficionados of baseball. But this equation simply does not work when it comes to Honduras. While baseball initially held more appeal for Hondurans than did soccer, by the 1920s soccer became the dominant sport in the country, as it did in Mexico, El Salvador, and Guatemala. Indeed, in much of Central America, baseball failed to have the lasting impact that it did in Cuba, Venezuela, and the Dominican Republic.

Nevertheless, baseball initially won many hearts in Honduras. Banana companies brought the sport and actively supported it, seeing the game as a way to provide healthy recreational activities to their employees. In fact, from the 1890s until the second decade of the twentieth century, soccer and baseball vied for popularity. Club Deportivo Olimpia, the oldest and winningest soccer club in the country, actually began as a baseball team in 1912. Although the precise year of the switch is unclear, by 1917, 1924, or 1926 Olimpia's main sport had become soccer. Indeed, the 1920s saw the rapid development of soccer clubs around the country, and by the 1930s soccer was the undisputed national sport. Club Deportivo Marathón and Real Club Deportivo España, in the northern town of San Pedro Sula, formed in the 1920s, as did Club Deportivo Motagua from Tegucigalpa. And the clubs—particularly those on the north coast—always had solid Afro-Honduran presence on the teams. Blacks, for example, composed more than half of the first soccer team of Motagua and played a prominent role in organizing many of the clubs in northern Honduras.[15]

The Honduran national team played its first match in 1921, traveling to Guatemala to celebrate the hundred-year anniversary of Central American independence. Little is known about this game other than the score—and even that is not fully agreed upon. We know that Guatemala dominated the encounter, beating the Bicolor 9–0 (some say that the score was 10–1). A lack of organization hurt the national

Salvador Bernárdez (*right*) and two teammates from the Honduran national team, circa 1982. By permission of *Proceso Digital*.

team's development, but sporadic visits by neighboring national teams kept fans cheering for La H. The next official competition that Honduras competed in was the 1930 North and Central American and Caribbean games in Havana. Honduras won two matches, against Jamaica and El Salvador, but lost badly to hosts Cuba and Costa Rica. Nevertheless, the tournament was considered a success due to the Catracho's first-ever official international victories and it's third-place finish.

Importantly for our story, at least four Afro-Hondurans played on the squad, and this at a time when Brazil would not field black players because it was still trying to present itself as a white nation. Honduran squads would continue to travel to tournaments around Central America and the Caribbean, with mixed teams and mixed success. If there was debate about including Afro-Hondurans on the national team, it has been lost to history: the authors of the only history of Honduran soccer make no mention of race.

Both internally and externally, however, Honduran soccer existed in a state of disorganization. As with other countries in the region, Honduran soccer began as a regional affair. For the first three decades of the twentieth century, local and provincial-level championships mattered much more than national ones. The national team relied on the strength of regional leagues and often selected the best club team as the national selección for international tournaments. But Honduran soccer was limited in international play due to the ineffectiveness of the national federation. Without one body capable of controlling the provincial leagues, Honduras could not gain FIFA affiliation and thus could not play in a World Cup. The Honduran government first attempted to implement a governing structure in 1936, creating the office of the director general of physical culture and sports, under the minister of education. Charged with overseeing sports at all levels of the country, the organization was ineffective. Only slowly did this change with the development of the first national Honduran league in 1948 and the creation of the Honduran Federation of Extracurricular Sports in 1951. The FNDEH, as it was known, immediately gained affiliation with FIFA, and from there international soccer in Honduras took off: in the first thirty years of the national team's existence, it played fewer than thirty matches; in the next thirty years, the Bicolor played over one hundred, including qualifying for the 1982 World Cup in Spain. Once there, they almost shocked the world. A young team made up of Hondurans of all races nearly beat hosts Spain in the first match.[16]

Honduras could have been excused for feeling nervous playing against the host nation in Valencia, Spain, in their first World Cup match. If the Catrachos felt anxious, however, it never showed in their play. To the contrary, the Honduran team, half of whom were Afro-Honduran, had Spain on its heels almost from the beginning of the match. Then, in the eighth minute, Hector Zelaya received a pass on the run as he entered the penalty area just ahead of a Spanish defender. After two dribbles he coolly slotted the ball under the Spanish goalkeeper, quieting the forty-five thousand people in the stadium and many more watching around the country. For the rest of the half Spain pressed forward to find the tying goal. Julio César Arzú, Honduras' Garifuna goalkeeper, seemed to have the net completely sealed. The second half played much the same way, with Spain pushing and Honduras launching effective counterattacks. In the sixtieth minute, however, the Argentine referee called a foul in the penalty area. Spaniard Roberto López Ufarte calmly walked to the spot as Arzú readied himself. Diving hard to his left, the Honduran goalie guessed correctly but the ball curled just beyond his outstretched fingertips. The game ended after one more close shave for the Spanish side: César Gutiérrez's free kick curled around the Spanish wall, but Spain's keeper, Luis Arconada, dove to reach the ball in time.

As far as World Cup debuts go, Honduras had performed admirably. And they would not go away easily. After falling behind to Northern Ireland, the Bicolor fought back to tie the game in the sixtieth minute. Two games, two points. Entering their last match of pool play, against Yugoslavia, Honduras had shown the world powers that it could play the game as well as any. With a win, the Bicolor would go through to the next round. It was not to be. A controversial penalty call in the eighty-eighth minute led to the only goal of the game. Honduras was out, but not without a fight. Equally importantly, Honduras represented itself on the world stage as a multiracial nation. Eleven of the twenty-two players who represented Honduras, including Julio César Arzú and César Gutiérrez, were of Afro-Honduran descent. This brings us back to the question asked at the outset of the chapter: why are there so many Afro-Honduran soccer players when they compose such a small portion of the population?

On Censuses and the Idea of Objectivity

Although we like to think of censuses as providing both objective and accurate snapshots of a nation's population, in fact this is not always the case. While successful in enumerating populations, in terms of race censuses fail the objectivity test in two ways. First, national governments decide what categories to include on a given census. In effect, by doing so they *create* different ethnic or racial groups. For example, the United States census of 1790 grouped people not by color but by status: free white, other free people, and slaves. By 1910 new ethnic groups appeared: white, black, mulatto, Chinese, Japanese, Indian, and "other" comprised the possible racial categories. Hispanic only became a potential answer in 1970, but it was separate from race. The 1990 census grouped people under one of five racial categories plus one ethnicity: white; black; American Indian, Eskimo, and Aleut; Asian and Pacific Islander; other; and Hispanic/Latino origin. The point here is that the racial categories can change for political or historical reasons—or for no apparent reason at all—and as a result, a nation's racial composition can appear to change when in reality it is only the labels that are changing.

Census data also fails the objectivity test for ethnicity and race because of *how* it places people in categories. What do I mean here? Who identifies a person's race can play as important a role as the categories themselves. Early censuses gave the census taker the role of identifying race and ethnicity, leaving the door open to inaccuracies and inconsistencies. One census taker might label someone black while another could label the same person mulatto, and vice versa. Moreover, the process relied on the enumerator's perception rather than any sort of objective fact. In 1887 the Honduran government made the subjective nature of the census explicit by instructing census takers to classify anyone of "questionable race" as ladino, a term that included both mestizos and mulattos.[17] This practice eventually shifted to a process of auto-identification, in which people described themselves on the census. However, self-classification is itself prone to inaccuracies: what box people check on a census may be influenced by social and cultural factors. For example, the 2005 Colombian census estimated that 10.5 percent of the population was of African descent while other estimates put the number of Afro-descendants at closer to 20 percent. Why the disparity? Because historically many have decided not to classify themselves as black due to discrimination faced by Afro-descended communities.

These two failures of objectivity help to explain how the African-descended population in Honduras dropped from roughly 30 percent of the population at the beginning of the 1800s to an estimated 6.7 percent in 1910 and less than 1 percent by 2001.[18] This precipitous drop did not result from low birthrates and high rates of intermarriage, though these may have affected demographic trends. Instead, active efforts to recast Honduras as a mestizo nation resulted in a redefinition of race, both on the basic level of the census and on the rhetorical level of political discourse.

Honduran censuses, like others, sought both to enumerate and to classify the nation's people. In so doing, they would literally redefine the racial composition of the nation multiple times. The 1910 Honduran census listed the population as predominantly mixed race: 61 percent of the population considered itself ladino (an umbrella term for mixed race); indigenous people composed over 16 percent; mestizos, (European/indigenous) 9.6; whites, 5 percent; black, 3.4 percent; mulatto, 3.3 percent; and "yellow," 1.3 percent. Yet by 1916 there were no mestizos, whites, mulattos, blacks, or yellows in the country because those categories no longer existed. In fact, only two did: indigenous and ladino. By 1926 no questions about race appeared on the census, though they would reappear in later enumerations. Not coincidentally, the change in census categories came at a time when Honduras began to reinvent itself racially.[19]

Changes in racial terminology played a major role in obscuring the African past in Honduras. For much of the colonial period and into the independence era, Honduran racial categories provided for a variegated definition of racial types. Along with the "pure" races (white, black, and indigenous), castas sought to place people into set categories. But alongside these groups, in Central America a catchall term existed as well: ladino. Used primarily in Guatemala and Honduras, the term ladino has subtle variations in meaning between the two countries. In Guatemala, ladino generally referred to indigenous and mestizos who have taken on the trappings of the European-dominated culture. Indigenous people who dressed in European clothing, for example, were considered ladinos. In Honduras, however, the term had a broader meaning, serving as an umbrella term that encompassed mestizos and mulattos. So in 1916 census questions replacing both mulatto and mestizo—specific terms that imply a particular mixing—with ladino raised no eyebrows. In the same way that a square is a type of rectangle, mulattos and mestizos are both ladino. Eventually the impact of this change would be vast. By 1945 Honduran censuses had no racial categories at all, implying the absence of race in the country. But in 1988 racial terms reappeared, and ladino had been replaced by the term mestizo.[20] No longer was there even a category that included people of African descent. Blacks had literally been written out of the country.

This process started as part of an intellectual project to erase blackness that began in the early twentieth century. At that time, the ideas of European superiority that had retained power in Latin America began to give way to more nativist impulses that saw the indigenous past as a powerful potential for uniting people behind the idea of the modern nation. As a result, a search for homegrown roots and heroes developed. No longer could Spaniards be held as the only forbearers of the nation. Instead, in much of Latin America nationalist leaders began to speak of their countries as mestizo. Since the European past had already been foregrounded, they looked now to elevate the indigenous past for inspiration. This drive had its most famous proponent in the Mexican José Vasconcelos. He wrote about the cosmic race born of racial mixing in Latin America that would lead the way to a greater human existence. Vasconcelos nevertheless retained a highly Eurocentric view of supposed racial characteristics. To form the cosmic race, European rationality mixed with African passion and Native American simplicity and honor.

In Honduras, intellectuals and government officials such as Alfonso Guillén Zelaya, Jesus Aguilar Paz, and Gregorio Ferrera followed Vasconcelos' lead. They began searching for indigenous heroes to add to the Honduran pantheon and to confirm the country's status as a mestizo nation. In the process they minimized the country's "primitive" African past by crafting historical narratives that excluded or vilified blacks. In the mid-1920s Honduran officials found their national "hero": Lempira. A warrior from the Lenca indigenous group, Lempira valiantly led the fight against Spanish invaders in the 1530s until his death at the hands of the conquistadors. Although no images of the indigenous leader existed, the Honduran government produced one that can still be seen today on the Honduran currency that bears his name. Lempira also appears in textbooks and is the source of countless myths about the indigenous past. He fit the bill: he represented the racialized ideal of the indigenous man as noble, strong, and honorable.[21] In embracing him Honduran nationalists of the early twentieth century consciously chose to create an image of the nation built on European and indigenous bases, thereby ignoring—and erasing from national history to the extent possible—the black population.

Why were the nationalist elites intent on destroying Honduras' African past? Though they were on the wane, nineteenth-century racial ideas held that the indigenous were backward but noble. Through training, education, and modernization, they could be made into productive, active citizens in modern nations. People of African descent, however, caused an altogether different reaction. Racist ideology of the day essentially made African blood incompatible with development or modern existence. Blacks were, according to Honduran thinkers of the era, "retarded ethnic elements" and were often classified as non-Honduran. Thus, for example, a 1915 newspaper classified workers on a banana plantation as "Honduran . . . moreno [black] . . . Italian . . . American." In this list the newspaper separated blacks from Hondurans, implying that to be black was to not be Honduran. Through the acceptance of the indigenous past Honduras invented itself as a biracial nation. But to do so it erased people of African descent, who nationalist elites saw as "a problem for the purity for the 'Honduran race.'"[22] So black Hondurans became invisible in most representations of the nation. Among the only places they were conspicuously represented was on the soccer field.

Carlos Costly

Carlos Jaír Costly Molina is a dynamic striker for the Honduran national team, a talisman of sorts. Son of Allan Anthony Costly—a star of Garifuna heritage on the Catracho team that represented the nation in the World Cup in Spain in 1982—Carlo, as he is known, is both a prolific scorer and tireless worker. A member of the national team since 2007, by 2013 Costly was already fourth on the Bicolor's all-time scoring list with thirty goals in sixty-eight games.

Yet it almost never came to be. Though not subject to the poverty of most Afro-Hondurans due to his father's profession, at age fifteen Costly moved with his mother to Mexico. There he could not sign on with a professional team and so played on reserve squads in the Mexican league until he returned to Honduras at age twenty-three. Even then he found it difficult to land a spot on a team. Rejected after a tryout with Club Real Deportivo España, Costly found a place on the smaller Club Deportivo Platense. In his first season Costly won the scoring title for the league. Since his professional debut in 2006 Costly has played with six teams in six countries. His longest stint, between 2007 and 2009, was with the Polish team Belchatów. He played in 2012 with the Veria F.C. of the Greek Superleague and transferred to Guizhou Zhicheng in 2013.

Costly, along with fellow Afro-Hondurans Osman Chávez, Maynor Figueroa, Hendry Thomas, David Suazo, and Carlos Pavón, played a crucial role in Honduran qualifying for the 2010 World Cup in South Africa, scoring six goals in the final round of CONCACAF qualification to lead Honduran scorers. He missed the World Cup, however, after breaking his foot while playing in Romania one month before the tournament began. Costly remained an integral part of the Honduran team, scoring seven goals in Honduras's sucessful campaign to qualify for the 2014 World Cup.

Looking Forward

Throughout this chapter we have looked back to explain the issue of race in Honduras and have highlighted the persistence of racism in the country by looking at soccer and construction of the mestizo nation. Yet perhaps there is a ray of hope. Generally speaking, in recent years Honduras has become more accepting of its racial minorities. New laws providing for bilingual education have helped considerably, though the government elected after the coup has failed to implement them. Attention brought by soccer players and others on racial discrimination has also helped. The redesigned Honduran census of 2001 included categories like Garifuna, negro inglés, and Miskito, among other recognized "ethnicities." But there is a still a problem of undercounting racial minorities. For example, the official Garifuna population is 98,000, while the more accepted number hovers around 250,000. Nevertheless, including African-descended populations on the census is a step in the right direction. In addition, indicators suggest that educational opportunities for Afro-Hondurans have surpassed those of their nonblack compatriots. Officially, levels of literacy are higher in the Garifuna and negro inglés populations than any other population in the country. So too Afro-Hondurans attend primary and secondary school at higher rates than their nonblack compatriots.[23] Afro-Hondurans are beginning to have a stronger presence in government and business, though still in very small numbers. Moreover, the continued visibility of Afro-Hondurans in the realm of popular culture such as soccer players, musicians, and actors may yet translate into greater understanding of black Hondurans' contributions to the country.

So why do national sporting icons who are black still suffer racist treatment at the hands of their compatriots? Why are there are no black coaches or referees in the Honduran first division? One answer is that after generations of being written out of the national narrative, Afro-Hondurans are still not considered fully Honduran. Regardless of the progress toward racial tolerance that the country may have made, Afro-Hondurans are still outside of "normal" Honduran identity due to their skin color. They challenge the dominant narrative that says to be Honduran is to be mestizo. By reinventing the country as mestizo in

The Honduran national team prior to its 2–0 loss to Spain in the 2010 World Cup. Honduras would defeat Spain in the 2012 Olympic Games. © Icon SMI/ZUMAPress.com

the early twentieth century, Honduran nationalist elites "purified" the nation of African influence, which was held at the time to be retarding to national development. Through government sponsored campaigns, Hondurans came to see themselves as the product of mixing, but the mixing was only between "rational" Europeans and "noble" indigenous people. Africans were not part of the story. People of African descent thus became national "others": Honduran by location of birth but not by culture. They were not exactly Honduran but not exactly foreign either. In effect, this further marginalized the already marginal population. Afro-Hondurans were relegated to living on the north coast in the minds of the average Honduran, even though they were everywhere in the country. They were invisible yet in plain sight.

Since 2009 the Honduran soccer team has had unprecedented success. True, Los Catrachos bowed out during the group stages of the

2010 World Cup. Still, to have qualified for the second time in Honduran history marked a signal achievement. Honduras continued its inspired play during the Gold Cup in 2011, beating archrival Costa Rica in the quarterfinals (a feat that La H would repeat in the 2013 Gold Cup) before falling in the semifinals to Mexico, 2–0 in extra time. The Bicolor also defeated Costa Rica in 2011 to win the Central American Championship. But most impressive and most promising for the future, Honduras took one of two qualifying spots for the 2012 Olympics, repeating its successes of 2000 and 2008. The Olympics marked the third straight major tournament that Honduras had reached (the 2008 Olympics, the 2010 World Cup, and the 2012 Olympics). And even more impressively, the Olympics saw Honduras beat Spain and reach the quarterfinals. There they twice led Brazil before falling 3–2 to the eventual silver medalists. This all bodes well for the future of Honduran soccer given that the Olympic team is made up of under-twenty-three-year-old players. And in October 2013, Los Catrachos qualified for the 2014 World Cup, continuing the team's run of sucess.

It is also a good omen for the deconstruction of the dominant racial narrative of the country. The Honduran soccer team continues to provide something of a history lesson each time it takes the field, suggesting a counternarrative to the idea of a mestizo nation. Honduran soccer reminds the country and the world of its multicultural nature, much like the multiethnic French team that won the 1998 World Cup. Yet there is a gap between the acknowledgement of multiculturalism and its embrace, which is visible in both Honduras and throughout Latin America. Until the grand narrative of Honduras, which represents the country as a mestizo nation changes, black Hondurans will continue to be considered "dark, expressive sportsmen of a distant continent," outsiders in their own land.

The Unfulfilled Promise
of Mexico

Mexican fans began to pour onto the field as the referee put the whistle to his lips. The year was 1970. The location was the Estadio Azteca, the monument to Mexican soccer that had been completed four years earlier. An ecstatic crowd of Mexican fans lifted a victorious player, shirtless in his euphoria, onto their shoulders and placed a mariachi sombrero on his head. As World Cup–winning celebrations go, it was nothing shocking, except that the player was not Mexican. Mexican dreams had been extinguished in the quarterfinals by Italy and the team had finished sixth. Instead, fans of El Tricolor adopted Brazil, feting Pelé and his Brazilian teammates after their 4–1 thrashing of Italy. To many fans, this celebration felt like a measure of revenge.

It would not be the last time that Mexican fans celebrated what, in essence, represented something other than success. In 1993 fans flocked around the Angel of Independence, a traditional celebratory spot, after Mexico *lost* to Argentina in the finals of the Copa América. Indeed, in Mexico, celebrating near misses suggests a deeper history of disappointment: until the 2012 London Olympics, the most successful

Pelé, wearing a sombrero, is carried on fans' shoulders after Brazil wins the World Cup in 1970. © Popperfoto/Getty Images

national team was the women's squad of 1970 and 1971, and their contributions have been largely ignored in Mexico and the world. The best generation of male Mexican players missed the World Cup because the national federation cheated in a youth qualifying tournament.

Perhaps an enduring narrative of Mexican soccer across the twentieth century was one of promise unfulfilled. And only now is a viable counternarrative in the process of construction: while still not the senior national team, gold for Mexico at the 2012 London Olympics has given Mexico's soccer dreams a shot in the arm. Or maybe that counternarrative will have to wait: in 2013 in both World Cup qualifying and the Gold Cup, Mexico played well below its potential. So too Mexico itself has inspired great hopes—from the Mexican Revolution to hope that the discovery of oil would bring wealth to its people—but has been unable to turn its potential into equitable economic growth and social development. According to Manuel Seyde, Mexico's few triumphs and "more common disappointments" result in the country and its soccer being "gripped by insecurities." Its fate, both in sports and otherwise, is to be "a giant in its region and a shadow in the rest of the planet."[1]

Mexico, 1970

The World Cup of 1970 stands out during discussions of lost opportunities in Mexican soccer. Not because Mexico had an exceptional team, though it was certainly a good one, but because the matches were played at home. It is often the case, though not always, that host nations advance farther in the World Cup than they might otherwise. Until South Africa's crash in 2010, no home team had failed to make it out of the first round. Sweden, for instance, lost the 1958 finals against Brazil. Four years later, Chile, which likely would not have qualified for the championship were it not the host, finished in third place. England, a perennial quarterfinalist, also won the trophy at home in 1966 but has only reached the semifinals one other time. So hosting the Cup and finishing sixth, as Mexico did in 1970, should be seen as a lost opportunity.

The Mexican team that contested the World Cup in 1970 hoped for better. A strong side, led by experienced goalkeeper Ignacio Calderón and Jorge Valdivia (star player Enrique Borja saw only limited action), the team raised expectations with a slate of games in early 1970. From February until April 1970, Mexico played twelve matches, winning five, drawing five, and losing only two. With one exception, all of the matches were against teams that had qualified for the World Cup. And Mexico started the tournament well, if uninspired, with a goalless draw against the Soviet Union. From there things began to look up. The Tricolor followed this match with two victories, over El Salvador and Belgium, to qualify for the knockout phase of the tournament for the first time. It was no small achievement. The team advanced with a certain amount of panache, scoring five goals and allowing none. And the quarterfinal match against Italy, played in Toluca, got off to a flying start for the Mexican team as the Tricolor took an early lead in the twelfth minute. Footage of the game shows the team celebrating the goal along with delirious fans. The joy would be short-lived. In the twenty-fifth minute Italy scored. A shot from twenty yards out

Hugo Sánchez (*left*) and Miguel España (*second from right*) against West Germany in the 1986 World Cup quarterfinals. West Germany would win in penalty kicks. © DPA/ZUMAPress.com

deflected off Mexican defenseman Javier Guzmán and escaped the grasp of goalkeeper Ignacio Calderón. It was only Italy's second goal of the tournament, and it appeared to shock the Mexican squad. In the second half Italy scored three more, ending Mexico's World Cup dreams.

But the hopes born from the 1970 World Cup related to more than soccer. Rather, as it had with the 1968 Mexico City Olympics, the Mexican government had hoped to use a world sporting event to project the image of a developed and modern Mexico. Both events highlighted Mexico's ability to plan a worldwide event and, to paraphrase historian Eric Zolov, temporarily replaced the myth that Mexico was a land of mañana—where tasks were put off indefinitely—with the notion that it was the land of an efficient and modern tomorrow. All of the advance planning for 1968, however, came to naught as the Mexico City Olympics are remembered not for the transformation of the capital city but for the massacre of student protesters in the Tlatelolco square and the black power salute of Tommie Smith and John Carlos.[2] By contrast, although the Mexican soccer team failed to make it past the quarterfinals in 1970, Mexico scored high marks for hosting one of the most memorable World Cups. Indeed, for Mexican commentators, the Cup suggested the country's potential to enter the ranks of developed nations. It represented, in other words, a promise for the future.

Labyrinths of Soccer

According to Octavio Paz, one of his country's preeminent thinkers of the last century, Mexico is not so much a country as a conglomeration of many "races" that each has its own culture and language. Others have called Mexico an assembly of *patrias chicas* (little fatherlands), while still others see it as a nation of regions. But while historians have used the idea of many Mexicos as an explanation for the country's inability to develop a coherent identity, in 1950 Paz used it as point of departure. For him, Mexico's goal was to forge one nation out of many, a task that had proven difficult over the first century of Mexican independence. Paz lamented this lack of unity as he pointed to its cause: a lack of history. Not, of course, that Mexico had no history but rather than Mexicans rejected much of their past. Not wanting to be either Spanish or indigenous, he explained, left Mexicans nowhere, since they were both.

Paz argued that Mexicans had always looked elsewhere to find answers to national problems—to Spain, to France, to the United States—and thus always came up empty. In this view, the Liberal era, from roughly 1857 to 1910 and personified by the dictator Porfirio Díaz, brought a great deal of development to the country but did little to unite it. The Mexican Revolution (1910–20) offered the promise of a new Mexico, but what that promise held was as yet unknown. Writing thirty years after the Revolution, Paz suggested that Mexico had not yet lived up to the revolutionary narrative in which all Mexicans, particularly the rural poor, would be given opportunity to succeed and thrive.[3]

Creation myths require a community of believers, but not all myths are created equal. Some may be less accurate but inspire more adherents while others may hew closer to the truth but be ignored. Veracity, in other words, is not a necessity. And in much of the world the myth persists that soccer instantly became the "national sport" after it arrived in Latin America virtually unchallenged in its supremacy. From here, the myth suggests, soccer became naturalized: Latin Americans love soccer because they are Latin American; it is as natural as the sun rising. Yet nowhere in the soccer nations of Latin America was this version of history true: at different times rowing, baseball, horseracing, cricket, and tennis all vied with soccer for the hearts and bodies of Latin American youth. The first soccer game in Argentina (and thus the region), after all, took place on the fields of the Buenos Aires Cricket Club. And in the soccer-playing nations of the region, perhaps nowhere was the supremacy of soccer less sure or more challenged than in Mexico.

In some ways sport in Mexico has a similar trajectory to that in the rest of the region. During the late nineteenth and early twentieth centuries, Mexico looked to Europe for its cultural models. The nation became dependent on European and North American trade and finance. With the money came experts, and the English engineers and Scottish managers who flocked to Mexico brought soccer with them. To this point the history of soccer parallels that of most of Latin America, but from here Mexican soccer history diverges slightly from the norm. Born at roughly the same time as elsewhere in the region, soccer in Mexico failed to capture the imagination of the nation as rapidly or as completely as in most other Latin American nations. Part of this can be put down to Mexico's location: "so far from God . . . so close to the United States," president Porfirio Díaz is supposed to have said. As a result, Mexico's northern neighbor dominated foreign investment. With money came influence, and baseball—as it did in other Latin American countries with close ties to the United States—played a crucial role in modernizing mindsets. In other words, soccer developed and grew in Mexico not as the dominant sport but as one among many.

Soccer arrived in Mexico during the neocolonial period, also known as the Porfiriato. From 1876 to 1911 Porfirio Díaz (hence the Porfiriato)

ruled the country either as president or as the power behind the throne. Over the course of thirty-five years in power, his regime centralized the government, modernized the country, and consolidated wealth in the hands of his political allies. In so doing, his policies marginalized the majority rural population and the nascent working class as he worked with the traditional elite and foreign investors at the expense of most Mexicans. In the late nineteenth century, then, Mexico followed the model of neocolonial Latin America: development and consolidation with an emphasis on influence from Europe.

And Mexican development was impressive. Mexico averaged 8 percent growth per year for a thirty-four-year period (1877–1911). Exports such as henequen, sugar, and minerals expanded by 900 percent. The Mexican government invested heavily in infrastructure, development, and education in order to foment this growth. The national railway network expanded from a scant 416 miles of track in 1876 to over 3,700 miles four years later and over 15,000 miles by the start of the Mexican Revolution in 1910. The railroad fed the export sector by opening up new territory to mining and agriculture. U.S. investment in mining grew from $3 million in 1884 to $55 million in 1892, while exports as a whole grew astronomically: between 1890 and 1900 Mexico experienced a 144 percent growth in exports, which would expand by another 75 percent until 1910. The technology required for Mexico's impressive export-led growth had other impacts as well. Railroads reduced travel time drastically, helping to bring the country closer together and creating a stronger sense of *mexicanidad*. Telegraph wires crisscrossed the nation and brought far-flung regions into more regular contact with the capital city and the world beyond. By 1910 there were over fourteen thousand miles of telegraph cable in Mexico.[4]

Perhaps nowhere was the dominance of foreign capital more prevalent than in the capital city. Although Mexico remained a largely rural country with over 70 percent of the population ("the real Mexico," in historian Alan Knight's words) remaining in the countryside at the turn of the twentieth century, Mexico City's population still doubled to five hundred thousand between 1850 and 1900. And Mexico City was the bellwether of national development. The redrawing of neighborhoods and streets, the installation of electric lights and tramlines—

all were built with Mexican sweat, U.S. dollars, and English pounds. Foreign companies based their expatriate employees in Mexico City during the late nineteenth century, and it became the center of modernizing impulses from around the world.

Sport came to Mexico with the modernizers. The foreigners who lived in Mexico City settled in their own sections of the city and established exclusive social clubs for members of their communities. British expatriates formed the Reforma Athletic Club in 1894 while U.S. citizens mingled in one of two locations: the Mexico City Country Club or the Reforma Country Club. These early meeting places soon became centers of sporting activity as well. For the British, cricket and lawn tennis predominated, while golf and baseball were the sports of choice at U.S. clubs.

Proximity to the United States and the prominence of U.S. capital in the development of the Mexican economy meant that soccer failed to monopolize the national sports scene the way that it did in other Latin American countries. Throughout the country, North American sports captured the imaginations of many Mexicans who dreamed of a modern life. In 1887 the three-team Baseball Association formed in Mexico City. Two of the teams took on Mexican names although they were composed of American players: Tenochtitlan and Toluca. Sonora had a state baseball championship tournament with teams from four towns in the 1890s while international matches between Mexican and American teams became a somewhat regular occurrence in the late 1890s. In the southern Yucatán peninsula baseball gained popularity in the 1890s, though it arrived with Cuban expatriates rather than American companies. By 1924 fifty-six baseball teams played throughout the country, and the Mexican Baseball League formed in 1925. It quickly became affiliated with the North American minor leagues. The cultural meaning of baseball in Mexico was much the same as that of soccer: by learning teamwork and playing a game with objective rules, Mexican players came to understand "modern" values of practice, teamwork, and fair play.[5]

Indeed, to many in Mexico baseball represented a modern counterpoint to archaic sports such as bullfighting. Closely tied to colonial era recreation, bullfighting was also seen as bloody and "barbaric." And it is likely for this reason that American football never caught on in the country, though not for lack of trying. In Mexico City in 1896 the University of Texas played the University of Missouri twice in American football. The two teams would play in Mexico on a semiregular basis until the turn of the century. In the English-language press, articles about football referred just as often to the American game as to the world game.[6] But in general, Mexicans never flocked to American football in the same way that they did baseball because the game lacked style and was considered too violent in nature. Eventually, although baseball and soccer early vied for popularity in Mexico, baseball would succumb to soccer.

Mexico shares many soccer creation myths with the rest of Latin America. As with other countries in the region, Mexican soccer history suggests two foundations of the sport: the foreign and the national. In Mexico, foreigners brought the game and spread it throughout the central valley. In the 1880s British and Scottish engineers in Pachuca formed the first teams as a recreational activity for employees of the Pachuca Mining Company and the Real del Monte Company. Compatriots in Mexico City soon did the same, and the game was on. In 1902 sufficient interest in soccer had developed in the foreign community for representatives of the five soccer-playing clubs to organize the Amateur League of Association Football, also known as the Primera Fuerza. The league's first game saw the British Club defeat Mexico Cricket Club.

For its first ten years the league allowed only clubs from the English-speaking community to participate, although Spanish expatriates were permitted to play starting in 1905. By 1908 the first Mexicans could be found representing Pachuca and the Reforma Athletic Club, but the teams remained firmly in British hands. Over the first decade of the twentieth century the sport began to spread to other foreign populations, to elite Mexican children through British *colegios* (high schools), and to working-age nationals through foreign companies. Company-based clubs also sponsored junior teams on which the children of Mexican employees could play. The sport was seen as a way to

build character and to create a sense of unity in high schools and factories, thus building loyalty. At the same time the sport began to diffuse
slowly into the streets. While the elite clubs kept Mexican teams from
playing in their league, they could not stop people from watching the
game and playing it on their own. When they did, the story goes, poor
youth in Mexico City played a different game—one based more on individuality and guile.

Outside of Mexico City foreigners also played a major role in intro-
ducing soccer, though they were not always successful. The town of
Orizaba's soccer narrative tells of a Scotsman who worked in a textile
factory and formed a team in 1902. It won the first league championship of the Amateur League, but the sport failed to spark interest and
so by 1904 the team disappeared. Soccer's time in Orizaba arrived a
few years later when Raoul Bouffier, a French executive for the Rio
Blanco Textile Company, founded Union Deportiva Rio Blanco in 1914.
In short order Club Cervantes, composed primarily of Spaniards, and
Asociación Deportiva Orizabeña, an elite Mexican team, formed. In
1915 a regional league developed in Veracruz. Club Iberia, in nearby
Córdoba, and the elite-based Veracruz Sporting Club joined the league
as well.

From foreign-based roots, the sport became increasingly Mexican-
ized by the second decade of the twentieth century. In Guadalajara a
Belgian employee of a merchant company brought the game and began gathering his fellow employees to play. They formed Club de Fútbol Union in 1906 out of a mixture of French, French-Mexican, and
Mexican players. In 1908 Club Union became Club Deportivo Guadalajara—more popularly known as Chivas—the only Mexican club that
still refuses to field players not of Mexican heritage. But it was not just
teams that formed among the urban elite and expatriates in Mexico.
In Guadalajara the Amateur League of Jalisco organized its first games
in 1908. So too Guanajuato and Veracruz had active leagues by 1915, in
the midst of the Revolution. That Mexican youth played soccer in the
throes of a violent internecine conflict serves to highlight the sport's
growing popularity throughout the country. More than that, however,
it foreshadows the use of the sport to pull the nation together after the
war.[7]

Revolutionary Promises

By the beginning of the twentieth century, the central government had consolidated its power in Mexico City, but for most Mexicans the nation had little impact on their daily lives. Of greater relevance to most were the vicissitudes of local and regional life that made Mexico more an agglomeration of regions, or "many Mexicos," than a nation. In 1910 the stability that had spurred development and growth crashed, and over the next ten years the country was wracked by war. Approximately 2 million Mexicans, or roughly one in fifteen people, died as a result of the conflict. Whole communities were displaced or wiped from the map. The Mexican social structure, with its minuscule upper class, vast lower class, and growing-but-still-small middle class, was exposed as deeply flawed.[8]

When Francisco Madero ran for president against Díaz in 1909 he did not seek to revolutionize the country. To the contrary, the scion of a wealthy landholding family in north-central Mexico merely sought honest government. His was an expression of frustration with the status quo, which had brought stability and economic growth as well as corruption, nepotism, and suppression of dissent. Yet Madero set in motion the first social revolution of the twentieth century, predating the Russian Revolution by some seven years. Begun essentially as an elite complaint against an aging dictator's refusal to give up power, the Mexican Revolution quickly evolved into a series of revolutions with competing aims. For rural landowners, it offered the opportunity to be free from meddling by Porfirio Díaz and his allies. The developing middle class hoped for increased political participation to match its growing influence in the economic sphere. Working-class activists sought better working conditions, higher wages, and an opportunity to raise the standard of living. For nationalists, it promised a break from dependency on Europe and the United States. And, most importantly, for poor rural Mexicans it promised access to lands that had been slowly taken away over the previous fifty years.

From the outset there was little cohesion among the revolutionary factions. Shortly after the Revolution began, Emiliano Zapata's call for "land and liberty" rallied a peasant fighting force in the South. In the north Pancho Villa's troops, recruited from cattle rustlers, cowboys, and others from the northern border regions, sought to break up the traditional landholding aristocracy. So too a conglomeration of elite politicians from the Díaz days, such as Venustiano Carranza and Álvaro Obregón, recloaked themselves as reformers. Once begun, the Revolution took on a logic of its own, sucking the entire nation into its vortex. The Revolution was victorious by the middle of the decade and the so-called Constitutionalists (the elite reformers who had shed their allegiance to the old regime) controlled of most of the country. But fighting continued between rival groups. Grassroots fighters like Villa in the North and Zapata in the South had considerable strength and loyal armies that would not disband until their aims were met.

Ultimately the factions created a new constitution intended to strike a compromise and provide direction to the nation. Although reformists had won on the battlefield, grassroots groups shaped a progressive document that, among other things, called for massive land reform, protected subsoil resources (oil, minerals, etc.), and severely limited foreign investment. In short, the Constitution of 1917 marked a radical break from the past, offering to create a vastly different society that would favor Mexicans over foreigners and the poor over the rich. The Revolution set lofty goals for itself and fell short of them more often than not.

Without doubt, the biggest promise of the Revolution was land reform. At the time of the Revolution, the majority of the population lived in rural areas and had seen their land systematically taken away by the modernizing efforts of the Díaz government. But once in power, the constitutionalist forces assassinated Villa and Zapata and stalled the land reform program. Instead, between 1920 and 1934 they chose to strengthen the grip of the old guard on power and land. What redistribution occurred often served to safeguard large landholdings by giving to the rural poor lands of marginal quality and allowing the wealthy to hold onto their fertile plots.

The inauguration of Lázaro Cárdenas as president in 1934 heralded a return to revolutionary hopes, particularly regarding land reform. Workers' standards of living rose, reforms modernized the Mexican educational system, and nationalist deeds began to follow nationalist

Hugo Sánchez Márquez

El Pentapichichi

In many ways, Hugo Sánchez Márquez embodies Mexico's unfulfilled potential. Called Hugol due to his prolific scoring touch, Sánchez represented Mexico sixty times over a twenty-one year period, playing in the 1978, 1986, and 1994 World Cups. Many consider Sánchez to be the best Mexican player ever.

Sánchez shined on the European stage, with stints leading both Atlético Madrid and Real Madrid to impressive heights. After scoring 99 goals in five seasons with the Mexican side Pumas, Hugol moved to Spain, a rare move for Mexican players in the 1980s. With Atlético, Sánchez won the first of his five *pichichis*—the award for the league's leading scorer—as well as the Copa de Rey and a Spanish Supercup. With Real Madrid, however, Sánchez exploded. He won three straight pichichis (and four overall), a FIFA Golden Boot, five league championships, one Copa de Rey, three Supercups, and the UEFA Super Cup. With Real he scored 253 goals in 283 games. Over the course of his career Sánchez tallied 479 goals. All of this for someone who had to beg his way onto the training field where his older brother was playing with the Mexican youth squad.

With El Tricolor he scored 28 goals, but generally his time with the national team is remembered for what could have been. A disappointing team performance in 1978 was followed by a stunning failure to qualify for the World Cup in Spain in 1982. And, at the peak of his game, Hugol was denied a chance in the 1990 World Cup as a result of the *cachirules* scandal that erupted when the Mexican Soccer Federation fielded overage players in a youth tournament.

After retiring as a player in 1997 Sánchez eventually became a coach, leading the UNAM Pumas to two Mexican league titles and taking over the Mexican national team coaching position in 2006. After a run of poor form he was fired in 2008. He returned to coaching with the Mexican team Pachuca in 2012 after a stint as commentator on Univision.

Hugo Sánchez, former star striker and coach of the Mexican national team from 2006 to 2008. Sánchez played during the era that Mexico was banned due to the cachirules scandal. © El Universal/ZUMAPress.com

words. Cárdenas began to distribute prime land to peasant farmers, which allowed agricultural cooperatives known as *ejidos* to be competitive with the remaining large landholdings. To support the peasant collectives, the Cárdenas government created special credit unions to support the new landowners while another branch of the land reform administration helped farmers with growing technologies and other technical issues. His regime distributed more than 44 million acres of land between 1934 and 1940, or more than double the amount distributed by all of his predecessors combined.[9] Perhaps the promise of the Revolution would be fulfilled after all.

Soccer Promises I

The Revolution brought with it promises for Mexican unity that were bolstered by the growth of soccer as the national game. The second decade of the twentieth century saw a sea change in Mexican soccer. While revolutionary fighting slowed the growth of the sport, it failed to stop soccer's development. Indeed, throughout the revolutionary decade, existing leagues continued to operate and new ones formed. The elite Mexico City Amateur League continued to operate throughout the conflict, holding its annual championship every year; some clubs prospered enough to expand their stadiums. Moreover, in Mexico City the number of lower-class teams grew during the era. These teams played on improvised fields, a far cry from even the rudimentary stadiums that elite teams were building. And even in the countryside, during breaks in the fighting or when the frontlines shifted far enough away, Mexican youth played soccer. When rebel forces occupied Pachuca in 1911, the commanding officer, Antonio Azuara, organized a soccer tournament and invited the British team, Pachuca Athletic Club, to play. Not wanting to anger the commander, they agreed.[10]

If the Revolution laid the groundwork for soccer becoming the most popular sport in Mexico, World War I helped to nationalize the game. Many English, French, and German players returned to Europe to fight, thus opening the field to other teams, including both Mexican and Spanish expatriate teams. In fact, soccer's growth during the decade 1914–24 resulted largely from the Spanish community resident in Mexico. In regions with sizeable Spanish populations—Veracruz, Puebla, and Tampico, among others—Spaniards also embraced the sport, and their influence is visible in the names of teams founded in this era: Club España, Deportivo Español, and Club Asturias are just a few. Club América, which remains a force in Mexican soccer, also formed out of the elite Spanish community while Club Iberia in Córdoba and Club Cervantes in Orizaba carried the Spanish passion for soccer in Veracruz.

While it would be a stretch to say that soccer alone brought the nation back together after ten years of internecine struggle, it definitely played a role. Certainly, national leaders saw enough potential in the sport to support it during the turbulent era. As early as 1916 soccer games were organized to raise funds to pay off government war debt. In 1919 Venustiano Carranza (president, 1917–20) saw enough value in sport to exempt all sporting goods from customs duties. Álvaro Obregón (president, 1920–24) organized the first nationwide soccer tournament in 1921 to celebrate the centennial of Mexican independence and gave the ceremonial first kick for the event. The event brought together thirteen teams from around the country, eight from the provinces and five from Mexico City, to play each other in a single-elimination competition. Clearly this was an effort on the part of the government to unite the country.

Obregón also played a major role in disseminating the sport throughout Mexico by exposing rural populations to the game. He initiated a physical education regimen on all army bases in the country and mandated that soccer be played regularly. This introduced many in the all-conscript army to the game for the first time. They, in turn, brought the game back to their villages, further spreading soccer both geographically and across social class. Indeed, Mexican presidents began to attend soccer matches on a regular basis, showing their approval for the new national sport. The Elimination Cup, begun in 1907 as the Tower Cup to honor the British minister, Reginald Tower, received newfound impetus from the federal government in the twenties. The championship, renamed the Copa México in 1933 when future president Lázaro Cárdenas donated a new trophy, played an important role in knitting "many Mexicos" into one by bringing teams from each region into competition with each other. A national tournament, the Copa pit teams from around the country against each other, bringing regions and people into contact with each other on a regular basis.[11]

Aside from state support for soccer, the 1920s saw deepening grassroots interest in the sport throughout the nation. In 1918 a second league formed in the capital city to accommodate teams from poorer neighborhoods who were excluded from the elite Amateur League. Formed by Pablo Alexanderson, a Swede who worked for a German insurance company in Mexico City, and sponsored by the sporting goods store Casa Spalding, the Liga Spalding exploded after its formation. By 1927 it had over two hundred affiliated teams in and around Mexico City. The league offered somewhere to play for teams that lacked the resources to purchase or rent their own fields. More importantly, it formalized competition for the burgeoning lower classes that had begun to move to the city after the Revolution. From the improvised games played by shoeless children on streets or in empty spaces around the city, the popular-class version of soccer emerged into full view for the nation to see. It was only a matter of time before the social barriers to playing in Mexico's elite league collapsed.

For nearly three decades, Mexico City's original Amateur League, by the mid-1920s called either the Liga Mayor or the Primera Fuerza, had kept lower-class teams from joining. Elite clubs argued that the Liga Spalding teams lacked the skill necessary to compete, thus justifying their exclusion. But in 1927 the club Atlante, nicknamed Los Prietitos (the little blacks) due to the players' largely indigenous and mixed-race backgrounds, lost a close match to the visiting Chilean team, Colo-Colo. The following year Atlante joined the Liga Mayor, bringing with it new fans. One historian has said that the stands became filled with straw sombreros and traditional sandals instead of the formal attire worn by elite spectators. Indeed, the entire tenor of the league changed. Teams began to worry less about a player's social class and put more importance on his skill, and the fan base spread significantly. It was not long before other non-elite teams joined the league, further expanding the fan base for the sport as the popular classes fully embraced the game.[12]

The formation of the Mexican Federation of Association Football (FMF) in 1927 gave further impetus to the sport. Formed to unite soccer organizations around the country, the centralizing process regularized league play and standardized the game around the country. Through the federation, Mexico officially joined the world soccer community by affiliating with FIFA two years later. This in turn opened the door for increased international play. With the Revolution less than a decade in the past, Mexican soccer now dominated the Mexican sporting scene. Although baseball and other sports remained popular in certain regions of the country, soccer had become the national sport. Like the Revolution itself, which started with the upper classes but was taken up by the masses, soccer had filtered from the top down. Its popularity, combined with government support in the 1920s and the growth of nationwide tournaments, had helped bring the nation together after years of conflict. And by joining FIFA, soccer would now represent the new Mexico to the world.

The Mexican national team disembarked in Montevideo on a chilly winter day in July 1930. The weather did not improve for the first game Mexico played in the inaugural World Cup, a 4–1 loss to France. If the national team blamed the weather for its initial defeat, it could not do the same for its next two games: a 3–0 loss to Chile and a 6–3 defeat at the hands of eventual runner-up Argentina. Called "primitive" by the Argentine press, Mexico finished last in the tournament and allowed the most goals. This certainly was an inauspicious start to Mexico's World Cup history. In truth, the federation should not have been surprised by the outcome. The Mexican team had practiced little before departing and arrived in Montevideo after a twenty-six-day voyage only two days before its first game.

This was not Mexico's first foray into international soccer. In fact, just as national leagues helped bring the country together after the Revolution, across the 1920s international play served to bring the nation together as well. In 1922 a Mexican team primarily made up of Club América traveled to Guatemala for a three-game series, defeating their hosts in two games and tying one.[13] A year later Mexico again defeated the guatemaltecos, this time at home. These successes created a surge in popularity for the sport. Tours by foreign teams to Mexico, which began in the late 1920s, also led to greater interest in the game as Mexicans turned out in droves to see how their teams would fare against those from Spain, Chile, and Uruguay. Generally Mexican teams lost. And while the Tricolor had success in regional championships such as the Central American Championships, in international play outside the region, Mexico lost too. The squad that represented Mexico in the 1928 Amsterdam Olympics lost both of its matches: 7–1 to Spain and 3–1 to Chile. It lost all of its games in the World Cup in 1930. Although the Tricolor met success in qualifier matches for the 1934 Cup in Italy, defeating Cuba three times, it failed to qualify for the finals, losing a play-in game in Rome to the United States. Indeed, the Tricolor rarely represented itself well in international tournaments. Between 1930 and 1958 Mexico participated in four of six World Cups, managing only one tie. In 1962 Mexico finally earned its first victory in the World Cup, but that hardly changed its fortunes. Mexico failed to win a game in 1966 and did not qualify for the 1974 or 1982 championships.

Nevertheless, notwithstanding Mexico's poor showings, international play helped to popularize soccer and forge a sense of identity based around cheering on eleven men representing the nation. Indeed, with the exception of nationalizing oil in 1938, soccer was perhaps the most important symbol around which all Mexicans could unite.

Oil Promises

It was a triumphant statement. In 1980, boasting of the vast oil reserves that had been discovered in Mexico and its offshore waters in the mid-1970s, President José López Portillo bragged that there were "two kinds of countries in the world today—those that do not have oil and those that do. We have it."[14] Oil promised to be Mexico's panacea. After the dislocation of the Revolution, the Mexican economy had taken some time to recover. But by the 1940s the country seemed to be emerging from the fog of war. Cárdenas had redistributed land and nationalized oil companies in the 1930s, laying the groundwork for economic development. In the 1940s and 1950s, like the rest of the region, Mexico embarked on a period of sustained growth based on import substitution industrialization, or ISI. Instead of importing goods from abroad, Mexico began to industrialize, making certain products itself—from cars and small appliances to steel. ISI proved successful, with periods of sustained growth and decreasing dependency on foreign trade. The gross domestic product averaged 6 percent growth per year between 1946 and 1980 as Mexico produced most of its own consumer goods and much of its own food. The middle class grew, and it appeared that the promise of the revolution might be met.

The solid economic growth of the mid-twentieth century helped grow soccer in Mexico and cemented its place as the national sport. The popularity of soccer as a spectator sport led the FMF to create the Segunda División in 1950, expanding both the professional ranks of Mexican soccer and the market for the game. As the economy grew, Mexicans began attending matches in larger numbers, as evidenced by the construction of a series of new stadiums. Prior to the 1940s most fields held between twenty thousand and twenty-five thousand fans, but starting with the opening of Estadio Olímpico (capacity thirty-five thousand) in 1947, capacity began to creep upward. Chivas de Guadalajara broke ground on the Estadio Jalisco in 1952. When it opened eight years later, it held over sixty thousand fans. So too the Estadio León and the Estadio Cuauthémoc held over thirty thousand when they opened in the late 1960s. Stadiums, in addition to signaling the growth of soccer, also became symbols of development and economic growth themselves.

The economic miracle, however, could not last. In order to support industrial growth, the government protected local manufacturers by raising tariffs on foreign goods and offering tax incentives to companies. While imports of consumer goods dropped, imports of capital goods (the expensive machinery needed to make consumer goods) increased. Mass industrialization led to urbanization as more and more Mexicans moved to cities to earn better wages. By the 1970s cracks began to appear in the façade. The Mexican market became saturated, meaning that companies produced more than the population could consume, and rising inflation caused prices to go up while Mexican products became uncompetitive on the global market. Moreover, the gains of the miracle had not been evenly distributed. While the rich got richer and a sizeable middle class developed, the poor had been largely left out. Oil, Portillo promised, was supposed to solve these problems.

In fact, oil had been Mexico's redemption once before. In 1938 a standoff between Mexican oil workers and Mexican Eagle—an oil company operated by Standard Oil and Royal Dutch Shell—reached an impasse. The company refused demands by workers to raise wages and then ignored a decision by the Mexican Supreme Court to improve pay and working conditions. In something of a shock move, President Lázaro Cárdenas nationalized the oil company on March 18, 1938, and subsequently created Petróleos Mexicanos, or PEMEX, to produce and refine oil. Angered by the nationalization, Standard and Shell organized a thirty-year boycott on Mexican oil that made it very difficult for PEMEX to refine its oil or buy equipment. Nevertheless, oil underwrote the Mexican miracle, providing a substantial percentage of Mexico's government revenue. Moreover, nationalizing oil meant—in theory—that Mexico would not have to import oil to run its industries and drive its cars, and oil sales would allow for a redistribution of wealth to Mexico's poor. Oil, in other words, was supposed to be the goose that laid the golden egg. It was not.

The new find announced by López Portillo prompted the government to take out massive loans in the late 1970s and early 1980s in order to stimulate production and subsidize many goods for the poor. It banked on increased oil revenue to pay down the debt. But like many promises of development, Mexico's oil riches failed to deliver their desired impact. After a spike in oil prices in the late 1970s and early 1980s that saw oil reach nearly eighty dollars per barrel, prices crashed. By 1988 oil hovered at twenty dollars per barrel. In seven years Mexico's oil reserves had lost 75 percent of their value. Mexico could no longer pay its debts. Inflation skyrocketed, reducing Mexican earnings to almost nothing overnight.[15] The promise of PEMEX—that the nationalist dream could raise standards of living across the country—had dissipated.

Soccer Promises II

In the midst of the "lost decade," as the economic crisis of the 1980s is known, Mexico hosted another mega event. The World Cup in 1986 was supposed to be held in Colombia, but missed construction deadlines and a simmering civil conflict caused the country to renege on its organizing responsibilities. FIFA reopened bidding for the right to host, and Mexico beat out bids from the United States and Canada. In so doing, it became the first country to host the Cup for the second time, causing a surge in nationalist pride and raising spirits in the midst of financial gloom. Moreover, the Mexican government invested millions of dollars to present the country as modern and developed once again.

In the year before the tournament Mexico's soccer star shone brightly even as its economy teetered. In June 1985, one year before the Cup, the Tricolor tied Italy and defeated England and Germany. Indeed, throughout 1985 the team appeared nearly invincible, losing only four of twenty-two games. Mexican hopes for a strong showing at the World Cup seemed attainable; a good showing in soccer would doubtless buoy the national sentiment. And then disaster struck. On the morning of September 19, 1985, eight months before the World

Cup was to begin, an 8.0 magnitude earthquake struck off the West Coast. Between ten thousand and forty thousand people died, and thousands of buildings were damaged in Mexico City alone. But none of the twelve existing stadiums had been damaged by the quake and all of the new structures built for the event had also escaped damage. Nevertheless, Mexico found itself having to run a World Cup in the midst of a massive reconstruction effort, just as Chile had done twenty-four years earlier. Strong aftershocks, over 7 on the Richter scale, could still be felt one month before the tournament began.

The 1986 World Cup is remembered mainly for the audacity of Diego Maradona. In the quarterfinal match against England he scored two goals: the infamous "hand of God" goal and his stunning run through the entire British defense to score what many say is the greatest goal of all time. But there are other stories from that Cup: Mexico's disallowed goal in the quarterfinal against Germany; Manuel Negrete's beautiful goal, which would have been the best of the tournament had it not been for Maradona. Here is another. The Mexican team took the field for its first game in the 1986 World Cup at the Estadio Azteca in front of more than one hundred thousand fans. As Hugo Sánchez, Tomás Boy, Manuel Negrete, and the rest of the Tricolor stood waiting for the national anthem to start, the sound system failed. Instead, the majority of the fans serenaded the national team.[16]

As a result of its excellent outcomes in the lead up to the World Cup, expectations for the Mexican team were high. Hugo Sánchez, then a twenty-eight-year-old phenomenon, had just won his second consecutive Spanish league scoring title (pichichi) with Real Madrid. Alongside him, Manuel Negrete, Javier Aguirre, Raúl Sevrin, and Tomás Boy formed a formidable team. And they performed well. Belgium posed no threat, with Mexico taking a 2–0 lead and holding on to win 2–1. A rough game against Paraguay ended in a 1–1 draw, and Mexico navigated around a weak Iraq, 1–0. For only the second time, Mexico was through to the knockout stages. There El Tri would meet Bulgaria, waltzing to a 2–0 win. In the quarterfinals, a hard-fought match against eventual runner-up West Germany showed Mexico's grit and determination. The game ended in a 0–0 draw—with a goal by Mexico controversially disallowed. After a goalless extra time, the

Javier Hernández Balcázar

El Chicharito

Along with Giovani dos Santos, Andrés Guardado, and Pablo Barrera, among others, Javier Hernández Balcázar represents the most dynamic and promising Mexican team in generations. Strong from back to front, this version of El Tricolor plays with a selfless style not common to Mexican teams from the past. It is, Mexicans hope, the team that will break the curse of unfulfilled promise. One member of the team who has already done so is its offensive leader and main goal-scoring threat, Javier Hernández. Hernández comes from a long line of soccer players. His maternal grandfather, Tomás Balcázar, played for the national team in the 1954 World Cup while his father, Javier "el Chicharo" Hernández, also played professionally and with the national squad in the 1986 World Cup.

Born in 1988 in Guadalajara, Chicharito (little pea)—so called because of his light green eyes—began playing in the Mexican league with Club Deportivo Guadalajara, better known as Chivas. He soon caught the attention of international scouts and amid great secrecy signed a transfer deal to Manchester United in 2010, just before the start of the World Cup in South Africa. It proved to be a coup for Manchester. Although laden with talent and with a promising future, at the time Chicharito was not yet a fixture on Guadalajara let alone on the national team. The little pea emerged from his shell in South Africa, however, scoring three goals in four games. Since then Hernández has continued to be a leader on El Tri. He scored seven goals during Mexico's gold medal campaign in the Gold Cup, winning Player of the Tournament honors. Although his second year at Manchester was less impressive than the first, he nevertheless trailed only Wayne Rooney in goals. In his first two years with Manchester, Chicharito scored thirty-two goals in eighty-one appearances.

On the Mexican national team, however, there can be no doubt about the number one striker. With thirty-five goals in fifty-seven games as of late 2013, Chicharito will be the main target for Giovani dos Santos and other

Javier "Chicharito" Hernández in action against Uruguay during the 2010 World Cup in South Africa. © Icon SMI/ZUMApress.com

distributors on the team. Moreover, with four years in the European soccer to toughen him, he will only be stronger when the team gets to Brazil.

Chicharito is one of the leaders of Mexico's so-called golden generation, who have already impressed but will need to do more to fulfill their potential. Winners of the 2005 and 2011 editions of the FIFA's Under-17 World Cup and the gold medal at the 2012 Olympics, Mexico has a surplus of talented youth. Nevertheless, as a lackluster 2014 World Cup qualifying campaign and a poor showing in the 2013 Gold Cup showed, the team needs to continue advancing to fulfill Mexican soccer dreams.

game went to penalty kicks. Mexico's leading offensive players were off the field injured, cramping, or substituted for and Mexico scored only one. Germany won easily. Once again, Mexico's soccer promises had gone unfulfilled.

Yet the future appeared to bode well for the Tricolor. They could not fail to build off the experience and improve their performances by the time that Italy hosted the next Cup in 1990. Indeed the 1990 competition was supposed to be a coming-out party for Mexico: Sánchez would be thirty-two, hardly an old man, while Negrete would just be thirty-one. Younger players like Carlos Hermosillo and Alberto García Aspe would be ready to take over. And the team wanted to prove that 1986 had been no fluke. The promise of the generation, of Mexican soccer finally arriving as a force to be reckoned with, awaited fulfillment.

The *cachirules* scandal is one of the biggest to ever hit a national team, ranking with the case of Chilean goalkeeper Roberto "el Condor" Rojas in terms of impact. In that incident, during a World Cup qualifier at the Maracaná in 1989, Rojas fell to the ground bleeding in the sixty-seventh minute, claiming that he had been hit by an exploding firework. Subsequent investigation showed that the firework had not landed anywhere near Rojas and that he had, in fact, cut his own face with a razor blade. Chile forfeited the match against Brazil and was banned from competing in the 1994 World Cup. Rojas, the Chilean coach, and trainer all received lifetime bans from FIFA. However, while the Rojas scandal was big, it was the act of a few. The cachirules scandal, on the other hand, involved the highest heights of Mexican soccer.

FIFA has organized the World Youth Championship, now known as the Under-20 World Cup, since 1977. Mexico has typically performed well there, winning the silver medal in Tunisia in 1977 and bronze in 2011. During the qualification process for the 1989 championship, hosted in Saudi Arabia, the Mexican newspaper *Ovaciones* published an article accusing the youth team of using overaged players during the qualification rounds. At first Mexican soccer officials, including the president of the Mexican Football Federation, Rafael del Castillo, denied the charges. But they would not go away. The Mexican press continued to run stories about the case and was only too happy to oblige when del Castillo demanded to see proof. Journalists disclosed that the FMF's own age registry showed that at least four of the players were overage. Two players exceeded the limit by two years, one by three years, and the fourth was seven years older than he claimed. The scandal grew. Other national soccer federations demanded that the regional confederation, CONCACAF, take decisive steps to punish Mexico. CONCACAF's disciplinary panel decided to ban the Mexican team from the Saudi tournament and imposed lifetime bans on the FMF executive council members.

Hoping for a more favorable hearing in front of the FIFA disciplinary board, del Castillo appealed the ruling to Zurich. There, however, he received a harsher rebuke. Instead of earning a reprieve for the Mexican youth team, FIFA banned *all* Mexican teams from FIFA tournaments for two years and upheld the ban on the FMF executive council. Mexico, with a stunningly talented squad, would miss the 1988 Olympics in Seoul—for which they had already qualified—and the 1990 World Cup in Italy. Both Mexicans and commentators around the world had expected the team to challenge for the Cup. Hugo Sánchez, fresh off tying the Spanish record for goals in a season (thirty-eight) for Real Madrid, would be back. Carlos Hermosillo, who had scored twenty-four goals the previous season in the Mexican leagues, was on the squad. With that tandem, Mexico would have been difficult to stop, a fact that they proved in the year prior to the tournament. While El Tri had been banned from official tournaments, it could still play friendly matches. Prior to the World Cup, other teams sought games with the talented Mexican squad to warm up against quality opposition. Mexico played five teams headed to Italy: Argentina, the reigning world champion; Colombia; South Korea; the United States; and Uruguay. El Tri won all five of these games. Another promise unfulfilled.[17]

The Promise of NAFTA

When the oil boom failed to deliver on its promise in the 1980s, the Mexican economy began a decades-long slowdown with rising inflation and unemployment, and increased urbanization and migration to the United States. It also caused Mexico to drop the import substitution model for neoliberal reforms that sought to open Mexico to foreign trade and reduce state involvement in the economy. Begun in 1986 when Mexico signed onto the General Agreement on Tariffs and Trade, the country's neoliberal turn was confirmed in 1990. In that year president Carlos Salinas de Gortari floated the idea for the North American Free Trade Agreement, better known as NAFTA. According to Salinas, NAFTA would create industrial jobs and help the agricultural sector modernize through the lowering of trade barriers and easing rules on investment. It would, he argued, resuscitate the dream of the Mexican Revolution and help the country to recover permanently from the lost decade of the 1980s.

NAFTA came with a series of new regulations and changes to the constitution designed to favor foreign investment. Gone were laws barring foreign ownership of land. Gone too were protections for the ejidos, the pride of the revolution and bulwark of rural Mexico. Ejido land could once again be bought and sold, opening the door for a consolidation of land in the hands of a few. With the disappearance of the trade barriers that protected Mexican industry, industrial production initially suffered. Unable to compete with now cheap imports from the United States, many Mexican businesses folded. It was an inauspicious start. To make matters worse, on January 1, 1994, the day that NAFTA went into effect, an armed rebellion erupted in the southern state of Chiapas. Drawing on revolutionary narratives, the Zapatista National Liberation Army questioned the premises of free trade and argued that it benefited the few at the expense of the many.

As with all narratives, those of NAFTA offer competing views of Mexico's past and present. Supporters of the free trade agreement point to increases in exports to the United States, which rose from nearly $50 billion in 1994 to $216 billion in 2008. They also point to Mexico's positive trade balance with its northern neighbor, reversing decades of trade deficits. Or they note the roughly 1.7 million industrial jobs created over between 1994 and 2012. On the other hand, critics say that NAFTA has increased dislocation in Mexican society. The benefits of free trade, according to this narrative, accrue mostly to the wealthy. In 2012, for example, the wealthiest 10 percent of Mexicans earned twenty-seven times more than the poorest 10 percent. Industrial job creation has occurred mostly in maquiladoras, low-skilled manufacturing positions with low pay and no worker protections. Moreover, critics argue, the increase in industrial jobs has been more than offset by the agricultural sector, which lost 1.3 million jobs by 2010. Those who have lost farm employment tend to be less educated and unskilled, meaning that they have few opportunities in other sectors. Likewise, agricultural growth has been in the export sector at the expense of Mexican self-sufficiency. By the 1970s Mexico produced most of its own staples; it is now a net importer of corn.[18]

There is, in other words, not yet a dominant Mexican narrative about NAFTA. The Mexican government points out that, in 2008, in absolute numbers poverty was approaching all-time highs. According to the National Council for the Evaluation of Social Development Policy, 44.3 percent of Mexicans lived in poverty, with a further 37.3 percent of the population "vulnerable," meaning that they stood the risk of becoming poor. Yet, while income inequality is still vast in Mexico, it has been improving steadily since 1994.[19] Regardless of how one interprets the narrative of NAFTA, however, it clearly has not accomplished all that it promised.

Redemption?

Teams from other years might have given up. Playing in the finals of the 2011 CONCACAF Gold Cup just one year after a disappointing departure from the World Cup in South Africa, El Tricolor fell behind quickly to the host United States. Eight minutes into the game, U.S. midfielder Michael Bradley got free near the front post on a corner kick and glanced a header into the goal. Less than fifteen minutes later Landon Donovan doubled the score after a pass filtered through the porous Mexican defense. The Mexican team looked in disarray. With each U.S. goal the crowd in the Rose Bowl became more silent; the vast majority had come to support El Tri in its bid to consolidate regional supremacy. In the previous Gold Cup final, Mexico had prevailed 5–0. That team, with many of the same players as tonight, had played a free-flowing game against an overmatched opponent. Tonight was

Mexican striker Aldo De Nigris (9) celebrates after scoring in the 2011 Gold Cup semifinals against Honduras. Mexico won the match 2–0 in overtime. © Luis Leyva/SCG/ZUMAPress.com

different. The United States was brimming with confidence, and two early goals only boosted U.S. morale.

In Mexico, television announcers relayed Donovan's goal in distinctly downtrodden tones and began to wax poetic about El Tricolor's unfulfilled potential. In the past, commentators knew, Mexican teams would have remained down. But then it happened. Pablo Barrera's first goal, just eight minutes after Donovan's, started the turnaround. "We have a game! We have a game!" announced Telefutura. The Mexican team was picking itself off the mat. Ten minutes before halftime, a Giovani dos Santos cross deflected into the path of Andres Guardado, who tucked the ball under Tim Howard to tie the score. Guardado's goal electrified the Rose Bowl. Mexican flags that had been draped forlornly over people's shoulders or on the backs of seats only ten minutes earlier now covered the stadium in a sea of red, white, and green. After halftime Pablo Barrera added a third goal, a stinging one-time shot that bent around Howard into the net.

But a one-goal lead in soccer is a precarious advantage. No matter how in control of a game one team seems, a goal is always attainable. Even against the run of play, as soccer commentators like to say, a swift counterattack can result in a tie game. And after Mexico's third goal, the United States began to press forward for the equalizer. But it was not to be. Instead, in the seventy-sixth minute, Giovani dos Santos scored not only the game winner but perhaps the goal of his life. Receiving the ball inside the eighteen-yard box with his back to the goal, dos Santos turned. As he did, the U.S. goalkeeper, Tim Howard, came out to cut off dos Santos' options. Instead of shooting, Gio dribbled backward, just evading Howard and keeping him on the ground scratching for the ball. With the goal empty, five U.S. defenders scrambled to get between dos Santos, now back near the eighteen-yard line, and the goal, leaving the Mexican with no clear sight of the goal. Without looking up, dos Santos shot. There was no power in the shot, only grace. The floated ball arced upward slowly, curling ever so slightly in the air before dropping into the top far corner of the net, just over the desperately outstretched head of a U.S. defender. Some commentators would say that it was a goal that shed years of Mexican inability to perform on the international stage, that signaled a change in attitude, a psychic shift in the way that Mexicans play soccer and look at themselves. It was an amazing goal, a goal for the ages.

This is Mexico's so-called golden generation, the latest in a line of promising teams with players of incredible skill. Many Mexicans believe that they represent the best chance that El Tri has to finally bring home the World Cup and to show that Mexico can compete on the world stage. But they have seen this promise before only to watch teams that should have excelled collapse under pressure. The generation of Hugo Sánchez and Carlos Hermosillo was supposed to go further than the quarterfinals. That generation lost its chance at redemption in 1990 due to inept and corrupt bureaucracy. So too the generation of 1994 (with Cuauhtémoc Blanco, Luis Hernández, and Jorge Campos) promised Mexican greatness. Indeed, this seems to be the narrative of Mexican soccer history and Mexico itself: destined for greatness that, sometimes through no fault of its own, remains just out of reach. Maybe the golden generation will lead Mexico to reach its potential and step out of the shadows on the world stage. Or maybe, like earlier teams and earlier promises, it will not. But it is not about winning. It has never been. It is only about performing up to its potential and showing that Mexico belongs at the table in soccer and beyond.

Anthropologist Roger Magazine has suggested that Mexico lacks a "prominent national mythology" about the national soccer team because national narratives had been constructed by the time soccer gained popularity. These narratives focused not on urban Mexico, where soccer developed, but on the rural Mexico that had spurred the Revolution. So, he says, Mexicans "closely scrutinize the performance of the national team" but do not use it as a measuring stick for the nation.[20] This may indeed be true. But perhaps this curiosity, the lack of investment in the team, comes from the expectations that, just as the national mythology that glorifies the Revolution as an equalizing force has never fully delivered on its promises, so too the Tricolor flatter to deceive. In other words, just like the narrative of the nation, the narrative of soccer is one of continual promise and unfulfilled potential.

Interlude 3

Counterpoint: Baseball in Venezuela

Soccer was not the only sport that captured the attention of Latin America in the late 1800s and early 1900s. At the same time as soccer, baseball—the hegemonic sport in the United States—arrived on the scene. And in much of the region the two sports vied for supremacy during the first decades of the twentieth century. Generally speaking, sports historians argue that those nations that fell under the U.S. sphere of influence became baseball nations, while those that were tied to England favored soccer. Mexico and Honduras show, however, that this was not always the case. Nevertheless, in countries like Cuba, the Dominican Republic, Panama, and Venezuela, baseball became king. Its arrival, like soccer's, coincided with the consolidation of nation-states, and the sport became a powerful force in the construction of national identities.

Baseball's arrival in Venezuela, as with most origin stories, is shrouded in myth. There is general agreement that the sport arrived in Caracas in 1895 in the bags of elite youth who had been studying in the United States, though some suggest that Cubans living in Caracas introduced the game to the country. Either way, baseball—like soccer—began as an elite sport. In May 1895 four brothers—Amenodoro, Emilio, Gustavo, and Augusto Franklin—organized the Caracas Base Ball Club. By November, one of the original members had convinced his father, who owned a brewery, to construct a rudimentary stadium.

Elite embrace of baseball in Venezuela helped the game become much more than mere sport and linked it to society, to business, and to the idea of the nation.

Paralleling the development of soccer elsewhere in the region, baseball quickly became a popular site for elite social outings. Wealthy families attended games to relax, often bringing a picnic lunch to eat while watching the action. By the 1920s bands began to come to newly constructed stadiums, bringing more members of the society elite to the park. At a ball game Venezuelans could watch baseball, mingle with friends, and listen to the latest music from around the region and the United States. To play or watch baseball, in other words, was to be a part of modern, cosmopolitan Venezuela.

So too baseball became the game of the political elite. Juan Vicente Gómez, Venezuelan dictator for twenty-seven years, supported the sport and unofficially sponsored two teams. But the sport became a refuge as well. In the late 1920s, when political protest and police brutality rocked the nation, people turned to the national pastime to take their minds off of the conflict in the streets.

Businesses soon tied themselves to the sport, sponsoring teams and advertising at ball fields. By linking brands with sports, manufacturers and merchants ensured that they were getting publicity. But companies sponsored teams for other reasons as well, primarily as a way to maintain a loyal workforce and inculcate workers into a new labor pattern where teamwork was essential. Beer companies, textile factories, and other businesses provided money for workers to buy uniforms and equipment and fielded teams in the amateur leagues. With the advent of semiprofessional and professional ball, these teams continued to provide outlets for workers to play and avenues for employers to train workers.

And, as with soccer, baseball and the media formed a mutually beneficial relationship. Newspapers carried scores and reports from games as early as 1895, and sports sections in newspapers began in the first decade of the twentieth century. Sports magazines and specialized sports journalists soon followed. In 1931 radio stations began to transmit baseball games live, linking the sport to modern technology and, more importantly, linking fans across the nation.

The sport also represented the nation abroad. In 1941 the Venezuelan baseball team attended the Fourth Amateur World Series, held in Havana. After winning seven games and losing only one, Venezuela found itself tied with the host nation and two-time defending champion, Cuba. A one-game tiebreaker was scheduled for October 22. That day Venezuelans crowded around their radios. School was suspended, shops closed. In a tightly played game, Venezuela prevailed 3–1 and the nation rejoiced. Venezuela would repeat the feat twice more, in 1945 and 1946.

Baseball's history as the national sport of Venezuela parallels that of soccer elsewhere in the region. Originally imported as a foreign game, it quickly became linked to the cultural elite, economic development, and the progress of the nation. Today, even though soccer is gaining popularity, Venezuela remains a baseball nation. Over one hundred Venezuelans play in Major League Baseball, including all-stars Johan Santana, Félix Hernández, Pablo Sandoval, and Miguel Cabrera. Venezuelan newspapers carry baseball box scores every day, and newscasts regularly recount the exploits of Venezuela's native sons. Venezuelan baseball also represents the nation in international tournaments. It won the now defunct Baseball World Cup three times, finished second twice, and won the bronze medal three times. In the new World Baseball Classic, Venezuela lost in the semifinals in 2009.

7

Left Out

Women's Soccer

It was a *golazo*, an extraordinary goal. Marta's second, and her team's final, goal in Brazil's 4–0 dismantling of the U.S. women's team in the semifinals of the 2007 Women's World Cup seemed pulled directly from her compatriot Pelé's playbook. Receiving a pass just outside the penalty box from near midfield, she flicked it to herself twice. The second time, Marta curled the ball around a U.S. defender, shook off an ill-disguised attempt to pull her down, and wrong-footed a second defender before blasting a shot into the net. Brazil went on to lose to Germany in the finals, but Marta's play—and the team's success—announced that Brazil, so long a force in the men's game, intended to make the same impact on the women's game.

If there is anywhere that women's soccer should catch on, it is Brazil. Brazilians often refer to their country as *o pais do futebol*—the country of soccer. It is the only country whose men's team has qualified for every World Cup, which it has won an unprecedented five times. The women's team is a world and regional power as well, finishing as silver medalists in the 2004 and 2008 Olympics as well as the 2007 World

Cup. One of the world's most well-known soccer players at present is Brazilian: Marta Vieira da Silva, who won FIFA's woman footballer of the year award five times in a row between 2006 and 2010.

Yet the success of the Brazilian women's team in dominating regional play and its increasing recognition on the international field has not translated into popularity at home. Women's soccer in Brazil has always survived on the fringe. It was illegal from 1941 and 1975 (though the ban was not fully lifted until 1979). Between 1999 and 2003 there were no official practices for the team, and only after the 2007 Women's World Cup did the Brazilian Soccer Confederation create a tournament for women's teams. Brazilian women who wish to play professionally do so outside of the country; Marta and most of her fellow Brazilian teammates played in the Women's Professional Soccer league in the United States until it folded in 2012. Many now play in Sweden.

The lack of support at home, however, belies the deep roots of women's soccer in the region, even if those roots are usually obscured. In Brazil and elsewhere in Latin America, women began playing soccer in the early twentieth century. Yet regional soccer histories suggest that women's interest in the game was limited to cheering on their husbands and friends, and ogling the male sex symbols of the day. Women, according to this version of history, had no desire to play. This narrative, however, veers somewhat from the truth. By the late 1910s and early 1920s reports began to appear of women stepping onto the field to play soccer. By the 1940s women played soccer from Costa Rica to Colombia, from Brazil to Mexico. These stories are crucial to understanding the broad reach of women's soccer in Latin America and act as an important counternarrative to the history of the sport, which has ignored women almost entirely.

Narratives occasionally miss things. These oversights can happen for a number of reasons, not all of them intentional: enough written sources may not exist, or interest may be on another realm of history (political instead of economic history for example). But part of a historian's work is to review and revise history, going back to include elements overlooked or left out of earlier versions of the story. Women's soccer in Latin America, however, was not simply overlooked. National leaders sought to suppress it. Sports authorities systematically closed down options for women to play the game with the support of public health "experts" who claimed that soccer damaged women's reproductive capacities. Ultimately the reason for banning women's soccer had little to do with the game itself and much more to do with the meaning of soccer and womanhood for Latin American nations. While men's soccer was—and remains—the national game throughout much of the region, women's soccer was seen as a threat, making the game almost antinational. The idea that women soccer players violated national ethos led to the near dismissal of the sport.

Although most countries had women's soccer in one form or another during the twentieth century, Brazil, Costa Rica, and Mexico represent compelling case studies. In each of these nations women played the sport earlier than the prevailing narrative would have us believe. In Brazil the national government closed avenues for women's soccer, claiming that the women's game risked the very survival of the nation. And if, given Brazil's love affair with soccer, we are not surprised by Brazilian women's desire to play, Mexico and Costa Rica highlight the popularity of the game throughout the region. In both countries women's soccer attained considerable success and international acclaim. Yet in all three countries and, indeed, around the region and the world, women continue to face both institutional hurdles and societal scorn in order to play.

The Start of Women's Soccer

Before we look at women's soccer in Latin America, however, it would be useful to examine what happened to the women's sport in the birthplace of the game: England. Women's soccer gained an early foothold in England, starting in the 1890s. By the 1920s, however, the governing body of the sport in England, the Football Association (FA), chose to restrict the women's game due to concerns over women's health. And just as Latin America adopted soccer from England, so too it adopted attitudes about the women's game from the cradle of the sport.

Soccer fans in England initially treated the women's sport as something of a joke. The field at Crouch-End in London surely was not meant to accommodate eleven thousand spectators, yet somewhere close to that number settled in to see the first match of the British Ladies Football Club in 1895. Formed near Aberdeen, Scotland, in 1894 by Nettie Honeyball, the club had been playing for about a year. As the ladies came out to play, they were treated to "a tremendous roar of mingled shouts and laughter," and the *Manchester Times* suggested that the twenty-one women and one boy who comprised the two teams treated the fans less to a game of soccer than to "a burlesque." The spectators, apparently, treated the entire game as a joke, focusing more on the "fair players" than on the game itself. While women took increasingly active roles in public spaces at the end of the nineteenth century, the idea of women playing soccer still rubbed many people the wrong way.[1]

Until the start of World War I, women's soccer remained little more than a spectacle in Europe. The war, however, opened up new opportunities for women players by eroding traditional boundaries between men's and women's work. As men went off to fight and die on the continent, women filled their jobs in factories, making the war materiel crucial to the fighting. Factories, for their part, had been missionaries of sport since at least the 1890s, when managers began to see the benefits of a healthy workforce that understood the value of teamwork and discipline. As a result, the number of workplace-sponsored sports teams exploded. And during World War I, as they had taken men's place in the factory, women replaced men on the soccer field as well. Women played charity matches to support the Red Cross, as raising money was a popular and patriotic activity during wartime. According to historian Jean Williams, charity events allowed women to remain in their traditional roles as caretakers even as they challenged assumptions about their ability to work in a factory or play a "rough" game like soccer.

Just as the war created new opportunities for women in work and sport, the end of hostilities heralded a return to prewar norms. Men wanted their jobs back—both in the factories and on the field—and wanted women to return to taking care of the home as wives and mothers. So, in a move that would be copied by soccer associations around the world, the FA engineered ways to prohibit women's soccer. The FA forbade male clubs from allowing women's teams to play on their fields and sought medical expertise to bolster its position that soccer was unsafe for women. While the ban was never completely successful in England or elsewhere, it effectively pushed women's soccer to the sidelines.

The idea that vigorous physical activity was unsafe for women was supported by medical ideas of the time. The turn of the century saw growing interest in physical fitness as way to strengthen both people and nations. Doctors and intellectuals advocated the belief that a healthy body led to a healthy mind, good citizenship, higher moral values, and greater intelligence. As a result of these attitudes governments all over the world began to include physical education in newly created public schools and to create parks and recreation grounds. But physical fitness meant different things for men and women. Educators and others encouraged men and boys to participate in vigorous activities such as rugby and soccer. These activities would help develop strong, virile men capable of succeeding in a competitive world and defending their nation. Girls and women, on the other hand, were to practice harmonious sports such as gymnastics and swimming in order to prepare them for lives as wives and mothers. These sports promoted balance and calm, which supposedly were more in tune with women's nature. Though some believed strenuous games to be beneficial to young girls' development, the majority thought that even mild competition and physical stress could damage their "fragile" constitutions.

Eventually *The Lancet*, a leading public health journal, established a panel of doctors and educators to study girls' sports in British schools. The group released its preliminary report in 1922, which argued that physical education offered concrete benefits to girls' physical and emotional health while also strengthening their morals and intellects. Moreover, the report found no link between physical sports and health problems among school-aged girls, nor any evidence of adverse effects on childbearing or labor. In fact, the experts broadly agreed that all competitive sports had a positive effect for girls and young women. All sports except one: soccer. Soccer, according to the report, entailed "too much strain." So while cricket, basketball, volleyball, field hockey, and lacrosse all met the panel's standards, soccer was "unsuitable" for girls to play.[2] The FA used the *Lancet* study to justify its restriction of girls' soccer. All soccer clubs affiliated with the FA risked expulsion for letting women play on their fields, which effectively ended the development of women's soccer in England for decades. Once women's soccer began in earnest in Latin America, national federations in the region explored following suit.

Those unfamiliar with the history of women's soccer in Latin America might think it is a relatively new phenomenon that began in the late 1980s or early 1990s when FIFA started to organize women's competitions. At that point national governing bodies of soccer in the region began to pay a nominal attention to the sport. But there is much more to the history than that. Women began playing soccer in the region in the early twentieth century, and in many ways the arc of women's soccer in Latin America parallels that of England: a start as spectacle, the development of recreational leagues, and the eventual suppression of women's teams. In fact, Latin American football associations used many of the same reasons for limiting girls' access to the field as their counterpart in England: the game was too violent and thus presented a risk to potential mothers. Nevertheless, Latin American women continued to play in the face of broad resistance from governments, associations, and family.

Threats to the Nation

Brazil may have had the earliest organized women's soccer in the region. It was not uncommon for girls to kick balls around with friends from the time that Charles Miller brought the rules of the game to Brazil in 1894. By the 1910s–1920s, clubs sponsored skills competitions for people who did not play organized soccer: women, children, and the elderly. For example, in 1920 Penha A.C. held a goal-scoring contest for girls. Indeed, according to Brazilian sports educator Eriberto José Lessa de Moura, competitions such as this were common as halftime amusement. In other words, women cultivated and exhibited soccer skills, which makes it likely that they played soccer as well. However, the difference between leisurely kicking a ball and competing in a game

Claudina Vidal

Claudina Vidal may be the most important women's soccer player that no one has heard of. She ranks near the top of the list of forgotten players of the twentieth century. For a few brief months in 1971 Claudina caused a major uproar in the soccer world when she was signed to play with a men's club. Although she never saw action in an official game, her presence in practice, in exhibition matches, and on the bench split opinions in Uruguay and around the world.

Women's soccer in Uruguay experienced a minor flowering in the early 1970s with the development of the Amateur Association of Women's Football (AAFF). The league formed in 1971 and had disbanded by 1976, but over the course of its six-year existence eighteen teams played at one point or another. In Paysandú, a small city to the northwest of Montevideo, women's soccer began to catch on as well. By 1971 six women's teams from in and around the city organized a league, and on one—Club Midland—played a young woman named Claudina Vidal.

Vidal, according to those who saw her play, was highly skilled. The leading scorer on her team, she was far superior to the other women with whom she played. She was also well known around a local men's team— the Institución Atlética Sud Americana Paysandú (IASA) (not to be confused with the Montevideo team of the same name)—because her cousin was the coach. She often attended club events and regularly went to the team's matches. As the story goes, one day Claudina stopped by the training grounds with her soccer bag. Her cousin asked if she was on her way to practice, then added half-jokingly that she could practice with the men if she wanted to. She accepted his offer, and within a few practices had convinced the coach that she could hold her own with the men on the club.

Complications arose as word got out that a woman was playing on a men's team. The league at first refused permission to sign her but eventually relented because league rules did not specify that players had to be men. Then the local press began to boycott team matches and refused to print the rosters and scores for IASA Paysandú's games. The newspaper did not believe that a woman could play on a men's team. Vidal's own brother thought that the signing was little more than a publicity ploy.

If signing Claudina was a stunt, it worked. Attendance at matches increased while international media covered the event. In late 1971 the British Broadcasting Corporation aired a twelve-minute segment on Vidal; newspapers from around the region came to interview her. IASA Paysandú traveled

CLAUDINA VIDAL
Una mujer que
ha conmovido
al mundo

Claudina Vidal, who in 1971 signed with IASA Paysandú, a men's soccer team in Uruguay. Although she played in exhibition matches in Uruguay, Argentina, and Brazil, due to protest she never played an official match for the club.

to Brazil and Argentina, playing exhibition matches with Vidal in front of packed stadiums.

In the end, however, Claudina Vidal never played an official match with the club. League officials, referees, and the Paysandú press opposed her presence on the team so much that she remained on the bench. Nevertheless, as her performance in exhibitions showed, she was more than capable of playing alongside men. As women's soccer in Uruguay disappeared below the surface in the 1970s, however, Vidal faded from view.

was vast. It took almost thirty years from the time the first men's game was played until the first reported match between two women's teams.

In 1921 two women's teams from the suburbs of São Paulo, Tremembe and Cantareira, played what many consider the first match between women's teams in Brazil. From then on, scattered reports of women playing soccer appear in the São Paulo and Rio press. By the early 1930s a number of Brazilian women and girls took to the game rapidly and they received a measure of support from sports clubs and the Brazilian press. Regular reporting on women's soccer began in 1931, appearing in *Jornal dos Sports*, a major Rio de Janeiro sports-only newspaper. According to the *Jornal*, a May 1931 women's soccer match provided an "attractive festival" that was "watched with great satisfaction" by those in attendance. Ten years later *O Imparcial*, another paper from Rio, noted the "intuition" with which women "thrilled" the audience. In other words, women knew how to play the game. Indeed, by the late 1930s women's soccer in Brazil received support from local and regional federations such as the Suburban Federation of Football in São Paulo state. The majority of women's soccer teams formed in São Paulo and Rio, with scattered games in Belo Horizonte and other regions of the country.[3]

As in England, the growth of sports was part of a culture of physical education that inundated Brazil and the rest of Latin America in the late nineteenth and early twentieth centuries. National leaders sought to create physical education curricula for boys and girls, and magazines promoted physical fitness through articles and advertisements. Women were encouraged to play sports, but only certain kinds. Sports that aided women's "harmony" and did not threaten her "fragile" nature were seen not only as desirable but as essential in helping Brazilian women develop healthy bodies and minds. Thus, experts argued that women should practice gymnastics, ride horses, play tennis, swim, and even play basketball and volleyball. Soccer, however, was the subject of a great deal of debate. Most agreed that women should be banned from playing. Others, however, argued that with the proper modifications and precautions, soccer could be perfectly healthful for women.

Debate about the women's game played out, among other places, in the magazine *Educação Physica*, an influential publication that lobbied for increased physical education in Brazilian schools. Hollanda Loyola, for example, suggested that soccer could be beneficial to Brazilian girls' and women's health. He pointed out the numerous benefits of the game—it developed "initiative, solidarity and discipline." At the same time, he recognized the sport's potential drawbacks: "morphological defects . . . excessive development of the legs . . . damage to certain organic functions." However, with the correct precautions, Loyola saw little danger for women playing the game. All female players should, he argued, have a full medical exam prior to playing to ensure that their bodies would be able to withstand the rough nature of the game. Loyola also suggested rules changes to "soften the natural violence of the game": smaller fields and shorter games would accommodate women's and girls' more fragile disposition. Indeed, Loyola argued for soccer to be incorporated into physical education programs for girls in schools as long as they did not play it too seriously.

On the other hand, Dr. Humberto Ballariny, a specialist in physical education, suggested that soccer would cause "pelvic damage . . . harmful to the female organs." Moreover, the sport was "anti-aesthetic" for girls and women as it caused women to become overly muscular while at the same time causing contusions, "deformed knees," and a loss of feminine "harmony." The sport brought about a certain aggressiveness that, in the mind of many, was "incompatible" with the "female character." In other words, under no situations should girls and women be allowed to play soccer. Dr. Leite de Castro shared Ballariny's opinion, arguing in the *Sports Gazette* that soccer brought with it "defects and vices," by which he meant "general alterations to women's delicate physiology" that could "seriously compromise" their reproductive capacity.[4] Medical experts argued—indeed, this argument remained popular through the 1970s—that being hit repeatedly with a soccer ball could harm the uterus and potentially cause infertility and breast or uterine cancer.

Public health and government officials were concerned about women's soccer in part because of its potential impact on the nation. While sports were seen as promoting the health of the nation, they were also gender specific. Rough sports that required physical exertion, body-to-body contact, and stamina were the domain of men. Women playing these sports were unnatural; their bodies were supposed to develop softness and suppleness in order to fulfill their "primordial duty": motherhood. Women who were not physically prepared for this task risked the "extinction of their descendants."[5]

But this concern was not aimed at *all* women. Hollanda Loyola noted that the majority of women playing in the Rio de Janeiro area belonged to "the most respectable clubs." National leaders at the time were heavily influenced by eugenic philosophies, which suggested that selective breeding could create stronger nations. Concern centered on the middle- and upper-class girls and young women who played soccer. Their play risked the very population that Brazil needed to develop and advance, and their fertility was conceived of as a matter of national importance. Any reduction in fertility among healthy, productive women meant that the future of the entire country could be at risk. In the early twentieth century, motherhood was seen as the patriotic duty of women—especially women with the "right" racial and socioeconomic profile. The nation needed healthy mothers to raise good citizens to benefit the patria.

The idea that women's soccer damaged women's ability to reproduce provided a convenient justification for the official suppression of the game. On April 25, 1940, a concerned citizen named José Fuzeira wrote a letter to the Brazilian president about a "calamity" threatening the nation: girls and young women playing soccer. The danger in women playing soccer, according to Fuzeira, stemmed from the inherent violence in the game, which could "seriously damage the physiological equilibrium" of women's "organic functions." Soccer, in other words, endangered girls' and women's reproductive capabilities. Furthermore, the girls would become "prisoners of a depressive mentality" leading to "rude and extravagant exhibitionism." Fuzeira worried that unless the government intervened to stop women's soccer, it could be ruinous to the country. If the game continued to expand from its base in the middle-class suburbs of Rio, São Paulo, and Belo Horizonte, he argued, within a year more than two hundred teams would form "destructive nuclei for . . . future mothers." Brazilian girls who played soccer, in other words, would make bad mothers. If they became mothers at all.

Less than a month later, in May 1940, President Getúlio Vargas' office charged the minister of health with protecting women from football. "There exists an interminable bibliography," noted the presidential directive, which suggested that soccer "caused trauma that can affect particularly important and delicate female organs." Within a year women's soccer was banned throughout the nation. Decree law 3199, which, among other things, created the National Council for Sports, passed on April 14, 1941. Article 54 of the law limited the sports that women could play. Soccer headed the list of sports, which included judo and rugby, that were considered incompatible with the nature of women. The ban would last thirty-four years.[6] One question we might legitimately ask is why? Why expend energy trying to keep women from playing soccer?

Women's soccer in Latin America did not develop in a vacuum but rather in the context of nations coming to terms with their own identities. Soccer arrived in Latin America in the context of rapid changes that swept the region in the late nineteenth century. As nations consolidated and economies modernized, regional leaders turned to Europe for political, economic, financial, and social models. And attitudes about gender played a critical role in the construction of modern nations. According to George Mosse, ideas about masculinity played a "determining role" in the creation of new national identities in the late nineteenth and early twentieth centuries. Nationalist thinkers "adopted the masculine stereotype as one of the means of national representation."[7] In other words, the nation itself was defined along masculine lines. And shortly after its arrival soccer became a prominent way to define both masculinity and the nation: it helped to crystallize the abstract idea of the nation around eleven players, created a space where men could express "national capabilities and potentialities," and served as an initiation ground into maleness in the same way that playing with dolls "trained" girls to be mothers. In other words, soccer was a male space par excellence.[8]

At the same time, the construction of new nations heralded changes in social structures as well, including those related to gender. Michael Messner termed the era from 1870–1920 as one of "crisis" for masculinity, marked by "drastic changes in work and family." Indeed, women's place in these emergent societies was hotly debated. Throughout Latin America in the early twentieth century, women agitated for increased rights both inside and outside the home. From expanding educational opportunities to changing divorce laws and granting suffrage, women from all political backgrounds took to the streets for their rights. In Brazil efforts begun in 1891 for voting rights came to fruition in 1932 with the passage of a suffrage bill granting literate women over the age of twenty-one the right to vote. This was a partial victory to be sure, but one that heralded deeper changes in gender relations. While the concrete successes of the Brazilian women were not paralleled by other women's movements in the region, nevertheless active and vocal women's movements developed in Mexico, Argentina, Cuba, and Chile. In Argentina, for example, women activists had staged strikes as early as the 1880s for improved working conditions, while in 1920s Mexico women agitated for and temporarily obtained voting rights in the Yucatán.

Political activism on the part of women in the region was only one element of women's expanding roles. Urbanization meant that women increasingly had roles outside of the home. Burgeoning industries in cities from Santiago to Montevideo and Rio Grande do Sul to Caracas employed increasing numbers of women. Women's place in the workforce grew—in some places more than doubling—while opportunities for education increased as well. Literacy rates jumped for both men and women in the region but went up more steeply for women. At the same time, however, expectations for women remained rooted in the home and the family. National leaders and intellectuals advocated for increased education for girls but only as a means to "modernize" the home. Women throughout the region were encouraged to understand home economics, to become more efficient housewives and mothers, and to inculcate their children with patriotic zeal.

Women saw their role in these changes not as passive observers but as active participants. From politics to education to sports, they sought to engage with society in new ways. But many national leaders interpreted women's increasing engagement in society as a threat and sought to close off avenues that would lead to an upsetting of the traditional order. Soccer was one such activity. Conceived of as a quintessentially male domain and tied intimately to the nation, women's soccer had the potential to alter social dynamics. Public health officials argued that the game endangered young women's reproductive capacity and thus threatened the nation. As a result, officials in Brazil sought to restrict women's access to the game. But women continued to play.

Indeed, if the ban on women's soccer effectively closed off the chance that the sport would grow, some clubs continued to support the women's game. For example, in the city of Pelotas, a small city in Rio Grande do Sul province, two clubs had women's teams in the 1950s. Vila Hilda and Corinthians Futebol Club (not to be mistaken for the São Paulo-based Corinthians Sport Club) both formed teams in April 1950. By July the two women's clubs played their first match against each other. Photos of the match show packed stands, signaling at the very least curiosity about the match. Indeed, according to Luiz Carlos Rigo, the sport retained popularity. The two Pelotas clubs played exhibition matches throughout Rio Grande do Sul state in 1950, including against other women's clubs. By November of that year, at least five women's teams played soccer in the province.[9] Nevertheless, the ban on women's soccer made it very difficult to develop the sport in any coherent manner.

Still, the game continued in the face of both the official and unofficial ban on women's soccer, and women and girls kept playing the sport wherever they could: in the streets, on the beach, in abandoned fields full of dirt. In Brazil, subterranean soccer made it possible for women's soccer to take off once the sport became legal again in the late 1970s. Leagues began developing all over the country, and by 1987 over two thousand teams with forty thousand women played the sport.[10] The women's team Radar, which initially trained on the beach in Rio while the ban on women's soccer was still in place, became the dominant team in Brazil once the sport was legalized, winning 39 games and losing 2 over a four-year period. Perhaps more astonishing, between the team's founding in 1981 and 1986, it had a record of 241 wins, 19 ties, and 5 losses.[11] Radar would go on to represent Brazil in FIFA's 1988 Women's Invitational, a precursor to the Women's World Cup, and would make up the majority of the national team as well as the inaugural Women's World Cup in 1991. But the exponential growth in women's soccer after the ban was lifted suggests two things: that soccer was immensely popular with women, and that they had continued to play despite the prohibitions against the game.

Spreading the Sport: Deportivo Femenino Costa Rica

By the second decade of the twentieth century, women played the game not only in Brazil but elsewhere in the region as well. In Chile the first women's teams appeared in the late 1910s, and Santiago counted at least ten teams by 1919. So too in Paraguay women became involved in soccer, with a member of the "fair sex" lining up with Club Nacional in a 1919 match against archrival Olimpia.[12] Photos in the popular Argentine sports newspaper *El Gráfico* displayed Argentine women as "enthusiastic futbolistas," kicking a soccer ball in white dresses that fell below the knee.[13] Women's soccer teams and leagues also developed in Panama and Cuba prior to World War II. By the late 1940s women in Costa Rica began to play.

Wherever women's soccer existed, consternation and discussions about its appropriateness ensued. In 1925, for example, the popular sports magazine *El Gráfico* suggested that while women should be physically active and participate in sports such as tennis, they should practice a "good deal of moderation." In Costa Rica the development of women's soccer teams led to congressional hearings about the public health threat posed by women's soccer. But, as in Brazil, public health concerns only served to paper over the true motivations of governments and concerned citizens: attitudes about gender norms and concern over the changing role of women in society.

Playing in front of three thousand to five thousand people, including government ministers, in San José's National Stadium, the women of Deportivo Femenino Costa Rica F.C. had reason to be nervous. Having struggled just to get to this point, they were unsure of what their reception would be. Indeed, just stepping onto the pitch signaled a victory of sorts. In order to get to practice some of the team lied to their parents, saying they were practicing basketball. Others sacrificed relationships and many were punished, even beaten, for traveling every Sunday to fields just outside the capital to practice the sport they loved. One player recalled that by the end of the first half, the "the crowd had to eat the tomatoes and oranges they had brought to hurl at us."[14] The exhibition match in March 1950 was the first women's soccer game in Costa Rica. After the success of the match, a second exhibition took place in June of the same year.

Costa Rica in 1950 was a nation in transition. Civil war in 1948 swept out the old oligarchy and ushered in a new government that sought to end the political infighting that had destabilized the country for decades. In 1949 Costa Rica ratified a new constitution, which among other things dissolved the army and gave women the right to vote. Although the women's movement had been active for decades prior, suffrage generated renewed debate about the role of women in Costa Rican society. In this context women's soccer developed in the country, in part reflecting a new openness and in part highlighting the limits of change.

Deportivo Femenino Costa Rica F.C. got its start in an unusual place. At their father's wake in 1949, brothers Fernando and Manuel Bonilla began discussing the idea of forming a women's soccer team with their sister and her friends. Within weeks they had transformed a field on the family's property into a soccer field, and soon more than thirty young women arrived to be molded into *futbolistas*. With enough players for two teams, the brothers began to search for venues in which to play exhibition matches, ultimately securing the National Stadium in San José. The women who composed Deportivo Femenino, far from being driven by a desire to change the face of soccer or challenge Costa Rican gender norms and dominant stereotypes, merely wanted to play a game that they loved. Yet challenge the status quo they did. The team acted as soccer missionaries, touring Central America and the Caribbean in the 1950s. Indeed Deportivo Femenino Costa Rica F.C. highlights the extent that women played soccer in much of the region.

Expectations for the first exhibition match were anything but high. Since the sport was one of "masculine ink," journalists believed that the women could not demonstrate skill approaching that of men, and most expressed surprise that the game was "a splendid sporting spectacle" instead of an arrhythmic "ballet on the field."[15] After the second set of exhibition matches in June, Deportivo Femenino went on extended tours of Central America and the Caribbean, playing very few games on Costa Rican soil. A photograph from 1950 shows the team about to board a plane to Panama for a series of exhibition matches dressed in uniforms favored by women in the military: skirts cut just below the knee, blazers and white shirts, and garrison caps. The team then traveled to Curaçao for ten days, where thousands of spectators watched a series of exhibition matches. In April 1951 the Honduran press lauded Deportivo Femenino, noting that many on the team played with more skill than the majority of men on Honduran professional teams. At the same time, one article noted that male fans made the women the "objects of their most loving gestures."[16]

Deportivo Femenino apparently inspired other countries to experiment with a women's version of the national game. In Guatemala, for example, Club Fútbol Femenino Cibeles formed and invited the Costa Rican women—*ticas*—to play a series of matches in May 1951. In Honduras, too, women's soccer developed in the wake of the Costa Rican tour, with women's leagues forming in both Tegucigalpa and San Pedro Sula. The Costa Rican team toured Colombia as well, and by the late 1960s a nighttime five-on-five women's soccer league had developed as a regular fixture in Bogotá. Wherever women played soccer, opposition to the game arose. While not precisely the same as that in Brazil twenty years earlier, many continued to see women's soccer as immoral and unfeminine. In Colombia, the Costa Rican team that toured in 1960 created a minor international incident: they were stopped at the border, causing the cancellation of games, because the team's uniforms did not conform to Colombia's morality laws. The shorts revealed too much of the young women's legs.

As in Brazil, the sight of women playing soccer caused concern among national leaders. Even if Deportivo Femenino proved an able team, the fact that women participated in the quintessentially male sport created a backlash. Acting on citizen concern, the Costa Rican Senate convened hearings on the threat posed to girls by soccer. Medical experts testified in San José to discuss a possible ban on the sport. Many believed in the potential deleterious effects soccer had on girls' health and considered the sport a threat to women's—and ultimately the nation's—health. However, not all in the court of public opinion condemned the game. For Luís Cartín, a Costa Rican coach and sports journalist, soccer was not only beneficial for girls and young women but was necessary. He noted that the women of Deportivo Femenino had a strict training regimen and diet, had all gained weight since beginning to play, and were generally healthier. Unlike Brazil, Costa Rica decided not to prohibit women's soccer.[17]

Nevertheless, although it remained legal, women's soccer in Costa Rica had a precarious existence. Shortly after Deportivo Femenino's formation, other teams began to develop. Femenino La Libertad (1950), Evita de Perón by (1952), América, Odeca, and Independiente (mid-1950s) all formed part of the new Women's Association of Costa Rican Soccer. These teams continued to play, on the margins and with passing mentions in the press, until the 1970s. Yet the women of Deportivo Femenino acted as pioneers of the game in the region and helped to develop the sport both in their own country and around the region. They would play the first women's international match in Latin America against Guatemala as well as the first international series (home and away) against Cuba. So too they played an important role in popularizing the game to Mexico, where women's soccer had a brief explosion of both popularity and visibility.

Estadio Azteca, 1971

According to the official annals of soccer, the biggest crowd ever to attend a women's soccer match was at the finals of the 1999 Women's World Cup in Los Angeles. Yet in 1971 nearly 110,000 people packed into the Estadio Azteca in Mexico City to watch Mexico and Denmark contest the finals of the second Women's World Championship. Special women's police units were stationed outside team changing rooms and around the field, dressed in pink uniforms for the occasion. Grainy footage from the finals shows the stadium packed with fans on hand to see Mexico lose 3–0 to Denmark. Despite the host country's loss, the tournament cannot be classified as anything other than a success. Match attendance for most games was over 15,000, while Mexico's matches more regularly reached over 50,000. The men and women who attended the games went not for a spectacle but to watch soccer. Well-documented though the match is, FIFA fails to recognize the Mexican women's championship as well as the women's championship in Italy the previous year—because the host associations were not a part of the international federation and women's soccer was not yet under its control. So we must live with a half-truth: those who attended the finals in the Estadio Azteca were the largest crowd never to have seen a women's soccer match. This is the story of women's soccer throughout Latin America: everyone knew it existed yet no one recognized it.[18]

Based on scattered references in the magazines *Afición* and *Esto*, Mexican women's soccer began in the 1950s but remained relatively isolated. It appears that the sport gained new impetus and popularity in 1963 after a tour by two Costa Rican teams spurred further interest in the game. From that point on women's soccer began to develop quickly in Mexico. By 1969 the Liga América held Mexico's first women's championship, boasting seventeen teams in and around Mexico City. Teams played sixty-minute games on public fields that were little more than dirt and rock, and they had no support to speak of from Mexico's soccer institutions. Instead, interest grew rapidly by word of mouth and volunteer activity, and by 1970 the Mexican Association of Women's Football (AMFF) formed to oversee the sport. That same year a second league formed, and Mexico was invited to Italy for the first Women's World Championship. The Mexican team finished a surprising third, defeating countries with more experience in the women's game: Austria (9–0) and England (3–2). On its return the team was welcomed as heroes by everyone except the Mexican Soccer Federation, and the sport took off. By 1971 a second federation had formed. The Mexican

Alicia "la Pelé" Vargas shows off her juggling skills. After the 1970 Women's World Championship in Italy, Vargas was offered a contract with Torino that would have provided food, housing, a per diem, and a scholarship. From the collection of Chris Unger. Used by permission of *La Prensa*.

Federation of Women's Soccer (FMFF) comprised associations from twenty-six states, with nearly one thousand affiliated teams.[19]

Mexico's performance in 1970 also led to the country's hosting of the second Women's World Championship in 1971. With opposition from the official Mexican Soccer Federation, which threatened to fine any of its clubs that provided field space to women's teams, the organizing committee nevertheless arranged for two of Mexico's biggest stadiums—Estadio Azteca and Estadio Jalisco—to be the venues for the tournament. The championship took place in August and September, with six teams participating: four from Europe and two from Latin America. Joining Mexico from the Americas was Argentina, while Denmark, England, France, and Italy represented Europe.

The championship was a rough affair, with newspaper articles noting the brutality of the players. In the semifinal match between Mexico and Italy, fights broke out toward the end of the game, and the Mexican team ran into the dressing room in fear after the match. In the finals between Denmark and Mexico, cooler heads prevailed. Critics of women's soccer pointed to the violent play both to highlight women's unfitness for the sport and to point to its masculinizing nature. On the other hand, supporters of the sport boasted of the large crowds and Mexico's place in the finals.

The tournament's success both on the field and in the ticket booth brought some popularity to the women's game, but it quickly faded. In 1971 over twenty thousand women played soccer around the country, and many in the women's soccer world must have imagined a bright future. It was not to be. Within the year, Mexican women's soccer was in a state of disarray, in part due to the effort required to organize the championship. Although 1972 saw a national league, with teams from sixteen states participating, attendance dropped precipitously and the league found itself relegated to public fields once again.

Why did women's soccer essentially drop from public view given its on-field success? For one thing, a lack of financial support helped to doom the sport. Unable to find sponsors or fields and barely able to afford balls for practice, the women's league was unable to sustain itself. The players themselves could not commit the time necessary to training because they had jobs and families. Moreover, women's soccer lacked organized administrative support. Mexican women's leagues depended completely on volunteers, who were fatigued after organizing the championship. And institutional support was not forthcoming. The Mexican Soccer Federation, the governing body of the sport in the country, refused to recognize women's leagues. The FMF tried to block the growth of the women's soccer by threatening teams with fines for allowing the use of fields. In fact, the soccer team Toluca received a twenty-thousand-peso fine in 1971 for allowing the use of its fields. Indeed, Joaquín Soria Terrazas, the head of the amateur division of the FMF, refused to congratulate the Mexican women for their third-place finish in Italy 1970, saying that even if they had won the world championship, "there was no [soccer] organization in Mexico that would recognize" the victory. FIFA itself weighed in on women's soccer in Mexico, sending a circular in February 1971 that threatened to revoke affiliation of "any club, association, or player that helps the organization of the Women's World Championship."[20]

Aside from the institutional barriers put in place by the governing bodies of both world and Mexican soccer, social stigma helped to keep women's soccer from making the jump into the mainstream. Articles and editorial cartoons throughout the late 1960s and early 1970s poked fun at women's soccer, suggesting that the sport was too rough for women and went against their nature. These images depicted women either as masculinized brutes or sexualized naïfs. Mexican women players from the 1970s also recall intense opposition from their parents and other family members. Elsa Salgado Pérez, for example, recalled being scolded and receiving harsh "punishments" for playing soccer. So too Patty Hernández fought bitterly with her sister over soccer until her sister began to play as well. Maria Silvia Zaragoza's father beat her when she played soccer because he thought "the sport was made only for men." And the mother of Alicia Vargas, one of the team's stars, also regularly punished "la Pelé" (as she was called) for playing.[21] Why were parents so opposed to their daughters being involved in soccer? In 1971 many Mexicans *still* believed that playing soccer caused damage to women's sexual organs. In addition, the "masculine" women and girls were accused of "not hav[ing] boyfriends," a subtle accusation that they were lesbian.[22]

The Mexican women's team could have created a groundswell for the women's sport in the region. After all, with roughly one thousand teams affiliated with the FMFF, at least twenty thousand women and girls played organized soccer in Mexico in the early 1970s. However, mismanagement, institutional barriers, and social stigma conspired to keep the sport from growing. While women's soccer was never a large part of the Mexican sporting scene, it is hard to say how important it could have become had it received greater support.

Backward or Forward?

What the foregoing has shown is that women's soccer has a much longer history in Latin America than might be thought. Throughout the region, from soccer powers like Brazil to nations like Costa Rica,

Marta Vieira da Silva

She has been called "Pelé in skirts" by Pelé himself. Perhaps no woman soccer player is as recognizable—and recognized—around the world as Marta Vieira da Silva, more commonly known as Marta. Averaging more than one goal per game across her international career, she is the unchallenged leader of the Brazilian women's team and has led the Verde-Amarela to gold medals in the Pan American Games (2004 and 2007) and the South American championships (2003 and 2010), as well as silver medals in the Olympics (2004 and 2008) and Women's World Cup (2007). First nominated for the Ballon d'Or, FIFA's player of the year award, at age eighteen in 2004, Marta has won the award five times (2006–2010), more than any other player, male or female.

Born in 1986 in a small town called Dois Rachos, in the rural northeast of Brazil, Marta began playing soccer with local boys on the dusty streets and fields of town at a young age. She went to play for club Vasco da Gama's women's team at age fourteen. But due to a lack of opportunity for women's professional soccer, Marta soon found herself on an itinerant journey. With few—if any—professional options at home, she was forced to play in struggling leagues in faraway places. After a four-year stay in Sweden, she moved to the United States to play in the Women's Professional Soccer League, where she played for three teams over two years: two of the teams for which she played folded, and the league ceased operations in 2012. So too the Brazilian side Santos F.C., with whom she won two women's Copa Libertadores, announced in 2012 that it would no longer fund its women's team. In 2012 she moved to Tyresö FF in Sweden.

Marta once claimed that she has the skill to play with men, and she is likely right. It seems that she can do anything with the ball at her feet, and her mere presence on the field opens up space for her teammates. In her professional career, up until mid-2013, Marta has scored 222 goals in 266 games with nine teams. With Brazil, however, she has been even more impressive, tallying 80 goals in her first 72 games with the Canarinhas.

Marta played a major role in beginning to reshape perceptions of the women's game in Brazil. She has been a vocal critic of the lack of media

Marta celebrates a goal in the 2007 Pan-American Games against Jamaica.
© EFE/ZUMAPress.com

coverage of women's soccer, arguing that fans would take to the game if
it were on TV more often. Indeed, many believe that due to Marta and her
teammates Brazilians have stopped laughing at women's soccer and are
beginning to take it seriously. While they may take it more seriously, however, Brazilians still sexualize women soccer players. For instance, Pelé noted
that Marta had one advantage over him. "Her legs," he once said, "are more
beautiful than mine."

women's involvement in the sport dates to the early twentieth century. This is not to say that women's soccer was as embedded in Latin American societies as the men's game was. Save for brief periods in the spotlight the sport remained marginal, important only to those who played. And for the most part, it has been written out of the dominant history of the sport. Yet given the importance of soccer in the region, this is no minor elision: since the sport is essential to national identity, excluding women's sports stories means excluding women from a crucial construct of the nation. The reasons for omitting women's play from the narrative of both soccer and the nation are many, but they all revolve around the concern that women who play transgress traditional roles.

Indeed, despite the success it has attained in the last two decades—the Brazilian women's team regularly finishes in the top five of world tournaments while Mexico, Chile, and Colombia have made great strides both in terms of national leagues and international play—women's soccer remains marginalized and stigmatized in much of the region. Official attitudes about women and girls who play soccer have evolved since the early days, when it was suggested that the sport was antipatriotic and threatened the future of the nation. No longer do Latin Americans think that women who play soccer risk their potential for motherhood or risk getting cancer. However, while public health concerns have dissipated, ideas about gender persist. Many still see soccer as masculinizing, and concerns over the sexuality of young women who play the sport remain a powerful barrier to the popularity of the game. Soccer remains tied to ideas of the nation, and the men's game plays an important role in underpinning national identities. Thus, continued opposition to women's soccer relates not only to the sport itself but to the continued role of soccer in constructing both nations and masculinity.

While not as common as it once was, teenage girls still face the stigma that playing soccer will over-develop their muscles and masculinize them. In Mexico, according to former Under-20 Women's National Team coach Andrea Rodebaugh, "women are supposed to be feminine, soft, sweet . . . look pretty and sexy," all traits that soccer players supposedly lack.[23] The perception remains that women's

Maribel Dominguez celebrates a goal against Japan in a
qualification match for the women's World Cup 2007 in China.
© Jorge Nunez/EFE/ZUMAPress.com

soccer, more than basketball or volleyball, is a fertile "recruiting
ground" for lesbians. Concerns over sexuality and the "masculinizing"
effects of soccer retain their grip on many in the region, restricting
the spread and popularity of the game. Players still face the assumption that they will get "strong legs," and begin to "develop into a male."
Since the early twentieth century women have contended with societal norms that dictate delicacy and fragility as ideals for feminine
beauty. These attitudes have led parents to punish their daughters for
playing the game. So it is that Maribel Dominguez, one of Mexico's
foremost women's players, began her soccer life as Mario Dominguez,
cutting her hair short so she would be able to pass as a boy. Her mother

feared that her daughter would be "masculinized," so she would hide Maribel's soccer shoes to make it more difficult for her to play.[24] In Brazil girls report fighting with siblings for the right to play soccer. One informant recounted to Brazilian psychologist Jorge Knijnik that she regularly fought with her brothers and father over her desire to play soccer. Others reported to Knijnik that they faced a good deal of opposition from their families even if they did not admit to facing physical abuse. "Dulce" noted that her mother begged her to find another sport. But it is not only unknown youth players who faced this resistance. Prentinha, for example, who played in four World Cups and four Olympic Games for Brazil, was beaten by both her mother and brothers for playing soccer.[25]

Alongside the fear that women will become more masculine through playing soccer runs the fear that women who play will become lesbian. "You can't talk about women's soccer," according to one former player, "without this [the issue of sexuality] coming up." Women who play soccer, she says, are considered "male-like, tomboys, dykes, lesbians, it is inevitable. It always comes up!"[26] It should be noted here that homosexuality remains taboo in men's soccer as well. In 2006, for example, a Brazilian judge suggested that homosexual men who wanted to play soccer should form their own league. The salient difference, however, is that male soccer players are assumed to be heterosexual, while the suspicion is that female players are gay. This attitude has existed in the region at least since 1970, when the official position of the Paraguayan government, in its representation to FIFA, held that "women who enjoyed playing soccer" went "against nature."[27]

The idea that more homosexuality exists in women's sports is one that continues to inhibit the growth of women's soccer in the region. In discussing her own history in soccer, one former Mexican women's player noted that she faced the same attitudes in Mexico in the 1990s that she had faced growing up playing soccer in the 1970s in the United States: women who played were "either tomboys or lesbians." In Brazil girls who play are mocked as *molequinhos*—little boys—and many face regular scorn at home and work for playing with "a bunch of dykes." Ana, a twenty-three-year-old Brazilian futebolista, recalled facing prejudice because people believed that "in football there are many lesbians, so they think that if you play you are one of them."[28]

To fight the image of masculinized women, players have resorted to a variety of tactics. An advertisement promoting the Mexican women's team campaign for the 2008 Beijing Olympics juxtaposes images of the team playing a hard-fought game with the women in evening gowns. The goal of the ad tried to highlight both the high quality of women's soccer and the team's femininity. To the same end, many members of the Brazilian women's have posed in *Playboy* and other magazines in various states of undress. Isabel Cristina Nunes, also known as Bel, first appeared in *Playboy* in 1995, shortly after leading the Brazilian women's team to the South American Championship.

Soccer institutions have also attempted to shed the masculine image of women's soccer in Latin America and around the world. In so doing, however, they have made the problem of sexism worse. In 2001, for example, the São Paulo Football Federation and Pelé Sports and Marketing decided to market the Paulista women's championship by highlighting the "beauty and sensuality of the women players to attract a male public." This meant, among other things, that the uniforms had short shorts. In 2004, Sepp Blatter suggested that that women's soccer would be more popular if the players wore "more feminine clothes" such as "tighter shorts." Since women players were "pretty," he argued, a "more female aesthetic" would benefit the sport. In other words, FIFA contends that reinforcing stereotypes about proper femininity and sexuality is an important way to promote the women's sport, even if studies suggest that sexualizing women athletes, instead of raising the status of sport, trivializes it.[29]

Throughout Latin America, from soccer powers like Brazil to nations like Costa Rica, women's involvement in soccer dates almost to its introduction to the region. And the sport has come a long way since the first games were played in 1921. While it experienced a brief period of semirespectability, for much of the last century women's soccer survived on the margins, played on makeshift fields in the face of

The Colombian women's national team with the Women's World Cup trophy, 2011. Former men's team star Carlos Valderrama is in the back row, second from right. Next to him is FIFA representative Steffi Jones. © El Tiempo/GDA/ZUMAPress.com

national scorn. But the grassroots nature of the sport helped it to keep going until it received recognition from the sport's governing bodies beginning in the 1990s. In the past twenty years top-down support has brought with it greater stability and respectability for women players. So too attitudes about women and girls who play soccer have evolved slightly since the early days that suggested the sport was antipatriotic and threatened the future of the nation. No longer do Latin Americans see soccer as risking potential motherhood or causing cancer. However, dominant patriarchal ideas about gender and "appropriate" womanhood persist. In much of the region women and girls still face the stereotype that women's soccer is a masculine sport.

The resilience of these ideas highlights the challenges faced by the sport, which have made it hard for women's soccer to gain ground in

Latin America. While FIFA has attempted to rectify this by funneling money to regional and national governing bodies—FIFA requires that all federations spend a percentage of their income on women's soccer—this support nevertheless has done little to change entrenched attitudes. Indeed, some of the tactics used by FIFA and others to promote the sport do more to marginalize the game. By promoting dominant images of beauty and womanhood that effectively sexualize the sport, soccer's governing body denigrates female athletes and the sport that they play. Until the stereotypes against women's soccer, both official and unofficial, are erased, women's soccer will continue its pattern of one dribble forward, two dribbles back.

Epilogue

New Narratives

According to Spanish explorers, El Dorado—a mythic city of gold—existed somewhere in the Americas. The fable inspired all manner of adventurers, from well-financed noblemen to delusional transients, to set out seeking the fabulous riches it offered. During their quests, some who were not mad became so; others found wealth and power on the way. None, however, found the legendary city. This book is ostensibly about why Latin Americans love soccer. As the most popular sport in the world, there are myriad reasons for its power. Some would say that searching for one explanation for soccer's popularity is a fool's errand, akin to searching for a mythical land of riches. I beg to differ. Finding multiple reasons for soccer's grip on Latin America suggests the depth of the bond between the sport and the peoples of the region. Over the course of this journey we have seen how history, sport, and society intersect to create narratives about both soccer and the nation.

But narratives are always in the process of formation and re-formation. That is, as the countries in the region continue to evolve, the narratives of both national history and soccer change to reflect new realities, whether increased acceptance of minority populations, changing economic circumstances, or political reordering. So, for example, Brazil's economic development over the past decade has brought many soccer players home from Europe, reversing the decades-long trend of the best talent migrating away. Nevertheless, changes in Latin

American societies will not likely break the bond between soccer and the nation: the two fused so long ago so that soccer's place as the national game is unassailable.

Soccer and nation grew up together. Soccer's arrival in Latin America coincided with a series of social changes, including the creation of modern nation-states. This was a happy coincidence, and one of crucial importance. Soccer landed in Latin America at the same time that nations were consolidated by national armies (instead of regional forces commanded by local leaders), educational systems, and state institutions. It also arrived in the midst of debates about who should be included as full citizens and what citizenship might look like. Questions about worthiness of indigenous peoples, people of African descent, people of mixed heritage, and immigrants galvanized intellectual and political leaders. The role of women outside of the home in newly emerging societies caused a great deal of consternation. In other words, soccer appeared and gained popularity as Latin American identities were in the process of being formed, and for that reason the sport became an integral part of those national stories.

And it remains so. As the countries of the region experienced political, economic, and social change across the twentieth century—modernizing, undergoing revolutions and military dictatorships, experiencing economic privation, and ultimately democratizing—soccer remained a crucial way to adapt to, reflect, and protest against those changes. The sport helped unite countries after conflict, bolstered national pride, reflected persistent inequalities, and served as a point of mobilization.

In exploring the meaning of soccer in the countries that qualified for the 2010 World Cup, this book highlights a reality for both Latin America and soccer in the United States. Much of the time, the countries of the region—with which we share increasing cultural and economic bonds—remain off Americans' radar. Only in times of crisis, and world sporting events, do the diverse countries of Latin America register to many in the United States. This is, of course, lamentable. But importantly, soccer offers a window onto Latin American society. As this book has argued, national teams are not all that matter in the soccer world, but they represent the nation much more visibly than club teams do or than an individual player can. Why? When international tournaments occur, focus turns to those countries participating in the event. In other words, international play provides the excuse to look deeper into the meaning of sport and the history, society, culture, and politics of the region.

For example, as the last round of World Cup qualifying for CONCACAF—known as the Hexagonal—got under way in February of 2013, eyes turned to the two presumptive favorites: Mexico and the United States. Commentators in both nations, assuming that their teams would qualify easily for Brazil 2014, almost completely overlooked their first opponents. Mexico, fresh from Olympic gold in 2012, seemed poised to walk over Jamaica at the Estadio Azteca. The match would highlight El Tri's offensive firepower over a theoretically much weaker Jamaican team. The two played to a listless draw, and Mexico looked either outclassed or disinterested for much of the contest.

The United States, for its part, prepared to play Honduras in San Pedro Sula. The U.S. opponent seemed something of an afterthought for the U.S. press. Most articles commented on Jürgen Klinsmann's lineup or the absence of veteran players such as Landon Donovan and Carlos Bocanegra. They noted talented Honduran players but suggested the technical superiority of the United States. Most American journalists predicted a draw, due not to Honduran skill but rather to the hostile playing environment. Commentators failed to mention that Honduras had acquitted itself well in the 2010 World Cup, or that the Catrachos had reached the quarterfinals of the 2012 Olympics, falling to eventual silver-medalist Brazil in a close-fought match. Instead, the press focused on the fact that the Honduran government declared a national holiday for the day of the game, and painted the country as violent and crime-ridden. Honduras thoroughly outplayed the United States in a 2–1 victory.

Why is this relevant? The coverage of the U.S. team in Honduras brought the country into the mainstream American press, providing an opportunity to examine Honduras more closely. Scratching just below the surface of reports on high murder rates and anti-American sentiment, we gain a much better understanding of the reasons behind the social crisis facing Honduras. Crime, in fact, spiked after the 2009 coup that ousted Manuel Zelaya. Since his overthrow the murder rate in the country has skyrocketed while human rights violations by the military and police have also risen sharply. We also discover that the sharp increase in violence coincided with the opening of a new front in the U.S. war on drugs in Honduras, bringing with it U.S. operatives and increased militarization. In other words, while Honduras remains outside of U.S. consciousness most of the time, World Cup qualifiers, the World Cup, and other international matches offer moments of recognition and opportunities for learning—not just about the sport but about society as whole.

In the same way, the summer 2013 street protests in Brazil, ostensibly over a rise in the price of public transportation, would not normally have become major international news. Yet because Brazilian ire erupted at the same time that the country hosted the 2013 Confederations Cup, the protests received sustained attention from the world media. Moreover, since some protestors explicitly tied soccer to Brazil's social ills, the mainstream media's gaze turned to these issues. These protestors argued that the money being allocated by Brazil to mega sporting events such as the 2014 World Cup and the 2016 Olympics in Rio would be better spent on solving some of the country's longstanding problems such as education or health care. Here, not only did a soccer tournament offer the opportunity to delve into deeper issues in Brazilian society but some of the debate revolved around the sport itself and the value of hosting the World Cup.

Soccer, in other words, will remain a critical way to examine the changing narratives of Latin American nations. The sport, for instance, can just as easily help to explain the racial reality of Ecuador or Colombia as it can Honduras or Brazil. The political and social conflict that tore Colombia apart for much of the last sixty years finds an outlet in soccer just as antigovernment protest in Chile did. To be sure, playing in the World Cup matters to Latin Americans, but soccer is embedded more deeply than that. Making the World Cup finals surely boosts the pride of each nation that qualifies, but it does not redefine national identity. In the same way, failing to qualify does not diminish Latin American love of the sport.

☉

From the time it arrived in the region, soccer has helped the nations of Latin America grapple with the thorniest challenges that they have faced. The sport has acted as a space both to assert identity and to question authority. It aided in creating a sense of unity in Uruguay after the decades of chaos resulting from independence as well as after the upheavals of modernization and development. So too soccer helped Brazil and Argentina forge national identities by integrating elements of their populations—whether poor immigrants, as in the case of Argentina, or people of African descent, in the case of Brazil. In the same way, soccer assists us in understanding the complexities of corruption in Paraguay, the many promises of development in Mexico, or changing ideas about gender throughout the region.

Indeed, the questions that we have addressed in this book—from corruption to political protest, from promises of national development to questions of race and gender—will continue to confront the region for the foreseeable future. But the direction that the countries take on these issues—how Latin American countries confront the issues and the way that soccer both informs and reflects their decisions—will continue to evolve. What this book has argued is that soccer elucidates the major issues that face the region. It helps to shape the narrative of nation and gender, of race and politics. Moreover, the sport often provides counterpoints to the dominant versions of history, creating spaces in which alternative stories about the nation can be told. Whether reinforcing national narratives or crafting counternarratives, soccer remains a way to explore, examine, and understand Latin America. It has this explanatory power because of how the sport and the nation have been tied together for more than a century. And it matters so much to many Latin Americans precisely because of these ties—to community, to nation, to history, and to other critical junctures of national history. In short, almost since its arrival soccer has served as a way to reflect reality and project the future aspirations of nations and people.

What the future holds for Latin America, and for Latin American soccer, is anyone's guess. Much of the region has begun a process of increasing economic integration exemplified by South America's Mercosur (Argentina, Brazil, Paraguay, Uruguay, and Venezuela), which seeks to reduce trade barriers. Politically, the Community of Latin American and Caribbean States, begun in 2011, looks to create political interconnection without the influence of the United States. These institutions speak to changing realities in Latin America and a growing recognition of the region's power on the world stage. No longer do Latin American leaders take the traditional economic and political power of the United States as unquestioned. Likewise, indigenous peoples and people of African descent continue to advocate for increased rights. In other words, new national and regional narratives are in the process of being written, and their end results are as yet unknown. Whatever their outcome, however, soccer will play a role in both crafting and explaining these new histories.

Soccer matters in Latin America not because of how well a club or nation performs but because soccer has come to reflect the identity of a community—be it national, regional, or local—in ways that other institutions cannot. These reflections of who a people are become the narratives that in turn supposedly describe where they come from and their essence. This makes soccer incredibly powerful, now and in the future.

Moreover, soccer will continue to be the face of Latin American nations to many in the world, whether through the players who migrate to Europe for economic opportunity or through world soccer events such as the World Cup. And the question will remain, as it has for more than a century: what will that face be? Will it represent the dominant narratives of the region or, to paraphrase Eduardo Galeano, will it suggest the multiplicity of histories that course through the veins of the region?

Acknowledgments

Acknowledgments are a bit like acceptance speeches at awards shows, often long-winded and apparently tangential. I will try to keep this brief, lest the microphone stand drop back into the stage and the band start to play. As with all books, this one could not have been completed without the support and guidance of others. I would like to thank Amy Gorelick for walking me through the process from proposal to completed work. Lou Pérez and John Chasteen advised me at different stages along the way, as did John French. A number of colleagues and friends from my days at the University of North Carolina provided me with tangible and emotional support over the course of this project: Matthew Brown, Enver Casimir, Oscar Chamosa, Jeffrey Erbig, Gerardo Garza, Ethan Kytle, Marko Maunula, Leah Potter, Joel Revill, Blain Roberts, and William Van Norman. I also would like to thank my colleagues in the History Department at North Carolina Central University. I have felt at home there since my first day, and they have served as inspirations for how to combine high-intensity teaching with high-level research. I would especially like to thank Carlton Wilson for finding creative ways to provide me more time to work on the project.

Over the course of researching and writing, many people gave generously of their time and insight. Thanks to Michael Francis for getting the ball rolling. Bill Wisser helped to shape the initial project and to distract me with dreams of woodworking and auto body repair. Jeff Richey served as an early sounding board for ideas about which he knew far more than I did and, with Katharine French-Fuller, hosted me in Argentina; I am grateful. During the research phase a number of current and former players, coaches, and administrators freely offered their knowledge and experiences: Andrea Rodebaugh, Diego Guacci, Manelich Quintero, and Patricio Kiblisky. Others helped dig up sources on women's soccer: Maritza Carreño Martínez, Eliézer Pérez, and Elizangela Silva Ribeiro. So too I would like to thank Chris Unger and Adalberto Villasana. In Argentina, María Otálora at the library of the Asociación de Fútbol Argentino offered her advice and knowledge of the holdings. At FIFA, Christa Bühler and Dominik Petermann made sure that I had more than I needed at all times. And thank you to Jean-Edouard Courcier and Astrid Carver-Courcier for their hospitality.

Those who commented on papers and read chapters provided me with more support and encouragement than they can know: Hans Muller, Jacob Bonenberger, Matt Andrews, Michael Huner, Hugo Ceron, Celso Castilho, Kay Schiller, Jeffrey Lesser, Raanan Rein, Hector Fernández L'Hoeste, Yago Colás, Robert Irwin, Roger Kittleson, Bryan McCann, John Nauright, and Wanderly Marchí Jr. The anonymous readers of my manuscript improved it immeasurably with their comments, and I sincerely thank them. A Duke University Humanities Writ Large fellowship provided me the time and space to complete the project, and I would like to thank everyone at the Duke Haiti Lab and the Franklin Humanities Institute for making my time there enjoyable and productive.

Without Katharine French-Fuller's editing and savvy, this project would have floundered long ago. I'm not sure how many times I've said it, but once more can't hurt: you rock! And the music is beginning to play. . . . My parents, for everything. It sounds cliché, I know, but if I do half as good a job raising my children as they did, I will be very happy. I promise to call more often. My amazing sister, Helen, whose eye for prose and ability to juggle my manuscript with the eighty million other things in her life reinforce to me once again how lucky I am.

And finally, to Evanthia Canoutas, who continues to captivate me with her intellect and wit. For supporting my work, for putting up with countless weekends of solo parenting, for lifting me emotionally and spurring me on—in short, for being a wonderful partner and mother—*s'agapo poli*. And to Sofia and Rafael, whom I have missed so much in this process, and whose love of soccer somehow has not diminished after losing their father to its history for so long. Now we have time.

Notes

Introduction

1. Nathan Irving Huggins, "The Deforming Mirror of Truth," introduction to *Black Odyssey: The African American Ordeal in Slavery* (New York: Vintage, 1990).

Chapter 1. Uruguayan Arrivals

1. José P. Varela, quoted in Enrique Méndez-Vives, *El Uruguay de la modernización: 1876–1904* (Montevideo: Ediciones de la Banda Oriental, 1975), 45.

2. José Pedro Barrán, *Apogeo y crisis del Uruguay pastoral y caudillesco* (Montevideo: Ediciones de la Banda Oriental, 1974). See also Fernando López-Alves, *State Formation and Democracy in Latin America, 1810–1900* (Durham, N.C.: Duke University Press, 2000), ch. 2; Juan A. Oddone, "The Formation of Modern Uruguay, c. 1870–1930," in *The Cambridge History of Latin America*, vol. 5, ed. Leslie Bethell (Cambridge: Cambridge University Press, 1986), 453; Raul Jacob, "Algunas consideraciones sobre la industrialización" in *La industrialización del Uruguay 1870–1925: 5 perspectivas históricas*, ed. Alcides Berreta et al. (Montevideo: Fundación de Cultura Económica, 1978), 9; Ana Frega, *El pluarlismo uruguayo* (Montevideo: CLAEH, 1987), 94–95; and Clarence Jones, "The Trade of Uruguay," *Economic Geography* 3, no. 3 (July 1927): 361.

3. Jones, "Trade of Uruguay," 374.

4. This is a paraphrase of Luís Prats. See Prats, *La crónica celeste: Historia de la Selección Uruguaya de Fútbol: triunfos, derrotas, mitas y polémicas (1901–2001)* (Montevideo: Editorial Fin de Siglo, 2001), 8.

5. See Benjamin Nahum, *La epoca batllista, 1905–1929* (Montevideo: Ediciones de la Banda Oriental, 1975); and Benjamin Nahum, coordinator, *Estadísticas históricas del Uruguay, 1900–1950*, vol. 4 (Montevideo: Universidad de la República, Facultad de Ciencias Sociales, 2007), 301–2.

6. Prats, 8.

7. Claudia Giaudrone, "El gaucho en el ámbito iconográfico del Centenario uruguayo (1925–1930)," *Revista Hispánica Moderna* 61, no. 2 (December 2008): 149–65.

8. "El football inglés y el rioplatense," *El Gráfico*, July 7, 1928, 15.

9. Ernesto Escobar Bavio, *El football en el Río de la Plata (desde 1893)* (Buenos Aires: Editorial Sports, 1923), 13. This thread is picked up by Richard Giulianotti, *Football: A Sociology of the Global Game* (Cambridge: Polity Press, 1999), 8; Chris Taylor, *The Beautiful Game: A Journey through Latin American Football* (London: Phoenix, 1998), 25; David Goldblatt, *The Ball Is Round: A Global History of Football* (London: Penguin, 2007), 130; and Eduardo Santa Cruz A., *Origén y futuro de una pasión: Fútbol, cultura, y modernidad* (Santiago: LOM-ARCIS, 1995), 29.

10. José I. Buzzetti and Eduardo Gutierrez Cortinas, *Historia del deporte en el Uruguay (1830–1900)* (Montevideo: Tall. Graïf Castro, 1965), 71; and Juan Carlos Luzuriaga, "La forja de la rivalidad clásica: Nacional-Peñarol en el Montevideo de 1900," efdeportes.com 10, no. 88 (Septiembre 2005). Eventually Albion changed its rules to permit foreign-born players, but the foreign presence on the team remained small.

11. Prats, 7.

12. Not all of these matches are official internationals, as some may have been played by teams that combined Uruguayan and Argentine players.

13. Juan Antonio Magariños Pittaluga and Mateo Magariños Pittaluga, *Del fútbol heroíco* (Buenos Aires: Talleres Gráficos de Alfonzo Ruíz, 1942), 266.

14. Juan Antonio Capelán Carril, *Nueve décadas de gloria* (Montevideo: Asociación Uruguayo de Fútbol, 1990), 16.

15. See Nahum, *Epoca*.

16. Quoted in Manuel Frau, "Fútbol e historia: La esquizofrenia oriental," *Caravelle* no. 89 (December 2007), 134.

Chapter 2. La Nuestra and Futebol Arte

1. The first use of the phrase "the beautiful game" is subject to debate. Stuart Hall, a British commentator, claims to have coined the phrase in 1958 while others credit Brazilian star Didi with its creation. In fact, Tómas Mazzoni, a Brazilian journalist, used the phrase in his 1938 book, *O Brasil na taça do mundo*.

2. "The Week in Quotes," FIFA.com, June 25, 2011, http://www.fifa.com/newscen tre/features/news/newsid=1460317/index.html, accessed July 1, 2011.

3. Stephen Wade, "Argentina's Top Export—Soccer Players," *Standard Examiner*, January 2, 2011, http://www.standard.net/topics/sports/2011/01/02/argentinas-top -export-soccer-players; and "Argentina Doesn't Benefit as Soccer Players Go Abroad," *New York Times*, January 1, 2011, http://www.nytimes.com/2011/01/02/sports/soccer /02argentina.html. Both accessed September 15, 2012.

4. Julio Frydenberg, *Historia social del fútbol: Del amateurismo a la profesionalización* (Buenos Aires: Siglo Veintiuno Editores, 2011), 113.

5. Roberto Di Giano, *Fútbol y discriminación social* (Buenos Aires: Leviatán, 2007), 18; and *La Nación*, February 13, 1913, p. 14.

6. Hector F. Ugazio, *La Vanguardia*, May 4, 1917, p. 4; *La Nación*, January 27, 1913, 11; and "David Weiss, manager del team checoeslovako hace una serie de declaraciones para el Gráfico," *El Gráfico*, August 18, 1922, p. 21.

7. Oscar Chamosa, *The Argentine Folklore Movement: Sugar Elites, Criollo Workers,*

and the Politics of Cultural Nationalism, 1900–1955 (Tucson: University of Arizona Press, 2010), 39–40.

8. Eduardo Archetti, "Playing Styles and Masculine Virtues in Argentine Football," in *Machos, Mistresses, Madonnas: Contesting the Power of Latin American Gender Imagery*, ed. Marit Melhuus and Kristi Anne Stølen (London: Verso, 1996), 38.

9. "Raza y sport," *El Gráfico*, November 27, 1926, p. 15.

10. Borrocotó, "Los Reos de fútbol," *El Gráfico*, February 18, 1928, p. 14.

11. Carlos Sturzenegger, *Football: Leyes que lo rigen y modo de jugarlo* (Montevideo: Talleres Gráfico El Arte, 1911), 15–16; and "Los ases del deporte uruguayo: Alfredo Foglino," *El Gráfico*, June 2, 1923, 15.

12. "Criollos," *El Gráfico*, August 4, 1928, 36.

13. Fábio Franzini, "As raízes do país do futebol: Estudo sobre a relação entre o futebol e a nacionalidade brasileira (1919–1950)" (M.A. thesis, Universidade de São Paulo, 2000), 30.

14. Gilberto Freyre, *New World in the Tropics: The Culture of Modern Brazil* (New York: Alfred A. Knopf, 1959), 111–12; Cesar Gordon and Ronaldo Helal, "The Crisis of Brazilian Football: Perspectives for the Twenty-First Century," in *Sport and Latin American Society*, ed. J. A. Mangan and Lamartine P. Costa (London: Frank Cass, 2002), 145.

15. Gilberto Freyre, *The Masters and the Slaves* (Berkeley: University of California Press, 1996), 278. For critiques of Freyre, see Florestan Fernandes, *The Negro in Brazilian Society* (New York: Columbia University Press, 1969). Fernandes also holds on to some of the racialized imagery of the era in his class-based analysis of Brazilian society. See also Alexandra Isfahani-Hammond, *White Negritude: Race, Writing, and Brazilian Cultural Identity* (New York: Palgrave Macmillan, 2008); Elsa Larkin Nascimento, *The Sorcery of Color: Identity, Race, and Gender in Brazil* (Philadelphia: Temple University Press, 2007); and Helena Bocayuva, *Erotismo à brasileira, o, Excesso sexual na obra de Gilberto Freyre* (Rio de Janeiro: Garamond, 2001).

16. Gilberto Freyre, *Correio de Manhã*, June 15, 1938, quoted in José Sergio Leite Lopes, "The Brazilian Style of Football and Its Dilemmas," in *Football Cultures and Identities*, ed. Gary Armstrong and Richard Giulianotti (Houndsmills and London: Macmillan, 1999), 94–95n1.

17. Roberto DaMatta, "Antropologia do óbvio: Notas em torno do significado social do futebol brasileiro." *Revista USP* 22 (1994): 10–17; Ariel Sander Damo, "Ah! Eu Sou Gaúcho! O Nacional e o Regional no Futebol Brasileiro," *Estudos Históricos* 23 (1999), 89, 91; Gilberto Freyre, preface in Mario Rodrigues Filho, *O negro no futebol brasileiro* (Rio de Janeiro: MAUAD Editora, 2003), 24–25; and Mazzoni, *Brasil no taça*, 21, 88.

18. See *Ginga: The Soul of Brazilian Football*, dir. Tocha Alves and Hank Levine (2005).

19. Mazzoni, *Brasil no taça*, 88.

20. Leite Lopes, "Brazilian Style," 90; José Lyra Filho, quoted in José Sergio Leite Lopes, "Transformations in National Identity through Football in Brazil: Lessons

from Two Historical Defeats," in *Football in the Americas: Fútbol, Futebol, Football*, ed. Rory M. Miller and Liz Crolley (London: Institute for the Study of the Americas, 2007), 100; and Manuel Bandeira, "De vario assunto do futebol," in *O Melhor da Crónica Brasileira, tomo 2* (Rio de Janeiro: Livraria José Olympio Editora, 1981), 85.

21. João Saldanha, *Os subteranneos do futebol* (Rio de Janeiro: Livraria José Olympio Editora, 1980), 118; and Ruy Castro, *Garrincha: The Triumph and Tragedy of Brazil's Forgotten Footballing Hero*, trans. Andrew Downie (London: Yellow Jersey, 2004), 76.

22. Saldanha, 118.

23. *Ginga: The Soul of Brazilian Football*, dir. Tocha Alves and Hank Levine (2005); John Lanchester, "Brazil," in *The Thinking Fan's Guide to the World Cup*, ed. Matt Weiland and Sean Wiley (New York: Harper Perennial, 2006), 73.

Chapter 3. Paraguay

1. "Influyente político acusa a Leoz de presionar a árbitros," *La Nación*, September 25, 2006. http://www.nacion.com/ln_ee/2006/septiembre/25/udeportes-la5.html, accessed April 19, 2012; and "Senador oficialista califica como 'capomafiosos' dirigentes mundiales," *Terra Argentina*, September 28, 2006, http://deportesar.terra.com.ar/futlatino/interna/0,,OI1164578-EI7786,00.html, accessed April 19, 2012.

2. Peter Lambert, "History, Identity, and Paraguayidad," in *The Paraguay Reader: History, Culture, Politics*, ed. Peter Lambert and Andrew Nickson (Durham, N.C.: Duke University Press, 2013), 385.

3. Miguel Angel Bestard, *Paraguay: Un siglo de fútbol* (Asunción: Editorial Litocolor, 1996), 7.

4. Jesus Amado Recalde Guanes, "Prologue," in Humberto Domínguez Dibb, *El fútbol paraguayo* (Asunción: Talleres Gráficos Cromos, 1977).

5. "El fútbol de Sudamérica se radica en Paraguay," *ABC Color* suplemento especial, January 23, 1998; and Nicolás Leoz, *Pido la palabra: I Request the Floor* (Buenos Aires: Ediciones Salvucci y Asociados, 2001), 190–96.

6. James Dingemans, "Review of Allegations of Misconduct in Relation to the FA's 2018 World Cup Bid: Summary Report to the FA," May 26, 2011. José Maria Troche lists Leoz's honors in *El libro de oro del fútbol paraguayo, 1901–2011*. Spain is not among those countries to have given Leoz an official honor. Those that have include Argentina, Bolivia, Brazil, Chile, China, Colombia, Ecuador, Japan, and Mexico. See José Maria Troche, *El libro de oro del fútbol paraguayo, 1901–2011* (Asunción: Alvaro Ayala Producciones, 2011), 196.

7. Dingemans; David Bond, "FIFA President Sepp Blatter Set for U-turn over Bribes Investigation," *BBC*, October 18, 2011. http://www.bbc.co.uk/sport/0/football/15357180, accessed January 25, 2012; "CONMEBOL Defies Reforms and Appoints Leoz 'President for Life,'" *Play the Game*, May 3, 2012, http://www.playthegame.org/news/detailed/conmebol-defies-reforms-and-appoints-leoz-president-for-life-5388.html, accessed May 18, 2012; and Carlos Bottasso, "'Estamos bien posicionados'" *Diario el Sol*, May 8, 2012, http://www.elsolquilmes.com.ar/notas/9069-estamos-bien-posicionados, accessed May 18, 2012.

8. Sid Lowe, "Nelson Valdez Hails a 'Dream Come True' as Hércules Shock Barcelona," *Guardian*, September 13, 2010, http://www.guardian.co.uk/football/blog/2010/sep /13/hercules-stun-barcelona-sid-lowe, accessed April 19, 2012; and "My Journey," *Nelsonhaedovaldez.com*, http://www.nelsonhaedovaldez18.com/journey.html, accessed April 19, 2012.

9. Peter Lambert and Andrew Nickson, eds., *The Paraguay Reader: History, Culture, Politics* (Durham, N.C.: Duke University Press, 2013), 453.

10. Maria Victoria Fazio, "Poverty and Inequality in Paraguay: Methodological Issues and Literature Review," CEDLAS-World Bank, 2005, 15; and Natalia Ruíz Díaz, "Land Conflicts Threaten to Boil Over," *Inter Press Service News Agency*, February 28, 2012, http://ipsnews.net/news.asp?idnews=106888, accessed May 18, 2012.

11. Lambert and Nickson, *Paraguay Reader*, 236.

12. "Paraguayans Living Abroad Closer to Voting in National Elections," *MercoPress*, October 10, 2011, http://en.mercopress.com/2011/10/10/paraguayans-living -abroad-closer-to-voting-in-national-elections, accessed November 11, 2011.

13. Hugo Oddone, Claudina Zavattiero, Cynthia González Ríos, Edith Arrúa Sosa, and Elizabeth Barrios, *Perfil migratorio del Paraguay* (Buenos Aires: OIM, 2011), 23; and Dannin M. Hanratty and Sandra W. Meditz, eds., *Paraguay: A Country Study* (Washington, D.C.: GPO for the Library of Congress, 1988), http://countrystudies. us/paraguay/.

14. Troche, 87 and 64; and Catalo Bogado Bordón and Gilberto Ramírez Santacruz, *Arsenio Erico, el ángel que jugó para los diablos: Historia del mejor futbolista de todos tiempos* (Asunción: Aranduã Editorial, 2006), 41.

15. Daniel Edwards, "Paraguay Legend José Luís Chilavert Allegedly Comes to Blows with Argentine Agent in Airport," *Goal*, October 18,2010, http://www.goal .com/en/news/1700/paraguay/2010/10/18/2172019/paraguay-legend-jose-luis -chilavert-allegedly-comes-to-blows, accessed April 10, 2012.

16. "Bulldog Spirit: Flamboyant Chilavert still Paraguay's biggest star," *Sports Illustrated*, April 25, 2002, http://sportsillustrated.cnn.com/soccer/world/2002/world _cup/news/2002/04/25/paraguay_chilavert_ap/, accessed April 20, 2012.

Chapter 4. "Y va a caer"

1. See, among others, Theodor Adorno and Max Horkheimer, "The Culture Industry: Enlightenment as Mass Deception," in *Dialectic of Enlightenment*, trans. Edmund Jephcott (Stanford, Calif.: Stanford University Press, 2002); Juan José Sebreli, *Fútbol y masas* (Buenos Aires: Editorial Galerno, 1983); Janet Lever, *Soccer Madness* (Chicago: University of Chicago Press, 1983); and Jean-Marie Brohm, *Sport: A Prison of Measured Time* (London: Ink Links, 1978). Others offer a bit more nuanced view of the relations between state control and sport, notably: Pierre Bourdieu, "Sport and Social Class," *Social Science Information* 17 (December 1978): 819–40; Richard Gruneau, *Class, Sport, and Social Development* (Amherst: University of Massachusetts Press, 1983); John Hargreaves, *Sport, Power, and Culture: A Social and Historical Analysis of Popular Sports in Britain* (New York: St. Martin's Press, 1988); and Allen

Guttmann, *From Ritual to Record: the Nature of Modern Sports* (New York: Columbia University Press, 1978), among others.

2. Quoted in Eduardo Santa Cruz A., *Origen y futuro de una pasión: Fútbol, cultura y modernidad* (Santiago: LOM-ARCIS, 1995), 16.

3. Ibid., 32–47.

4. See Brenda Elsey, *Citizens and Sportsmen: Fútbol and Politics in Twentieth Century Chile* (Austin: University of Texas Press, 2011).

5. Ibid., 32.

6. Ibid., 28–32.

7. Alex Pickett, *Moscú, 26 de septiembre 1973, URSS o-Chile o: El partido de los valientes* (Santiago: Aguilar, 2003), 47–70.

8. Ibid., 43.

9. Arturo Valenzuela, *The Breakdown of Democratic Regimes: Chile* (Baltimore: Johns Hopkins University Press, 1988), 6–13 and 34–38; and Brian Loveman, *Chile: The Legacy of Hispanic Capitalism* (New York: Oxford University Press, 1988), 270–80.

10. The question of how Allende died was a hotly debated topic until September 2012. Some said that he committed suicide as the military took the palace while others claimed he was killed by the forces storming the palace. In 2012 a government commission that had exhumed Allende's body declared his death a suicide.

11. Rear Admiral Carlos Chubretovic, quoted in Daniel Matamala, *Goles y autogoles: La impropria relación entre fútbol y el poder político* (Santiago: Planeta, 2001), 73.

12. Luis Godoy Ortíz, "Pinochet, Colo-Colo y la Digeder," *La Nación*, December 11, 2006, http://www.lanacion.cl/prontus_noticias/site/artic/20061210/pags/2006 1210225605.html.

13. *Analisis, diagnóstico, y formulación de una estrategia de desarrollo para el fútbol chileno* (Santiago: DIGEDER, 1987), 7–8.

14. There is little agreement about the numbers of Chileans who attended soccer matches. Edgardo Marín places the attendance numbers at roughly 104,000 for 1937, 480,000 for 1939, and 297,000 for 1940. Daniel Matamala estimates 192,129 in 1937 and 826,231 in 1940. Either way, there was massive growth in spectatorship. See Edgardo Marín Méndez, *Centenario: Historia total del fútbol chileno, 1895–1995* (Santiago: Editores y Consultores REI).

15. Matamala, 47.

16. "Brazil, Yugoslavia, Play to Soccer Draw," *Redlands Daily Facts*, June 14, 1974, 23.

17. Wolfgang Kraushaar, "Chile Si, Junta No! Political Protests at the 1974 FIFA World Cup," trans. Toby Axelrod, *Eurozine*, July 8, 2008, http://www.eurozine.com/ articles/2008-08-07-kraushaar2-en.html, accessed December 28, 2011; "Australia v. Chile, 1974," *Youtube*, http://www.youtube.com/watch?v=wtlFqI_3uE4&feature=rel ated, accessed December 28, 2011; and "Fußball WM 1974: DDR-Chile 1:1," *Youtube*, http://www.youtube.com/watch?v=om8xiJxaIMQ, accessed December 28, 2011.

18. Carlos Huneeus, *The Pinochet Regime*, trans. Lake Sagars (Boulder, Colo.: Lynne Rienner Publishers, 2007), 272, 365.

19. Thomas Miller Klubock, "Copper Workers, Organized Labor, and Popular Protest to Military Rule in Chile, 1973–1986," *International Labor and Working Class History* 52 (Fall 1997), 117.

20. Matamala, 146.

21. The spot is available on the web: "Franja política por el No!, (parte 4 de 5), *Youtube*, http://www.youtube.com/watch?v=C8rp3tureCU&feature=related, accessed December 20, 2011; it is also recounted in Matamala.

Chapter 5. Dark, Expressive Sportsmen of a Distant Continent?

1. "Honduran Garifuna Culture Threatened by Coup," *New America Media*, September 4, 2009, http://news.newamericamedia.org/news/view_article.html?article_id=9bf0fc2b744767885a293093a23f7e3c, accessed May 15, 2012.

2. Mark Anderson, *Black and Indigenous: Garifuna Activism and Consumer Culture* (Minneapolis: University of Minnesota Press, 2009), 66.

3. Quoted in ibid., 106.

4. Some reports claim that Moncada used the term "negro de mierda"—"fucking black."

5. On the Palacios incident, see "Johnny Palacios acusó a un árbitros de insultas racistas en la liga de Honduras," *Univision Deportes*, October 4, 2011, http://futbol.univision.com/centroamerica/honduras/article/2011-10-04/johnny-palacios-acusa-a-arbitro-de-racista#axzz2PAEReq2X, accessed May 10, 2012. For more on John Terry and Luis Suárez, see "Unreliable and Inconsistent: FA's Verdict on Luis Suarez's Evidence in Race Row," *Mail Online*, January 1, 2012, http://www.dailymail.co.uk/news/article-2080751/Luis-Suarez-gave-unreliable-inconsistent-evidence-FAs-verdict-race-row.html, accessed April 23, 2012; and Derek Hunter, "I believe it was racist! Rio breaks his silence while brother Anton stands firm in Terry race row," *Mail Online*, October 30, 2011, http://www.dailymail.co.uk/sport/football/article-2055159/Rio-Ferdinand-breaks-silence-John-Terry-row-I-believe-racist.html, accessed April 23, 2012. On Blatter's comments, see "Sepp Blatter Says On-pitch Racism Can Be Resolved with Handshake," *BBC*, http://www.bbc.co.uk/sport/0/football/15757165, accessed April 23, 2012.

6. Jairo Landa, "Deportistas: blanco del racismo," *Proceso Digital*, http://www.procesodigital.hn/reportajes/050605_etnias06.php#, accessed May 17, 2012.

7. "Futbolistas de Honduras 'Contra el racismo,'" *El Heraldo.hn*, November 5, 2011, http://archivo.elheraldo.hn/Ediciones/2011/05/22/Noticias/Futbolistas-de-Honduras-Contra-el-racismo, accessed May 17 2012; and Christian Girón, "Osman Chávez: 'Al llamarnos negros demuestran odio,'" *Diez.hn*, November 14, 2011, http://m.diez.hn/Secciones/Legionarios/Jugadores/Osman-Chavez/Noticias/Osman-Chavez-Al-llamarnos-negros-demuestran-odio, accessed May 17, 2012.

8. Ivonne Rodríguez, "Racismo: Parlamentario confiesa su desprecio por los negros," *Proceso Digital*, March 29, 2006, http://www.procesodigital.hn/2006/03/29_racismo.php, accessed May 18, 2012; "Racismo y deporte, enemigos irreconciliables," *La Tribuna*, December 1, 2011, http://www.latribunadeportiva.hn/2011/12/01/racismo-y-deporte-enemigos-irreconciliables/; and "Esto es repudiable," *La Prensa*, March

10, 2009, http://archivo.laprensa.hn/Deportes/Ediciones/2009/03/11/Noticias/ Esto-es-repudiable, accessed May 17, 2012.

9. "Racismo, flagelo a erradicar en el fútbol," *El Heraldo.hn*, May 31, 2011, http:// archivo.elheraldo.hn/Zona%20Deportiva/Ediciones/2011/06/01/Noticias/Racismo-flagelo-a-erradicar-en-el-futbol, accessed May 17, 2012; and Landa.

10. Anderson, 43.

11. República de Honduras, *Características generales de los Garifunas conforme a los resultados del XI censo nacional y de vivienda, año 2001* (Tegucigalpa: INE, 2001), 10–13, 26. Green is quoted in "Racismo y deporte, enemigos irreconciliables" (see n. 7).

12. Chris Taylor, *Black Carib Wars: Freedom, Survival, and the Making of the Garifuna* (Jackson: University Press of Mississippi, 2012), 154–57.

13. The foregoing discussion on race, slavery, and mining comes from the following sources: Luz María Martínez Montiel, ed., *Presencia Africana en Centroamérica* (Mexico City: Dirección General de Culturas Populares, 1993), 9; and Rafael Leiva Vivas, "Presencia negra en Honduras," in *Presencia Africana en Centroamérica*, ed. Luz María Martínez Montiel (Mexico City: Dirección General de Culturas Populares, 1993), 123. Gold peaked in production prior to 1565, after which it declined. But between 1540 and 1542, more than 200,000 pesos worth of gold came from Honduran mines. See Linda Newson, "Labor in the Colonial Mining Industry of Honduras," *Americas* 39, no. 2 (October 1982), 186, 193. See also William L. Sherman, *Forced Native Labor in Colonial Central America* (Lincoln: University of Nebraska Press, 1972). Sherman notes that black slaves were "more desirable" than indigenous people, and cost more—between 100 and 200 pesos in 1550. See ibid., 232–33 and note 387; and Robinson A. Herrera, "'Por que no sabemos firmar': Black Slaves in Early Guatemala," *Americas* 57, no. 2 (October 2000), 247 note. See also Robinson A. Herrera, *Natives, Europeans, and Africans in Sixteenth-Century Santiago de Guatemala* (Austin: University of Texas Press, 2003); Mario Felipe Martínez Castillo, *La Intendencia de Comayagua* (Tegucigalpa: Litografía López, 2004), 12.

14. José S. García Ch., Mario Griffin Cubas, and Héctor Miguel Maradiaga, *Historia del fútbol y su desarrollo en Honduras* (Tegucigalpa: FENEFUTH, 1993), 19–21.

15. García, et al. (1993), 33–63; and José S. García Ch., Mario Griffin Cubas, and Héctor Miguel Maradiaga, *Historia del fútbol y su desarrollo en Honduras*, 2nd ed. (Tegucigalpa: FENEFUTH, 2000), 45. See also "Historia," *Clubolimpia.com*, http://www. clubolimpia.com/historia/, accessed May 1, 2012; "Nace el equipo mimado," *Club Deportivo Motagua*, http://www.motagua.com/1928/08/nace-el-equipo-mimado/, accessed May 1, 2012.

16. García, et al. (1993), 23–25; and "Honduras—List of International Matches," http://www.rsssf.com/tablesh/hond-intres.html.

17. Dario Euraque, *Conversaciones históricos con el mestizaje y su identidad nacional en Honduras* (San Pedro Sula: Centro Editorial, 2004), 22.

18. Newson; and Euraque, *Conversaciones*, 19. This number is taken from Linda Newson's estimates, which are cited in Euraque. She estimates that approximately 40–45 percent of the population was ladino, a 3:1 ratio of mulatto to mestizo. Thus, somewhere on the order of 30–35 percent would be mulatto, with a further 10

percent either black or white. See also Mark Anderson and Sarah England, "¿Auténtica cultura Africana en Honduras? Los afrocentroamericanos desafían el mestizaje," in *Memorias del mestizaje: Cultura política en Centroamérica de 1920 al presente*, ed. Dario Euraque, Jeffrey Gould, and Charles Hale (Guatemala: CIRMA, 2005), 257.

19. Anderson and England, 270.

20. Euraque, *Conversaciones*, 262.

21. Dario Euraque, *Estado, poder, nacionalidad y raza en la historia de Honduras* (Choluteca: Ediciones Subirana, 1996), 79–81; and Breny Mendoza, "La desmitologización del mestizaje en Honduras," *Mesoamérica* 42 (December 2001): 266–68.

22. Anderson, *Black and Indigenous*, 86, 25.

23. Anderson, *Black and Indigenous*, 22 note; and República de Honduras, *Características generales*, 15 and Annex 3.

Chapter 6. The Unfulfilled Promise of Mexico

1. Manuel Seyde, in Greco Sotelo, *Crónicas del fútbol mexicano*, vol. 3, *El oficio de las canchas (1950–1970)* (Mexico City: Editorial Clio, 1998), 14; and Ramón Márquez C., "Introducción," in Carlos Calderón Cardoso, *Crónicas del fútbol mexicano: Por amor de la camiseta*, vol. 2 *(1933–1950)* (Mexico City: Editorial Clio, 1998), 10.

2. Eric Zolov, "Showcasing the 'Land of Tomorrow': Mexico and the 1968 Olympics," *Americas* 61, no. 2 (October 2004): 163. See also Keith Brewster and Claire Brewster, "Cleaning the Cage: Mexico City's Preparations for the Olympic Games," *International Journal for the History of Sport* 26, no. 6 (April 2009): 790–813; and Kevin B. Witherspoon, *Before the Eyes of the World: Mexico and the 1968 Olympic Games* (DeKalb: Northern Illinois University Press, 2008).

3. Octavio Paz, *The Labyrinth of Solitude*, tran. Lysander Kemp (New York: Grove Press, 1961). The quotations from Paz are from pages 9–20. The idea of many Mexicos is from Lesley Byrd Simpson, who argued that geography, topography, and language made Mexico difficult to define as a unity. "Patria chica" is the term used by Alan Knight in his two-volume work on the Mexican Revolution. See Lesley Bird Simpson, *Many Mexicos* (Berkeley: University of California Press, 1960); Alan Knight, *The Mexican Revolution*, vol. 1, *Porfirians, Liberals, and Peasants*; and vol. 2, *Counter Revolution and Reconstruction* (Omaha: University of Nebraska Press, 1990).

4. Colin Maclachlan and William Beezley, *Mexico's Crucial Century, 1810–1910* (Lincoln: University of Nebraska Press, 2010), 138–56.

5. William Beezley, *Judas at the Jockey Club and Other Episodes of Porfirian Mexico* (Lincoln: University of Nebraska Press, 2004), 21–25. See also William Schell, *Integral Outsiders: The American Colony in Mexico City, 1876–1911* (Wilmington, Del.: SR Books, 2001), 46–50; and Gil Joseph, "Forging the Regional Pastime: Class and Baseball in the Yucatan," in *Sport and Society in Latin America*, ed. Joseph Arbena (Westport, Conn.: Greenwood Press, 1997), 29–62.

6. *Mexican Herald*, December 27, 1896, 8; *Mexican Herald*, December 28, 1896, 4; *Mexican Herald*, December 30, 1896, 5; and *Mexican Herald*, January 7, 1897, 4.

7. Jesús Galindo Zárate and Gustavo Abel Hernández Enríquez, *Historia general del fútbol mexicana: FMF 80 años* (Mexico City: Federación Mexicana de Fútbol

Asociación, 2007), 20–28; and Javier Bañuelos Rentería, *Crónicas del fútbol mexicano: Balón a tierra (1896–1932)* (Mexico City: Editorial Clio, 1998), 12–31.

8. See Knight, *Mexican Revolution*, vol. 1.

9. See Knight, *Mexican Revolution*, vol. 2, esp. 463–520; Thomas E. Skidmore, Peter H. Smith, and James N. Green, *Modern Latin America,* 7th ed. (New York: Oxford University Press, 2010), 59–61; and Teresa Meade, *A History of Modern Latin America, 1800 to the Present* (New York: Wiley Blackwell, 2009), 203–4.

10. Galindo and Hernández, 30–38.

11. On Spanish influence, see Bañuelos Renteria, 17–27; and on government use of soccer, see ibid., 64–65; Galindo and Hernández, 47; and Calderón Cardoso, 46.

12. Bañuelos, 43–47; and Galindo and Hernández, 42.

13. There is some debate about the tour. RSSSF, the statistical database for soccer, shows that the tour took place in early January 1923 and that Mexico lost one game 3–1. Galindo and Hernández, however, claim that the tour occurred in December 1922, and that Mexico won two games and tied one. See Galindo and Hernández, 49; and http://www.rsssf.com/tablesm/mex-intres.html. On the 1930 World Cup, see Galindo and Hernández, 65–66.

14. Quoted in Skidmore, Smith, and Green, 69.

15. Emily Edmonds-Poli and David Shirk, *Contemporary Mexican Politics*, 2nd ed. (Lanham, Md.: Rowman and Littlefield, 2012), 211; and Jorge G. Castañeda, *Mañana Forever: Mexico and the Mexicans* (New York: Alfred A. Knopf, 2011), 40.

16. Leon Krauze, *Crónicas del fútbol mexicano*, vol. 5, *Moneda en el aire (1986–1998)* (Mexico City: Editorial Clio, 1998), 14.

17. "Los Cachirules: Escándalos Deportivos," *Televisa Deportes*, http://www.you tube.com/watch?v=so1gW3LuClg, accessed December 20, 2011; Krauze, 28–29; and "Caso 'cachirules': negro recuerdo," *El Universal*, April 20, 2008, http://www.eluniver sal.com.mx/deportes/99513.html, accessed December 20, 2011.

18. M. Angeles Villareal, *NAFTA and the Mexican Economy* (Washington, D.C.: Congressional Research Service, 2010), 10; Edmonds-Poli and Shirk, 308; and OECD, *Divided We Stand: Why Inequality Keeps on Rising* (Paris: OECD Publishing, 2011), 22.

19. CONEVAL, *Informe de Pobreza Multidimensional en Mexico, 2008* (Mexico City: CONEVAL, 2011), 33; Tracy Wilkinson, "Poverty Grew in Mexico to Nearly Half the Population," *Los Angeles Times*, July 29, 2011, http://articles.latimes.com/2011/jul/29/world/la-fg-mexico-poverty-20110730, accessed May 5, 2012; and OECD, *Divided We Stand*, 22.

20. Roger Magazine, *Golden and Blue Like My Heart: Masculinity, Youth, and Power among Soccer Fans in Mexico City* (Tucson: University of Arizona Press, 2007), 17.

Chapter 7. Left Out

1. *Manchester Times*, March 29, 1895, 2.

2. "Report of the Joint Committee on the Physical Education of Girls," *Lancet* 200, no. 5163 (August 12, 1922): 365.

3. On soccer clubs hosting skills competitions, see Eriberto José Lessa de Moura, "As Relações entre Lazer, Futebol, e Gênero," (M.A. thesis, Universidade Estadual de

Campinas, 2003), 30; *Jornal dos Sports*, May 3, 1931, and *Jornal dos Sports*, May 16, 1931, quoted in Ludmila Mourão and Marcia Morel, "As narrativas sobre o futebol feminino," *Revista Brasileiro de Ciencia do Esporte* 26, no. 2 (January 2005): 76; and Lessa de Moura, 33.

4. Hollanda Loyola, "Pode a mulher praticar o futebol?," *Educação Física* 46 (September 1940), 20; and Humberto Ballariny, "Por que a mulher não deve praticar o futebol," *Educação Física* 49 (December 1940), 36, 52. Leite de Castro is quoted in Fábio Franzini, "Futebol é 'coisa para macho': Pequeno esboço para uma história das mulheres no país do futebol," *Revista Brasileira de História* 25, no. 50 (December 2005), 321.

5. Loyola, 41; and Orlando Rangel Sobrinho, *Educação Physica Feminina*, (Rio de Janeiro: Typografica do Patronato, 1930), 7, quoted in Silvana Goellner, "'As mulheres fortes são aquelas que fazem uma raça forte': Esporte, eugenia e nacionalismo no Brasil no início do século XX," *Revista de História do Esporte* 1, no. 1 (June 2008): 15.

6. Quoted in Franzini, 319–20. There is some debate about when the ban ends. Ludmila Mourão and Marcia Morel say 1976 while an earlier article by Mourão and Sebastião Votre says 1979.

7. George L. Mosse, *The Image of Man: The Creation of Modern Masculinity* (New York: Oxford University Press, 1996), 7–9.

8. Michael A. Messner, "Sports and Male Domination: The Female Athlete as Contested Ideological Terrain," *Sociology of Sport Journal* 5 (1988): 199. The idea of soccer serving to crystallize the nation is a close paraphrase of Eric Hobsbawm, in Eric Hobsbawm, *Nations and Nationalism Since 1780* (Cambridge: Cambridge University Press, 2012), 143. The quotation about national capabilities is from Eduardo Archetti, *Masculinities: Football, Polo and the Tango in Argentina* (Oxford: Berg, 1999), 15 and 42. Finally, the notion that soccer trained boys and dolls prepared girls is taken from Umberto Eco, *Viagem na Irrealidade Cotidiana* (Rio de Janeiro: Nova Frontera, 1984), 231, quoted in da Marcos Alves da Souza, "'A Nação em chuterias': Raça e masculinidade no futebol brasileiro" (M.A. thesis, University of Brasilia, 1996), 47.

9. See Luiz Carlos Rigo, Flávia Garcia Guidotti, Larissa Zanetti Thiel, and Marcela Amaral, "Notas acerca do futebol feminino pelotense em 1950: Um estudo genealógico," *Revista Brasileira de Ciências do Esporte* 29, no. 3 (May 2008): 173–88.

10. Ramon Missias Moreira, "A mulher no futebol brasileiro: uma ampla visão," *efedeportes.com* 13, no. 120 (May 2008).

11. Milton Costa Carvalho, "Conquistando o Mundo," *Placar* 848 (August 25, 1986): 70.

12. *El Mercurio*, May 8, 1919, 6; and Miguel Angel Bestard, *Paraguay, un siglo de fútbol* (Asunción: Liga Paraguaya de Fútbol, 1981), 41.

13. *El Gráfico*, January 31, 1920, 17.

14. Betty Rojas López, in Elías Zeledón Cartín, comp., *Deportivo Femenino Costa Rica, F.C.: Primer equipo de fútbol femenino del mundo* (San José: Ministerio de Cultura, Juventud y Deportes, 1999), 191.

15. "Las futbolistas dieron gran lección a los futbolistas," *La Prensa Libre*, March 27, 1950, in Zeledón Cartín, 22.

16. *La Nación* (Honduras), April 19, 1951, quoted in Zeledon Cartín, 87.

17. In Zeledon Cartín, 31–33.

18. Attendance spiked for games involving Mexico, with between 80,000 and 110,000 attending each of its four matches. See Maritza Carreño Martínez, "Fútbol femenil en Mexico, 1969–1971," (M.A. thesis, Universidad Autónoma de Mexico, 2006), ch. 8 and 10; and "Mundial (Women) 1971," http://www.rsssf.com/tablesm/mundo-women71.html. There is some discrepancy in attendance numbers. Maritza Carreño, for instance, cites 25,000 for the semifinal for Denmark v. Argentina, while Rec.Sport.Soccer Statistics Foundation (RSSSF) cites 50,000. Similarly, Carreño cites 90,000–100,000 for the final while RSSSF cites 110,000. See also ITN Source (1971) BGY508090098 "Mexico Women's Soccer: Denmark v. Mexico," personal collection of the author.

19. Carreño, 105. In Mexico women's soccer is called "fútbol femenil" instead of "fútbol femenino."

20. Ibid., 69. The FIFA circular is quoted in ibid., 98–100.

21. Ibid., 42, 38, 36.

22. Ibid., 14.

23. See, for example, Mourão and Morel; Goellner; Carreño; Zeledón Cartín; and correspondence with Andrea Rodebaugh, March 15, 2010.

24. "Estoy casada con el balón," BBCMundo.com, September 9, 2005, http://news.bbc.co.uk/hi/spanish/deportes/newsid_4717000/4717411.stm, accessed April 3, 2010.

25. Jorge Dorfman Knijnik, "Femininos e Masculinos no Futebol Brasileiro" (Ph.D. diss., University of São Paulo, 2006), 148, 113.

26. Correspondence with Andrea Rodebaugh, March 15, 2010.

27. "Deportes de aquí y de allá," *La Nación*, October 4, 1970, 110.

28. Quoted in Knijnik, 164–80, 220, 451.

29. Marcus Christenson and Paul Kelso, "Soccer Chief's Plan to Boost Women's Game? Hotpants," *Guardian*, January 16, 2004, http://www.guardian.co.uk/uk/2004/jan/16/football.gender. Accessed April 2, 2010. A good deal of research has been done recently on the impact of sexualized images on women's sports. See, for example, Mary Jo Kane, "Sex Sells Sex, Not Women's Sports," *Nation*, August 15–22, 2011, http://www.thenation.com/article/162390/sex-sells-sex-not-womens-sports, accessed October 29, 2012. See also Neal Christopherson, Michelle Janning, and Eileen Diaz McConnel, "Two Kicks Forward, One Kick Back: A Content Analysis of Media Discourses on the 1999 Women's World Cup Soccer Championship," *Sociology of Sport Journal* 19 (2002), 170–88; Mary Jo Kane and Heather D. Maxwell, "Expanding the Boundaries of Sport and Media Research," *Journal of Sport Management* 25 (2011): 205, 214; Elizabeth Daniels and Heather Wartena, "Athlete or Sex Symbol: What Boys Think of Media Representations of Female Athletes," *Sex Roles* 65, no. 7–8 (October 2011): 576; and Jennifer L. Knight and Traci A. Giuliano, "He's a Laker, She's a 'Looker': The Consequences of Gender-Stereotypical Portrayals of Male and Female Athletes by the Print Media," *Sex Roles* 45, no. 3–4 (August 2001), 227.

Bibliography

IVº Campeonato Mundial de Futebol Taça Jules Rimet. São Paulo: Confederação Brasiliera de Desportos, 1950.

77 años de fútbol en el Paraguay. Asunción: Editorial Veloz, 1977.

100 años. Asunción: Asociación Paraguaya de Fútbol, 2006.

Adelman, Miriam. "Mulheres no Esporte: Corporalidades e Subjetividades." *Movimiento* 12, no. 1 (2006): 11–29.

Adorno, Theodor, and Max Horkheimer. "The Culture Industry: Enlightenment as Mass Deception." In *Dialectic of Enlightenment*. Translated by Edmund Jephcott. Stanford: Stanford University Press, 2007.

Aguilar, Jesus Paz. *Tradiciones y leyendas de Honduras*. Tegucigalpa: Museo del Hombre Hondureño, 1989.

Alabarces, Pablo. "Boundaries and Stereotypes (or What Is the Use of Football, if Any Indeed?)." *Sociedad* 1 (2006): 12.

———, comp. *Futbologias: Fútbol, identidad y violencia en América Latina*. Buenos Aires: CLACSO, 2003.

———. *Fútbol y Patria: El fútbol y las narrativas de la nación en la Argentina*. Buenos Aires: Prometro Libros, 2002.

———. "Post-Modern Times: Identities and Violence in Argentine Football." In *Football Cultures and Identities*. Edited by Gary Armstrong and Richard Giuliannotti, 77–85. Houndmills, U.K.: Macmillan, 1999.

Alabarces, Pablo, and Maria Graciela Rodríguez. *Cuestion de pelotas: Fútbol/deporte/sociedad/cultura*. Buenos Aires: ATUEL, 1996.

Ali, Kecia. "The Historiography of Women in Modern Latin America." Duke-UNC Program in Latin American Studies, Working Paper Series, 18. Durham, N.C.: Duke University, 1995.

Amaya, Jorge Alberto. "Los negros ingleses o creoles de Honduras: Etnohistoria, racismo, y discursos nacionalistas excluyentes en Honduras," *Sociedad y Economía* 12 (2007): 115–29.

Anderson, Mark. *Black and Indigenous: Garifuna Activism and Consumer Culture*. Minneapolis: University of Minnesota Press, 2009.

Anderson, Mark, and Sarah England. "¿Auténtica cultura Africana en Honduras? Los afrocentroamericanos desafían el mestizaje." In *Memorias del mestizaje: Cultura política en Centroamérica de 1920 al presente*. Edited by Dario Euraque, Jeffrey Gould, and Charles Hale. Guatemala: CIRMA, 2005.

Arbena, Joseph. "Sport, Development, and Mexican Nationalism, 1920–1970." *Journal of Sport History* 18, no. 3 (Winter 1991): 350–64.

———, ed. *Sport and Society in Latin America: Diffusion, Dependency, and the Rise of Mass Culture*. New York: Greenwood Press, 1988.

Archetti, Eduardo. "Argentina 1978: Military Nationalism, Football Essentialism, and Moral Ambivalence." In *National Identity and Global Sports Events: Culture, Politics, and Spectacle in the Olympics and the World Cup*. Edited by Alan Tomlinson and Christopher Young, 133–48. Albany: State University of New York Press, 2006.

———. *Fútbol y ethos*. Buenos Aires: FLACSO, 1984.

———. *Masculinities: Football, Polo and the Tango in Argentina*. Oxford: Berg, 1999.

———. "Playing Styles and Masculine Virtues in Argentine Football." In *Machos, Mistresses, Madonnas: Contesting the Power of Latin American Gender Imagery*. Edited by Marit Melhuus and Kristi Anne Stølen, 34–55. London: Verso, 1996.

Argentina Mundial: Historia de la Selección. 1902–2002. Buenos Aires: Clarín, 2002.

Aroncena Olivera, Enrique. *De la aristocrácia y del poder: El Uruguay de los años 20*. Montevideo: Linardi y Rossi, 2004.

Balderston, Daniel, and Donna J. Guy, eds. *Sex and Sexuality in Latin America*. New York: New York University Press, 1997.

Ballariny, Humberto. "Por que a mulher não deve praticar o futebol." *Educação Física* 49 (December 1940).

Bandeira, Manuel. "De vario assunto de futebol," *O Melhor da Crónica Brasileira*, tomo 2. Rio de Janeiro: Livraria José Olympio Editora, 1981.

Bañuelos, Javier, Carlos Calderón, Greco Sotelo, and León Krauze. *Crónica del fútbol mexicano*. Vol. 4, *Los años dificiles (1970–1986)*. Mexico City: Editorial Clio, 1998.

Bañuelos Rentería, Javier. *Crónicas del fútbol mexicano*, Vol. 1, *Balón a tierra (1896–1932)*. Mexico City: Editorial Clio, 1998.

Barnade, Oscar, and Waldemar Iglesias. *Mitos y creencias del fútbol argentino*. Buenos Aires: Ediciones el Arco, 2006.

Barrán, José Pedro. *Apogeo y crisis del Uruguay pastoral y caudillesco*. Montevideo: Ediciones de la Banda Oriental, 1974.

Bayces, Rafael. "Cultura, identidades, subjetividades, y estereotipos: Preguntas generales y apuntes específicos en el caso de fútbol uruguayo." In *Fútbologias: Fútbol, identidad, y violencia en América Latina*. Edited by Pablo Alabarces, 163–77. Buenos Aires: Clacso, 2003.

Beezley, William. *Judas at the Jockey Club and Other Episodes of Porfirian Mexico*. Lincoln: University of Nebraska Press, 2004.

Bellos, Alex. *Futebol, Soccer the Brazilian Way*. New York: Bloomsbury, 2002.

Besse, Susan K. *Restructuring Patriarchy: The Modernization of Gender Inequality in Brazil, 1914–1940*. Chapel Hill: University of North Carolina Press, 1996.

Bestard, Miguel Ángel. *Paraguay: Un siglo de fútbol.* Asunción: Editorial Litocolor, 1996.

———. *80 años de fútbol en el Paraguay.* Asunción: Litograf, 1981.

Bocayuva, Helena. *Erotismo à brasileira, o, Excesso sexual na obra de Gilberto Freyre.* Rio de Janeiro: Garamond, 2001.

Bogado Bordón, Catalo, and Gilberto Ramírez Santacruz. *Arsenio Erico, el ángel que jugó para los diablos: Historia del mejor futbolista de todos tiempos.* Asunción: Aranduã Editorial, 2006.

Bourdieu, Pierre. "Sport and Social Class." *Social Science Information* 17 (December 1978): 819–40.

Braun Barillo, Emilio, ed. *Historia official de la selección nacional.* Bosque de las Lomas: Red W, 2002.

Brewster, Keith, and Claire Brewster. "Cleaning the Cage: Mexico City's Preparations for the Olympic Games." *International Journal of the History of Sport* 26, no. 6 (2009): 790–813.

Brohm, Jean-Marie. *Sport: A Prison of Measured Time.* London: Ink Links, 1978.

Bruhns, Heloisa Turini. *Futebol, carnival e capoeira: Entre as gingas do corpo brasileiro.* Campinas, SP: Papirus Editora, 2000.

Brun, Diego Abente. *El Paraguay actual, 1a. parte, 1989–1998.* Asunción: El Lector, 2010.

Bruni, José Carlos. "Apresentatação." *Revista USP* 22 (1994): 7–9.

Burkholder, Mark, and Lyman Johnson. *Colonial Latin America,* 2nd ed. New York: Oxford University Press, 1994.

Buzzetti, José I., and Eduardo Gutierrez Cortinas. *Historia del deporte en el Uruguay (1830–1900).* Montevideo: Tall. Graif Castro, 1965.

Caetano, Gerardo, and José Rilla. *Historia contemporánea del Uruguay: De la colonia al Mercosur.* Montevideo: Fin de Siglo, 1996.

Caldas, Waldenyr. "Aspectos sociopolíticos do futebol brasileiro." *Revista USP* 22 (1994): 41–49.

Calderón Cardoso, Carlos. *Crónica del fútbol mexicano,* vol. 2, *Por amor a la camiseta (1933–1950).* Mexico City: Editorial Clio, 1998.

Capelán Carril, Juan Antonio. *Nueve decadas de gloria.* Montevideo: Asociación Uruguayo de Fútbol, 1990.

Capitanio, Ana Maria. "Mulher, gênero e esporte: A análise da auto-percepção das desigualdades." M.A. thesis, Universidade de São Paulo, 2005.

Carboneli Debali, Arturo, ed. *Primer Campeonato Mundial de Football, Montevideo Julio de 1930: Coupe de Monde.* Montevideo: Impresora Uruguaya, n.d.

Carreño Martínez, Maritza. "Fútbol femenil en México 1969–1971." M.A. thesis, Universidad Autónoma de México, 2006.

Castañeda, Jorge G. *Mañana Forever: Mexico and the Mexicans.* New York: Alfred A. Knopf, 2011.

———. "Mexico." In *The Thinking Fan's Guide to the World Cup.* Edited by Matt Weiland and Sean Wilsey, 190–95. New York: Harper Perennial, 2006.

Castro, Ruy. *Garrincha: The Triumph and Tragedy of Brazil's Forgotten Footballing Hero*. Translated by Andrew Downie. London: Yellow Jersey, 2004.

Chamosa, Oscar. *The Argentine Folklore Movement: Sugar Elites, Criollo Workers, and the Politics of Cultural Nationalism, 1900–1955*. Tucson: University of Arizona Press, 2010.

Chaponick, Hector, ed. *Historia del Fútbol Argentino*, tomo 1. Buenos Aires: Editorial Eiffel, 1955.

Christopherson, Neal, Michelle Janning, and Eileen Diaz McConnel. "Two Kicks Forward, One Kick Back: A Content Analysis of Media Discourses on the 1999 Women's World Cup Soccer Championship." *Sociology of Sport Journal* 19 (2002): 170–88.

Cid, Gabriel, and Alejandro San Francisco, eds. *Nacionalismos e identidad nacional en Chile: Siglo XX*, vol. 1. Santiago: Ediciones Centro de Estudios Bicentenario, 2010.

———. *Nacionalismos e identidad nacional en Chile: Siglo XX*, vol. 2. Santiago: Ediciones Centro de Estudios Bicentenario, 2010.

Cien Años con el fútbol. Buenos Aires: Manrique Zago Ediciones, 1993.

Collier, Simon, and William Slater, *A History of Chile, 1808–1994*. Cambridge: Cambridge University Press, 1996.

CONEVAL. *Informe de Pobreza Multidimensional en Mexico, 2008*. Mexico City: Consejo Nacional de Evaluación de la Política de Desarrollo Social, 2011.

Constable, Pamela, and Arturo Valenzuela. *A Nation of Enemies: Chile under Pinochet*. New York: Norton, 1996.

Cordeiro de Azevedo, Tânia Maria. "A Mulher é a Atividade Desportiva: Preconceitos e estereótipos (Analize de periódicos especializados em Educação Física 1932–1987)." M.A. thesis, Universidade Federal Fluminese, 1988.

Costa, Francisco. "O futebol na punta da caneta." *Revista USP* 22 (1994): 84–91.

Costa Carvalho, Milton. "Conquistando o Mundo." *Placar* 848 (August 25, 1986): 70.

DaCosta, Lamartine P., and Ana Miragaya, eds. *Worldwide Experiences and Trends in Sport for All*. Aachen: Meyer and Meyer Sport, 2002.

D'Almeida Lima, Ruy. "Uruguay, 2—Brasil, 1." *Magazine 1950 del Campeonato*. Madrid, 1950.

DaMatta, Roberto. "Antropologia do óbvio: Notas em torno do significado social do futebol brasileiro." *Revista USP* 22 (1994): 10–17.

———. *Carnivals, Rogues, and Heroes: An Interpretation of the Brazilian Dilemma*. Translated by John Drury. Notre Dame, Ind.: University of Notre Dame Press, 1990.

Damo, Arlei Sander. "Ah! Eu Sou Gaúcho! O Nacional e o Regional no Futebol Brasileiro." *Estudos Históricos* 23 (1999): 87–117.

Daniels, Elizabeth, and Heather Wartena. "Athlete or Sex Symbol: What Boys Think of Media Representations of Female Athletes." *Sex Roles* 65, no. 7–8 (October 2011): 566–79.

D'Ávila, Lívia Bonafé, and Osmar Moreira de Souza Júnior. "Futebol feminino e sexualidade." *Revista das Facultades Integradas Claretianas* 2 (2009): 30–41.

DIGEDER. *Analisis, diagnóstico, y formulación de una estrategia de desarrollo para el fútbol chileno.* Santiago: DIGEDER, 1987.

Di Giano, Roberto. *Fútbol y discriminación social.* Buenos Aires: Leviatán, 2007.

Dingemans, James. "Review of the Allegations of Misconduct in Relation to the FA's 2018 World Cup Bid: Summary Report to the FA." May 26, 2011.

Domínguez, César Cristaldo. *Francisco S. López.* Asunción: El Lector, 2010.

Dosal, Paul J. *Doing Business with the Dictators: A Political History of United Fruit in Guatemala, 1899–1944.* Wilmington, Del.: Scholarly Resources, 1993.

Dunning, Eric, and Chris Rojek, eds. *Sport and Leisure in the Civilizing Project.* Hampshire, U.K.: Macmillan, 1992.

Eco, Umberto. *Viagem na Irrealidade Cotidiana.* Rio de Janeiro: Nova Frontera, 1984.

Edmonds-Poli, Emily, and David Shirk. *Contemporary Mexican Politics,* 2nd ed. Lanham, Md.: Rowman and Littlefield, 2012.

Edmundson, William. *A History of the British Presence in Chile: From Bloody Mary to Charles Darwin and the Decline of British Influence.* New York: Palgrave Macmillan, 2009.

Eisenberg, Christiane. "From Political Ignorance to Global Responsibility: The Role of the World Soccer Association (FIFA) in International Sport during the Twentieth Century." *Journal of Sport History* 32, no. 3 (2005): 379–93.

Elias, Norbert, and Eric Dunning. *Quest for Excitement.* Dublin: University College of Dublin Press, 2008.

Elsey, Brenda. *Citizens and Sportsmen: Fútbol and Politics in Twentieth Century Chile.* Austin: University of Texas Press, 2011.

Escartín, Pedro. *Lo de Brasil fué así. . . .* Madrid: Editorial Pueyo, 1950.

———. *Suecia, apoteosis de Brasil.* Madrid: Imp. Samarán, 1958.

Escobar Bavio, Ernesto. *El football en el Río de la Plata (desde 1893).* Buenos Aires: Editorial Sports, 1923.

Esquivel Horno, Diego, José Pedro del Solar Navarro, Rodrigo Vilensky Kuppermann, and Nicolás Vargas Merino. "Radiografía del fútbol femenino; Copa Mundial Femenina FIFA Sub-20, Chile 2008 y su trascendencia en una sociedad como la chilena." Santiago de Chile: Universidad del Pacífico, 2008.

Euraque, Dario. *Conversaciones históricos con el mestizaje y su identidad nacional en Honduras.* San Pedro Sula: Centro Editorial, 2004.

———. *Estado, poder, nacionalidad y raza en la historia de Honduras.* Choluteca: Ediciones Subirana, 1996.

———. *Reinterpreting the "Banana Republic": Region and State in Honduras, 1870–1972.* Chapel Hill: University of North Carolina Press, 1996.

Euraque, Dario, Jeffrey Gould, and Charles Hale, eds. *Memorias del mestizaje: Cultura política en Centro América de 1920 al presente.* Guatemala: Cirma, 2004.

Fernandes, Florestan. *The Negro in Brazilian Society.* New York: Columbia University Press, 1969.

Ferreira Borges, Carlos Nazareno, Simone Magalhãos Lopez, Claudia Aleixo Alves, and Fábio Padilha Alves. "Resiliência: Uma Posibilidade de Adesão e Permanência na Prática do Futebol Feminino." *Movimiento* 12, no. 1 (2006): 105–31.

Filho, Mario. *O negro no futebol Brasileiro*. Rio de Janeiro: Editôra Civilização Brasilei-ra, 1964.

Finn, Gerry P. T., and Richard Giulianotti. *Football Culture: Local Contests, Global Visions*. London: Frank Cass, 2000.

Foer, Franklin. *How Soccer Explains the World: An [Unlikely] Theory of Globalization*. New York: Harper Collins, 2004.

Franzini, Fábio. "Futebol é 'coisa para macho': Pequeno esboço para uma história das mulheres no país do futebol." *Revista Brasileira de História* 25, no. 50 (December 2005): 315–28.

———. "As raízes do país do futebol: Estudo sobre a relação entre o futebol e a na-cionalidade brasileira (1919–1950)." M.A. thesis, Universidade de São Paulo, 2000.

Frau, Manuel. "Fútbol e Historia: La esquizofrenia oriental." *Caravelle*, no. 89 (December 2007): 129–37.

Frega, Ana. *El pluralismo uruguayo (1919–1933): Cambios sociales y política*. Montevideo: CLAEH, 1987.

Freyre, Gilberto. *The Masters and the Slaves: A Study in the Development of Brazilian Culture*. Translated by Samuel Putnam. Berkeley: University of California Press, 1986.

———. *New World in the Tropics: The Culture of Modern Brazil*. New York: Alfred A. Knopf, 1959.

Frydenberg, Julio. *Historia social de fútbol: Del amateurismo al profesionalismo*. Buenos Aires: Siglo XXI Editores, 2011.

Gaffney, Christopher T. *Temples of the Earthbound Gods*. Austin: University of Texas Press, 2008.

Galeano, Eduardo. *Soccer in Sun and Shadow*. London: Verso, 1998.

Galindo Zárate, Jesús, and Gustavo Abel Hernández Enríquez. *Historia general del fútbol mexicano: FMF 80 años*. Mexico City: Federación Mexicana de Fútbol Aso-ciación, 2007.

García, José S., Mario Griffin Cubas, and Héctor Miguel Maradiaga. *Historia y desar-rollo del fútbol en Honduras*. Tegucigalpa: FENAFUTH, 2000.

———. *Historia y desarrollo del fútbol en Honduras*, vol. 2. Tegucigalpa: FENAFUTH, 1993.

Giaudrone, Carla. "El gaucho en el ámbito iconográfico del Centenario uruguayo (1925–1930)." *Revista Hispánica Moderna* 61, no. 2 (December 2008): 149–65.

Giménez Rodríguez, Alejandro. *La pasión laica: Una breve historia del fútbol uruguayo*. Montevideo: Rumbo Editorial, 2007.

Gimlette, John. *At the Tomb of the Inflatable Pig: Travels through Paraguay*. London: Hutchinson, 2003.

Giovannini, Eduardo, ed. *Cien años de historias*. Montevideo: Ediciones del Décano, 1999.

Giulianotti, Richard. *Football: A Sociology of the Global Game*. Cambridge: Polity Press, 1999.

Goellner, Silvana Vilodre. "'As mulheres fortes são aquelas que fazem uma raça forte': Esporte, eugenia e nacionalismo no Brasil no início do século XX." *Revista de História do Esporte* 1, no. 1 (June 2008): 1–28.

————. "Bela, maternal e feminina: imagens da mulher na Revista *Educação Physica*." Ph.D. diss., Universidade Estadual de Campinas, 1999.

————. "Mulheres e futebol no Brasil: entre sombras e visibilidades." *Revista Brasileira de Educação Física e Esporte* 19, vol. 2 (April/June, 2005): 143–51.

Goksøyr, Matti, and Hans Hognestad. "No Longer Worlds Apart? British Influences and Norwegian Football." In *Football Cultures and Identities*. Edited by Gary Armstrong and Richard Giuliannotti. Houndmills, U.K.: Macmillan, 1999.

Goldblatt, David. *The Ball Is Round: A Global History of Football*. London: Penguin, 2007.

González, Javier. *El beisbol en Venezuela*. Caracas: Fundación Biggott, 2003.

González, Lidia. *Fútbol, cultura y sociedad: imágenes y palabras*. Buenos Aires: Instituto Histórico de la Ciudad de Buenos Aires, 2001.

González, Michael J. *The Mexican Revolution, 1910–1940*. Albuquerque: University of New Mexico Press, 2002.

Gordon, Cesar, and Ronaldo Helal. "The Crisis of Brazilian Football: Perspectives for the Twenty-First Century." In *Sport and Latin American Society*. Edited by J. A. Mangan and Lamartine P. Costa, 139–58. London: Frank Cass, 2002.

Gordon, Robert S. C., and John London. "Italy 1934: Football and Fascism." In *National Identity and Global Sports Events: Culture, Politics, and Spectacle in the Olympics and the World Cup*. Edited by Alan Tomlinson and Christopher Young, 41–63. Albany: State University of New York Press, 2006.

Goussinsky, Eugenio, and João Carlos Assumpção. *Deuses da Bola: Histórias da seleção brasileira de futebol*. São Paulo: DBA, 1998.

Graf, Hans, and Javier Minniti. *La vinotinto: De pasión de pocos a delirio de millones*. Caracas: Alfadil Ediciones, 2004.

Graham, Richard, ed. *The Idea of Race in Latin America*. Austin: University of Texas Press, 1997.

Groba, César. *Emperadores del gol*. Montevideo: Ediciones El Galeón, 2005.

Gruneau, Richard. *Class, Sport, and Social Development*. Amherst: University of Massachusetts Press, 1983.

Gualberto, Marcio Alexandre. "Human Rights and the Afro-Brazilian Populace." In *Dignity and Human Rights: The Implementation of Economic, Social, and Cultural Rights*. Edited by Berma Klein Goldewijk, Adalid Contreras Baspineiro, and Paolo César Carbonari. Antwerp: Intersentia, 2002.

Gudmundson, Lowell, and Justin Wolfe. *Blacks and Blackness in Central America: Between Race and Place*. Durham, N.C.: Duke University Press, 2010.

Guttmann, Allen. *Games and Empires: Modern Sports and Cultural Imperialism*. New York: Columbia University Press, 1994.

————. *From Ritual to Record: The Nature of Modern Sports*. New York: Columbia University Press, 1978.

Hanratty, Dannin M., and Sandra W. Meditz, eds., *Paraguay: A Country Study*. Washington, D.C.: GPO for the Library of Congress, 1988. http://countrystudies.us/paraguay/.

Hargreaves, Jennifer. *Sporting Females: Critical Issues in the History and Sociology of Women's Sports*. London: Routledge, 1994.

Hargreaves, John. *Sport, Power and Culture: A Social and Historical Analysis of Popular Sports in Britain*. New York: St. Martin's Press, 1986.

Herrera, Robinson A. *Natives, Europeans, and Africans in Sixteenth-Century Santiago de Guatemala*. Austin: University of Texas Press, 2003.

———. "'Por que no sabemos firmar': Black Slaves in Early Guatemala," *Americas* 57, no. 2 (October 2000): 247–67.

Hetherington, Kregg. *Guerilla Auditors: The Politics of Transparency in Neoliberal Paraguay*. Durham, N.C.: Duke University Press, 2011.

Hilton, Isabel. "Paraguay." In *The Thinking Fan's Guide to the World Cup*. Edited by Matt Weiland and Sean Wilsey, 206–14. New York: Harper Perennial, 2006.

Hobsbawm, Eric. *Nations and Nationalism since 1780*. Cambridge: Cambridge University Press, 2012.

Huggins, Nathan Irving. "The Deforming Mirror of Truth," introduction to *Black Odyssey: The African American Ordeal in Slavery*. New York: Vintage, 1990.

Hughson, John, David Ingliss, and Marcus Free. *The Uses of Sport: A Critical Study*. London: Routledge, 2005.

Huizinga, Johan. *Homo Ludens: A Study of the Play Element in Culture*. Boston: Beacon Press, 1971.

Huneeus, Carlos. *The Pinochet Regime*. Translated by Lake Sagars. Boulder, Colo.: Lynne Rienner Publishers, 2007.

Isfahani-Hammond, Alexandra. *White Negritude: Race, Writing, and Brazilian Cultural Identity*. New York: Palgrave Macmillan, 2008.

Iwanczuk, Jorge. *Historia del fútbol amateur en el Argentina*. n.p.: Autores Editores, 1992.

Jacob, Raul. "Algunas consideraciones sobre la industrialización en el Uruguay (1870–1885)." In *La industrialización del Uruguay, 1870–1925: 5 perspectivas históricas*. Edited by Alcides Berreta, Raul Jacob, Silva Rodriguez Villamil, and Graciela Sapriza, 5–22. Montevideo: Fundación de Cultura Universitaria, 1978.

Janson, Adolfina. *Se acabo ese juego que te hace hacia feliz*. Buenos Aires: Aurelio Rivera, 2008.

Jones, Clarence F. "The Trade of Uruguay." *Economic Geography* 3, no. 3 (1927): 361–81.

Jones, Thomas. "Argentina." In *The Thinking Fan's Guide to the World Cup*. Edited by Matt Weiland and Sean Wilsey, 49–55. New York: Harper Perennial, 2006.

Joseph, Gil. "Forging the Regional Pastime: Class and Baseball in the Yucatan." In *Sport and Society in Latin America*. Edited by Joseph Arbena, 29–61. Westport, Conn.: Greenwood Press, 1997.

Junior, Luiz Seabra. "O Futebol feminino no pais do futebol." *Movimiento & Percepção* 10, no. 14 (2009): 3–5.

Kane, Mary Jo. "Sex Sells Sex, Not Women's Sports." *Nation* 293, no.7–8 (August 15, 2011): 28–29.

Kane, Mary Jo, and Heather D. Maxwell, "Expanding the Boundaries of Sport and Media Research." *Journal of Sport Management* 25 (2011): 202–16.

Karush, Matthew. "National Identity in the Sports Pages: Football and the Mass Media in 1920s Buenos Aires." *Americas* 60, no. 1 (2003): 11–32.

Kenealy, Arabella. *Feminism and Sex Extinction*. London: T. Fisher Unwin, Ltd., 1920.

Klein, Herbert, and Marcello Carmagnani, "Demografía histórica: La población del obispado de Santiago, 1777–1778." *Boletín de la Academia Chilena de la Historia* 72 (1965).

Klubock, Thomas Miller. "Copper Workers, Organized Labor, and Popular Protest to Military Rule in Chile, 1973–1986." *International Labor and Working Class History* 52 (Fall 1997): 106–33.

———. "Working Class Masculinity, Middle Class Morality, and Labor Politics in the Chilean Copper Mines." *Journal of Social History* 30, no. 2 (Winter 1996): 435–63.

Knight, Alan. *The Mexican Revolution*, vol. 1, *Porfirians, Liberals, and Peasants*. Lincoln: University of Nebraska Press, 1990.

———. *The Mexican Revolution*, vol. 2, *Counter-revolution and Reconstruction*. Lincoln: University of Nebraska Press, 1990.

Knight, Jennifer L., and Traci A. Giuliano, "He's a Laker, She's a 'Looker': The Consequences of Gender-Stereotypical Portrayals of Male and Female Athletes by the Print Media," *Sex Roles* 45, no. 3–4 (August 2001): 217–29.

Knijnik, Jorge Dorfman. "Femininos e Masculinos no Futebol Brasileiro." Ph.D. diss., Universidade de São Paulo, 2006.

Kornbluh, Peter. *The Pinochet Files: A Declassified Dossier on Atrocity and Accountability*. New York: New Press, 2003.

Krauze, León. *Crónica del fútbol mexicano*, vol. 5, *Moneda en el aire (1986–1998)*. Mexico City: Editorial Clio, 1998.

Krotee, March L. "The Rise and Demise of Sport: A Reflection of Uruguayan Society." *Annals of the American Academy of Political and Social Science* 445 (1979): 141–54.

Lacey, Josh. *God Is Brazilian: Charles Miller, the Man who Brought Football to Brazil*. Stroud, Gloucestershire: Tempus, 2005.

LaFeber, Walter. *Inevitable Revolutions: The United States in Central America*. New York: W. W. Norton and Sons, 1993.

Lambert, Peter. "History, Identity, and Paraguayidad." In *The Paraguay Reader: History, Culture, Politics*. Edited by Peter Lambert and Andrew Nickson. Durham, N.C.: Duke University Press, 2013.

Lambert, Peter, and Andrew Nickson, eds. *The Paraguay Reader: History, Culture, Politics*. Durham, N.C.: Duke University Press, 2013.

———. *The Transition to Democracy in Paraguay*. Houndmills, U.K.: Macmillan, 1997.

Lanchester, John. "Brazil." In *The Thinking Fan's Guide to the World Cup*. Edited by Matt Weiland and Sean Wilsey, 69–77. New York: Harper Perennial, 2006.

Langley, Lester, and Thomas David Schoonover. *The Banana Men: American Merce-naries and Entrepreneurs in Central America*. Lexington: University of Kentucky Press, 1995.

Lara Pinto, Gloria. *Perfíl de los pueblos indígenos y negros de Honduras*. Tegucigalpa: Ruta/Banco Mundial, 2002.

Leguizamón, Luis Martín, comp. *Fútbol. Pasión e identidad: Derivas de la simbología de una práctica*. Buenos Aires: Proyecto Editorial, 2002.

Leite Lopes, José Sergio. "The Brazilian Style of Football and Its Dilemmas." In *Football Cultures and Identities*. Edited by Gary Armstrong and Richard Giuliannotti, 86–95. Houndmills, U.K.: Macmillan, 1999.

———. "Class, Ethnicity, and Color in the Making of Brazilian Football." *Daedalus* 129, no. 2 (2000): 239–70.

———. "Transformations in National Identity through Football in Brazil: Lessons from Two Historical Defeats." In *Football in the Americas: Fútbol, Futebol, Football*. Edited by Rory M. Miller and Liz Crolley. London: Institute for the Study of the Americas, 2007.

Leiva Vivas, Rafael. "Presencia negra en Honduras." In *Presencia Africana en Cen-troamérica*. Edited by Luz María Martínez Montiel. Mexico City: Dirección Gen-eral de Culturas Populares, 1993.

Leonard, Thomas. *The History of Honduras*. Santa Barbara: Greenwood Press, 2011.

Leoz, Nicolás. *Pido la palabra: I Request the Floor*. Buenos Aires: Ediciones Salvucci y Asociados, 2002.

Lessa de Moura, Eriberro José. "As Relações entre Lazer, Futebol, e Gênero." M.A. thesis, Universidade Estadual de Campinas, 2003.

Lever, Janet. *Soccer Madness*. Chicago: University of Chicago Press, 1983.

Levine, Robert. "Sport and Society: The Case of Brazilian Futebol." *Luso-Brazilian Review* 17, no. 2 (Winter 1980), 233–52.

Lewis, Paul. *Paraguay under Stroessner*. Chapel Hill: University of North Carolina Press, 1980.

Lisi, Clemente Angelo. *A History of the World Cup, 1930–2006*. Lanham, Md.: Scare-crow Press, 2007.

Little, Cynthia Jeffress. "Education, Philanthropy, and Feminism: Components of Argentine Womanhood, 1860–1926." In *Latin American Women: Historical Per-spectives*. Edited by Asunción Lavrin, 235–53. Westport, Conn.: Greenwood Press, 1978.

Llonto, Pablo. *La vergüenza de todos*. Buenos Aires: Ediciones Madres de Plaza de Mayo, 2005.

Longman, Jere. *The Girls of Summer: The U.S. Women's Soccer Team and How It Changed the World*. New York: Harper Collins, 2000.

López-Alves, Fernando. *State Formation and Democracy in Latin America, 1810–1900*. Durham, N.C.: Duke University Press, 2000.

Lotina, Juan A., and Hernández Luján. "El fútbol femenino en Cuba en cuatro etapas." *CubAhora* 11 (July 13, 2010).

Loveman, Brian. *Chile: The Legacy of Hispanic Capitalism*. New York: Oxford University Press, 1988.

Lovit, Jho. "Por primera vez actuarán en provincias las señoritas futbolistas del 'Femenino Costa Rica.'" *La Nación*, October 6 1950.

Loyola, Hollanda. "Pode a mulher praticar o futebol?," *Educação Física* 46 (September 1940).

Luzuriaga, Juan Carlos. "La forja de la rivalidad clásica: Nacional-Peñarol en el Montevideo de 1900," efedeportes.com, 10, vol. 88 (Septiembre 2005).

Macías, Anna. *Against All Odds: The Feminist Movement in Mexico to 1940*. Westport, Conn.: Greenwood Press, 1982.

Macías, Julio. *Quien es quien en la selección argentina: Diccionario sobre los futbolistas internacionales (1902–2010)*. Buenos Aires: Corregidor Deportes, 2011.

Maclachlan, Colin, and William Beezley. *Mexico's Crucial Century: 1810–1910*. Lincoln: University of Nebraska Press, 2010.

Magariños Pittaluga, Juan Antonio, and Mateo Magariños Pittaluga. *Del fútbol heroíco*. Buenos Aires: Talleres Gráficos de Alfonzo Ruíz, 1942.

Magazine, Roger. *Golden and Blue Like My Heart: Masculinity, Youth, and Power among Soccer Fans in Mexico City*. Tucson: University of Arizona Press, 2004.

Maldonado, Julio Cesar. *Historial del fútbol paraguayo*. Asunción: EMASA, 1965.

Mangan, J. A., and Lamartine P. DaCosta, eds. *Sport in Latin American Society*. London: Frank Cass, 2002.

Marimón, Antonio. *Ultimo tango en Buenos Aires: Poetas, púgiles, futbolistas, mitos*. Mexico City: Cal y Arena, 1999.

Marini, Hugo. *Veinte años de football sudamericano*. Buenos Aires: Editorial Aire Libre, 1936.

Marín Méndez, Edgardo. *Centenario historía total del fútbol chileno, 1895–1995*. Santiago: Editores y Consultores REI, 1995.

Martínez Castillo, Mario Felipe. *La Intendencia de Comayagua*. Tegucigalpa: Litografía López, 2004.

Martínez Montiel, Luz María, ed. *Presencia Africana en Centroamérica*. Mexico City: Dirección General de Culturas Populares, 1993.

Martorelli, Horacio. *Urbanización y desruralización en el Uruguay*. Montevideo: Centro Latinoamericano de Economia Humana, 1977.

Mason, Tony. *Passion of the People? Football in South America*. London: Verso, 1995.

Matamala, Daniel. *Goles y autogoles: La impropia relación entre fútbol y el poder político*. Santiago: Planeta, 2001.

Mayne-Nicholls, Harold. *Historias sudamericanas en la Copa del Mundo, 1930–2006*. Asunción: Editorial Gráfica Mercurio, 2006.

Mazzoni, Tómas. *Historia de futebol no Brasil, 1893–1950*. São Paulo: Edições Leia, 1950.

———. *O Brasil na Taça do Mundo 1938*. São Paulo: Edições e Pulicações Brasil, 1938.

Meade, Teresa. *A History of Modern Latin America, 1800 to the Present*. New York: Wiley Blackwell, 2009.

Medina Perez, Gonzalo. *¡Prohibido Perder! Y otros juegos de poder alrededor del fútbol, la cultura, y la politica*. Medellin: Hombre Nuevo Editores, 2007.

Melià, Bartomeu, and Sergio Caceres. *Historia cultural del Paraguay*, 1a parte. Asunción: El Lector, 2010.

Méndez-Vives, Enrique. *El Uruguay de la modernización, 1876–1904*. Montevideo: Ediciones de la Banda Oriental, 1975.

Mendoza, Breny. "La desmitologización del mestizaje en Honduras." *Mesoamérica* 42 (December 2001): 256–78.

Merrell, Floyd. *The Mexicans*. Boulder, Colo.: Westview Press, 2003.

Merrill, Christopher. *The Grass of Another Country: A Journey through the World of Soccer*. New York: Henry Holt, 1993.

Messner, Michael A. "Sports and Male Domination: The Female Athlete as Contested Ideological Terrain." *Sociology of Sport Journal* 5 (1988): 197–211.

———. *Taking the Field: Women, Men, and Sports, Sport and Culture Series*. Minneapolis: University of Minnesota Press, 2002.

Morales, Juan Carlos. *Fútbol argentino: 80 años de professionalismo*. Buenos Aires: Corregidor Deportes, 2010.

Moreira, Ramon Missias. "A mulher no futebol brasileiro: uma ampla visão." *efedeportes.com* 13, no. 120 (2008).

Mosse, George L. *The Image of Man: The Creation of Modern Masculinity*. New York: Oxford University Press, 1996.

Moura, Eriberro José Lessa de. "As Relações entre Lazer, Futebol, e Gênero." M.A. thesis, Universidade Estadual de Campinas, 2003.

Mourão, Ludmila, and Marcia Morel. "As narrativas sobre o futebol feminino." *Revista Brasileira de Ciencia do Esporte* 26, no. 2 (2005): 73–86.

Nahum, Benjamin, coord. *Estadísticas históricas del Uruguay, 1900–1950*, vol. 4. Montevideo: Universidad de la República, Facultad de Ciencias Sociales, 2007.

———. *La epoca batllista, 1905–1929*. Montevideo: Ediciones de la Banda Oriental, 1975.

Nascimento, Elsa Larkin. *The Sorcery of Color: Identity, Race, and Gender in Brazil*. Philadelphia: Temple University Press, 2007.

Needell, Jeffrey. "Rio de Janeiro and Buenos Aires: Public Space and Public Consciousness in Fin-de-Siecle Latin America." *Comparative Studies in Society and History* 37, no. 3 (July 1995): 519–40.

Neri Farina, Bernardo, and Alfredo Boccia Paz. *El Paraguay bajo el Stronismo, 1954–1989*. Asuncion: El Lector, 2010.

Newman, Kathleen. "The Modernization of Femininity: Argentina, 1916–1926." In *Women, Culture, and Politics in Latin America*. Edited by Emilie Bergmann, Janet Greenberg, Gwen Kirkpatrick, Francine Masiello, Francesca Miller, Marta Morello-Frosch, Kathleen Newman, and Mary Louise Pratt, 74–89. Berkeley: University of California Press, 1990.

Newson, Linda. "Labor in the Colonial Mining Industry of Honduras." *Americas* 39, no. 2 (October 1982): 185–203.

Oddone, Hugo, Claudina Zavattiero, Cynthia González Ríos, Edith Arrúa Sosa, and Elizabeth Barrios, *Perfil migratorio del Paraguay*. Buenos Aires: OIM, 2011.

Oddone, Juan A. "The Formation of Modern Uruguay, c. 1870–1930," in *The Cambridge History of Latin America*, vol. 5. Edited by Leslie Bethell. Cambridge: Cambridge University Press, 1986).

OECD, *Divided We Stand: Why Inequality Keeps on Rising*. Paris: OECD Publishing, 2011.

Oliven, Ruben G., and Arlei S. Damo. *Fútbol y cultura*. Translated by Florencia Fragasso. Buenos Aires: Grupo Editorial Norma, 2001.

Paim, Maria Cristina Chimelo. "Visões esterotipicas sobre a mulher no esporte." *efedeportes.com* 10, no. 75 (2004).

Paim, Maria Cristina Chimelo, and Marlene Neves Strey. "Percepção de corpo da mulher que joga futebol." *efdeportes.com* 10, no. 85 (2005).

Panizza, Francisco. "Late Institutionalisation and Early Modernisation: The Emergence of Uruguay's Liberal Democratic Political Order." *Journal of Latin American Studies* 29, no. 3 (October 1997): 667–91.

Pardue, Derek. "Jogada lingüística: Discursive Play and the Hegemonic Force of Soccer in Brazil." *Journal of Sport and Social Issues* 26, no.4 (November 2002): 360–80.

Paredes, Roberto. *Entidades y personajes de la transición*. Asunción: AGR, 2001.

Paz, Octavio. *The Labyrinth of Solitude: Life and Thought in Mexico*. Translated by Lysander Kemp. New York: Grove Press, 1961.

Paz Aguilar, Jesus. *Tradiciones y leyendas de Honduras*. Tegucigalpa: Museo del Hombre Hondureño, 1989.

Pendle, George. *Paraguay: A Riverside Nation*. London: Oxford University Press, 1967.

Pereira, Leonardo Affonso de Miranda. *Footballmania: Uma história social do futebol no Rio de Janeiro, 1902–1938*. Rio de Janeiro: Editora Nova Fronteira, 2000.

Perez-Maricevich, Francisco, Ignacio Roldan Martinez, Rodrigo Colmán Llano, Carlos Sosa Rabito, and Amalia Ruiz Diaz. *Historia Cultural del Paraguay*, 2a. Parte. Asunción: El Lector, 2010.

Pérez Pérez, Eliézer Sebastián. *80 tragos de vinotinto: La historia de la selección venezolana de fútbol desde 1926*. Caracas: Editorial Melvin, 2006.

Petrucelli, José Luis. *La dinamica migratoria del Uruguay del ultimo siglo, 187–1975*. Montevideo: CIESU, 1977.

Pickett, Axel. *Moscú, 26 de septiembre, 1973, URSS 0-Chile 0. El partido de los valientes*. Santiago: Aguilar, 2003.

Pippo, Antonio. *Obdulio, desde el alma*. Montevideo: Editorial Fin de Siglo, 1993.

Plá, Josefina. "Los Británicos en el Paraguay (1850–1870)." *Revista de Historia de América* 70 (July–December 1970): 339–91.

———. "Los Británicos en el Paraguay (1850–1870), Continuación" *Revista de Historia de América* 71 (January–June 1971): 23–65.

Pope, S. W. "Introduction: American Sports History—Toward a New Paradigm." In *The New American Sport History*. Edited by S. W. Pope. Urbana: University of Illinois Press, 1995.

————. *Patriotic Games: Sporting Traditions in the American Imagination, 1876–1926.* Knoxville: University of Tennessee Press, 1997.

Prats, Luís. *La crónica celeste: Historia de la Selección Uruguaya de Fútbol: triunfos, derrotas, mitas y polémicas (1901–2001).* Montevideo: Editorial Fin de Siglo, 2001.

Preston-Werner, Theresa. "In the Kitchen: Negotiating Changing Family Roles in Costa Rica." *Journal of Folklore Research* 45, no. 3 (September–December 208): 329–59.

Ramírez Gallegos, Jacques Paul. "Fútbol e identidad regional en Ecuador." In *Fútbologias: Fútbol, identidad, y violencia en América Latina.* Edited by Pablo Alabarces, 101–18. Buenos Aires: Clacso, 2003.

Rangel Sobrinho, Orlando. *Educação Physica Feminina.* Rio de Janeiro: Typografica do Patronato, 1930.

Recalde Guanes, Jesus Amado, "Prologue." In *El fútbol paraguayo.* Edited by Humberto Domínguez Dibb. Asunción: Talleres Gráficos Cromos, 1977.

Regalado, Jesús García. *Venezuela y sus selecciones de fútbol, 1964–1999.* Caracas: Federación Venezolano de Fútbol, 2000.

"Report of the Joint Committee on the Physical Education of Girls." *Lancet* 200, no. 5163 (August 12, 1922): 365.

República de Honduras. *Características generales de las Garífunas conforme a los resultados del XI censo nacional y de vivienda, año 2001.* Tegucigalpa: INE, 2001.

Rey, Alfonso. *El fútbol Argentino.* Buenos Aires: Ediciones Nogal, 1947.

Rigo, Luiz Carlos, Flávia Garcia Guidotti, Larissa Zanetti Thiel, and Marcela Amaral. "Notas acerca do futebol feminino pelotense em 1950: Um estudo genealógico." *Revista Brasileira de Ciências do Esporte* 29, no. 3 (May 2008): 173–88.

Rios, Carlos. *Historia de los campeonatos sudamericanos de football.* Montevideo: Taller Gráfico Prometeo, 1944.

Riveros, Nicolás. *Retazo de la patria, cultura y balón.* Asunción, 2000.

Rivet, Paul, and Verónica Sans. "Los últimos charrúas." *Guaraguao* 8, no. 19 (Winter 2004): 165–88.

Rodriguez, José Carlos. *El Paraguay bajo el Nacionalismo, 1936–1947.* Asunción: El Lector, 2010.

Rovira Mas, Jorge. "Del desarrollo de Costa Rica y su crisis en el período de postguerra, 1948–1984." *Anuario de Estudios Centroamericanos* 11, no. 1 (1985): 23–42.

Ruíz, Armando Ramos. *Nuestro fútbol, grandeza y decadencia.* Buenos Aires: ISA, 1973.

Russell, David. "Associating with Football: Social Identity in England, 1863–1998." In *Football Cultures and Identities.* Edited by Gary Armstrong and Christopher Young, 15–28. Houndmills, U.K.: Macmillan, 1999.

Saldanha, João. *Os subterraneos de futebol.* Rio de Janeiro: Livraria José Olympio Editora, 1980.

Santa Cruz A., Eduardo. *Origén y futuro de una passion: Fútbol, cultura, y modernidad.* Santiago de Chile: LOM-ARCIS, 1995.

Scapinaches, Luis. *Gambeteando frente al gol.* Montevideo: Barreiro y Ramos, 1964.

Schell, William. *Integral Outsiders: The American Colony in Mexico City, 1876–1911.* Wilmington, Del.: SR Books, 2001.

Seabra, Daniel, and Joana Rodrigues, "Futebol com um Ritual," *Antropolíogicas* 2 (1998): 15–34.

Sebreli, Juan José. *Fútbol y masas*. Buenos Aires: Editorial Galerno, 1983.

Sevcenko, Nicolau. "Futebol, metrópoles, e desatinos." *Revista USP* 22 (1994): 30–37.

Sharrat, Sara. "The Suffragist Movement in Costa Rica, 1889–1949: Centennial of Democracy?" In *The Costa Rican Women's Movement: A Reader*. Edited by Ilse Abshagen Leitinger, 61–83. Pittsburgh: University of Pittsburgh Press, 1997.

Sherman, William L. *Forced Native Labor in Colonial Central America*. Lincoln: University of Nebraska Press, 1972.

Shorris, Earl. *The Life and Times of Mexico*. New York: W. W. Norton, 2004.

Silverstein, Jake. "Ecuador." In *The Thinking Fan's Guide to the World Cup*. Edited by Matt Weiland and Sean Wilsey, 112–20. New York: Harper Perennial, 2006.

Simpson, Lesley Bird. *Many Mexicos*. Berkeley: University of California Press, 1960.

Skidmore, Thomas E., Peter H. Smith, and James N. Green. *Modern Latin America*, 7th ed. New York: Oxford University Press, 2010.

Sotelo, Greco. *Crónica del fútbol mexicano*, vol. 3, *El oficio de las canchas (1950–1970)*. Mexico City: Editorial Clio, 1998.

Souza, Marcos Alves de. "A 'Nação em chuteiras': Raça e masculinidade no futebol Brasileiro." MA thesis, Universidade de Brasilia, 1996.

Spagnolo, Mauro. "Apuntes sobre la filosofía política del fútbol." In *Fútbol, pasión e identidad: Derivas de la simbología de una práctica*, 25–33. Buenos Aires: Proyecto Editorial, 2002.

Sturzenegger, Carlos. *Football: Leyes que lo rigen y modo de jugarlo*. Montevideo: Talleres Gráfico El Arte, 1911.

Sussekind, Hélio. *Futebol em dois tempos*. Rio de Janeiro: Relume Dumará, 1996.

Taylor, Chris. *The Beautiful Game: A Journey through Latin American Football*. London: Phoenix, 1998.

———. *Black Carib Wars: Freedom, Survival, and the Making of the Garifuna*. Jackson: University Press of Mississippi, 2012.

Tomlinson, Alan, and Christopher Young, eds. *National Identity and Global Sports Events: Culture, Politics, and Spectacle in the Olympics and the World Cup*. Albany: State University of New York Press, 2006.

Troche, José María. *El libro de oro del fútbol paraguayo, 1901–2011*. Asunción: Alvaro Ayala Producciones, 2011.

Urbina Gaitán, Chester. "Cohesión social, desorganización y manipulación política. Historizando el fútbol en Costa Rica." *efdeportes.com* 14, no. 133 (2009).

Uruguay, 2002. Montevideo: AUF, 2002.

Uruguay, Campeón de Football Mundial: La Olimpiada de París, 1924. Montevideo: Talleres Gráfico Rossi, 1926.

Valenzuela, Arturo. *The Breakdown of Democratic Regimes: Chile*. Baltimore: Johns Hopkins University Press, 1988.

Vazquez Montalbán, Manuel. *Fútbol: Una religion en busca de un Dios*. Barcelona: Arena Abierta, 2005.

Vera, Antonino. *Fútbol en Chile*. Santiago: Editora Nacional Gabriela Mistral, 1973.

Verón, Luis. *Carlos A. López*. Asunción: El Lector, 2011.

Villareal, M. Angeles. *NAFTA and the Mexican Economy*. Washington, D.C.: Congressional Research Service, 2010.

Vinotinto es Venezuela. Caracas: Sánchez Editores, 2003.

Votre, Sebastião, and Ludmila Mourão. "Women's Football in Brazil: Progress and Problems." In *Soccer, Women, Sexual Liberation: Kicking off a New Era*. Edited by Fan Fong and J. A. Mangan, 254–67. London: Frank Cass, 2004.

Wade, Peter. *Race and Ethnicity in Latin America*. London: Pluto Press, 2010.

Warren, Harris Gaylord. *Rebirth of the Paraguayan Republic: The First Colorado Era, 1878–1904*. Pittsburgh: University of Pittsburgh Press, 1985.

Weiland, Matt, and Sean Wilsey. *The Thinking Fan's Guide to the World Cup*. New York: Harper Perennial, 2006.

Whigham, Thomas. *The Paraguayan War*. Vol. 1, *Causes and Early Conflict*. Lincoln: University of Nebraska Press, 2002.

Williams, Jean. *A Beautiful Game: International Perspectives on Women's Football*. Oxford: Berg, 2007.

———. *A Game for Rough Girls?* London: Routledge, 2003.

Williams, John Hoyt. *The Rise and Fall of the Paraguayan Republic, 1800–1870*. Austin: Institute of Latin American Studies, 1979.

———. "Foreign Tecnicos and the Modernization of Paraguay, 1840–1870." *Journal of Interamerican and World Affairs* 19, no. 2 (1977): 233–57.

Winn, Peter. "British Informal Empire in Uruguay in the Nineteenth Century." *Past & Present* 73 (1976): 100–126.

Witherspoon, Kevin B. *Before the Eyes of the World: Mexico and the 1968 Olympic Games*. DeKalb: Northern Illinois University Press, 2008.

Yeager, Gertrude M., ed. *Confronting Change, Challenging Tradition: Women in Latin American History*. Edited by William H. Beezley and Colin M. Maclachlan. Jaguar Books on Latin America. Wilmington, Del.: Scholarly Resources, 1994.

Yeomans, Matthew. "Costa Rica." In *The Thinking Fan's Guide to the World Cup*. Edited by Matt Weiland and Sean Wilsey, 78–85. New York: Harper Perennial, 2006.

Zeledón Cartín, Elías, comp. *Deportivo Femenino Costa Rica F.C.: Primer equipo de fútbol femenino del mundo (1949–1999): reseña histórica*. San José, Costa Rica: Ministerio de Cultura, Juventud, y Deportes, 1999.

Zolov, Eric. "Showcasing the 'Land of Tomorrow': Mexico and the 1968 Olympics." *Americas* 61, no. 2 (October 2004): 159–88.

Index

JOSHUA H. NADEL is assistant professor of Latin American and Caribbean history at North Carolina Central University in Durham. His research focuses on soccer, food and identity, and North American cultural influence in the Caribbean.

The University Press of Florida is the scholarly publishing agency for the State University System of Florida, comprising Florida A&M University, Florida Atlantic University, Florida Gulf Coast University, Florida International University, Florida State University, New College of Florida, University of Central Florida, University of Florida, University of North Florida, University of South Florida, and University of West Florida.